Magic Guidebooks
Walt Disney World
2022

The BEST Walt Disney World Tips, Virtual Queue Tips, Disney Genie+, Disney Dining Guide, Magic Kingdom, Epcot, Disney's Hollywood Studios, Star Wars: Galaxy's Edge, and Disney's Animal Kingdom, Hidden Mickeys, & more!

ISBN: 978-1-7340792-8-9

Magic Guidebooks
Walt Disney World 2022

✦ Covers the entire Walt Disney World Resort including the Magic Kingdom, Epcot, Disney's Hollywood Studios, Disney's Animal Kingdom, Disney Springs, and more!

✦ Learn the BEST Virtual Queue tips and line-skipping strategies *without* needing to pay for Disney Genie+ or Lightning Lane!

✦ Celebrate Walt Disney World's 50th Anniversary with new attractions and special offerings around the Resort!

✦ A complete Star Wars: Galaxy's Edge guide with reviews and tips for visiting Disney's largest expansion!

✦ Covers new attractions including Remy's Ratatouille Adventure, Tron Lightcycle Run roller coaster, Guardians of the Galaxy: Cosmic Rewind, and more!*

✦ Discover the BEST food with unbiased restaurant coverage, delicious fan-favorite menu choices, and a review of the Disney Dining Plan!*

✦ Must-know tips for visiting with kids, tweens, teens, and even Disney World fun just for adults!

✦ Money- and time-saving tactics for worry-free planning!

✦ Explore secrets, histories, and magical details found around the Walt Disney World Resort—including lists of Hidden Mickeys!

✦ Event recommendations and tips for Disney After Hours, Halloween, the Holidays, Epcot festivals, & more!

BONUS: Guide to Universal Studios Orlando!

* Some experiences and products may be unavailable at the Walt Disney World Resort.

Table of Contents

GET UPDATES!

Sign up for our FREE e-mail list!

www.magicguidebooks.com/list
(We promise no spam!)

Wishing you a magical vacation!
Magic Guidebooks

Important Health and Safety Note:

By reading this book, you acknowledge that Magic Guidebooks and its contributors are not responsible for your health and safety. If you are traveling during a global pandemic, you could potentially expose yourself to COVID-19 or other illnesses. While the Walt Disney World Resort has taken certain precautions, it is still no exception. COVID-19 is a serious global pandemic and it is important that you review local health and safety guidelines before visiting. The Centers for Disease Control's website (cdc.gov) may also offer valuable tips for staying healthy. Additionally, WaltDisneyWorld.com posts safety guidelines for visiting its theme parks, hotels, and other attractions. This guidebook is not a replacement for guidelines found at the previously mentioned sources or medical recommendations. Magic Guidebooks is not suggesting that you take a vacation during a pandemic, no matter how excited we appear to be about theme parks and travel.

INTRODUCTION

ABOUT THIS GUIDE

When writing and designing this book, we had *you* in mind. Maybe you're a first-time visitor to the Walt Disney World Resort, or perhaps you've frequented it for many years. Wherever you come from and whatever your experience, we wanted to provide a complete guide from start to finish. In fact, the entire purpose of this guide is to give real advice covering the many attractions, restaurants, and hotels from the Disney World Resort and beyond.

Who are we? Well, we're theme park enthusiasts who spend a lot of time gathering first-hand knowledge and experiences from all around the world. In fact, we've visited every single Disney Resort, including the new Shanghai Disneyland, because we love them so much. In other words, advice in this guide is crafted from trial and error—and we're passing the fruits of our hard work on to you!

The Walt Disney World Resort is a constantly changing place. From exciting themed dining to limited-time thrilling attractions, sometimes we can never imagine what might be coming next! Since experiences come and go, we also invite you to subscribe to our free e-mail list for up-to-date travel information.

Keep in mind that this guide is an "unofficial edition," meaning that we are not sponsored or employees of the Walt Disney Company, the Disneyland Resort, or the Walt Disney World Resort, nor have we ever been. We are simply fans of the Walt Disney World Resort who are giving an honest opinion on what it has to offer!

FOR DISNEY WORLD NEWBIES

If you've never been to the Walt Disney World Resort before, this book is perfect for you! We've crammed our guide with tidbits about the best food, attraction recommendations, hotel pros and cons, and so much more. We'll fill you in on Disney lingo, history, and what's coming next. In the end, you'll have the knowledge of a pro!

FOR RETURN VISITORS

The Walt Disney World Resort is a constantly changing place. If you haven't been to Disney World in ten years, this guide is a great fit. Even if you visited just a few years ago, you will discover tidbits about how vacation planning has changed.

However, if you go every week, you probably won't learn much. That, of course, doesn't mean that you won't learn *anything*, but you're likely already a pro and a guide to a park that's basically your second home won't be much use. Still, if you're curious, we welcome you along for the ride!

A WORD FOR ALL

Since Walt Disney World Resort updates its experiences so frequently, some of the items in this guide will change even weeks after its publication. For example, restaurants in Disney Springs might close, attractions may be re-themed, and popular food items could become discontinued. To cover this, we send updates via our free e-mail newsletter to our readers. If you'd like to be updated, visit our website and sign up today: **www.magicguidebooks.com/list** (don't worry, we won't spam you). On our website, we also keep a list of ride and attraction refurbishments, so you'll learn which experiences might be unavailable during your vacation—check it out!

THE HISTORY

Four years after opening his iconic Disneyland Resort in Southern California, Walt Disney started a new dream: to create something bigger to enchant the globe. In essence, he wanted to build more than a *land*—Walt wanted a *world*!

In 1964, that dream was planted like a seed which would eventually grow into the massive, enchanting tree of reality. Originally nicknamed the covert "Florida Project," Disney secretively bought nearly 30,000 acres of marsh, swamps, and groves in Central Florida. Unfortunately, the next year, Walt Disney passed away. Luckily for all of us, his brother Roy kept Walt's dream alive.

By 1969, the secret was out, and construction began on the Magic Kingdom, Florida's version of Disneyland. Orlando's massive 189-foot (56 meters) Cinderella Castle towers far beyond Disneyland's Sleeping Beauty Castle—which is only 77 feet (23 meters). In October of 1971, Walt Disney World opened its gates to visitors, bringing classic attractions like Peter Pan's Flight, "it's a small world," and the Jungle Cruise!

The flat, Floridian lands just outside of Orlando now had a center of magic for all to behold. It wouldn't be long before thousands of visitors turned into millions, making it the most successful theme park resort in history (and it still is today). Nearly 20 million people visit the Walt Disney World Resort annually to live out the stories from classics like *Snow White and the Seven Dwarfs*, experience the frosty magic of *Frozen*, and to meet Mickey Mouse himself.

Disneyland fans will notice the wider streets of the Magic Kingdom and the spacious, interactive queues. Since it rains in Orlando more than Southern California, many of the queues are indoor and some of the classic rides have covers, like the Mad Tea Party. Florida makes an ideal spot for the Walt Disney World Resort as there is plenty of space for dozens of Disney hotels, four world-class theme parks, a shopping center, water parks, golf courses—the list goes on seemingly forever! With warm weather nearly year-round, it's the ideal destination for vacationers of all ages to experience the massive, endless magic that Walt Disney has brought to the world.

Soon after the construction of the Magic Kingdom, Walt Disney World continued its mission to become the massive theme park resort that it is today by adding the futuristic Epcot (which stands for Experimental Prototype Community of Tomorrow) in 1982, followed by MGM Studios (now called Disney's Hollywood Studios) in 1989, and Disney's Animal Kingdom in 1998. Walt Disney World also has two themed water parks, Disney's Typhoon Lagoon (opened in 1989) and Disney's Blizzard Beach (opened in 1995). There is also a downtown shopping area known as Disney Springs, a boardwalk, and the ESPN Wide World of Sports Complex.

THEME PARK BREAKDOWN

Magic Kingdom
This is Walt Disney World's most visited theme park. During the holidays and weekends, this park is a crowd favorite and draws the most visitors. In fact, the Magic Kingdom pulls in roughly 20 million visitors a year, doubling the number of guests for Disney's Animal Kingdom.

Epcot
Built over a decade after the Magic Kingdom in 1982, Epcot is one of Walt Disney World's most iconic parks. With a world travel theme and a massive, golf ball-looking centerpiece, Epcot brings in over 11 million visitors annually. Epcot is popular for its food and unique attractions like Soarin' Around the World and Frozen Ever After. Epcot picks up at night with locals looking to drink along its beautiful lake.

Disney's Hollywood Studios
Disney World never quite hit its expectations with its movie-themed park, Hollywood Studios. The new additions of Toy Story Land (2018) and Star Wars: Galaxy's Edge (2019) have greatly added to the park's appeal in recent years. Hollywood Studios is home to thrilling attractions like the Twilight Zone Tower of Terror and the Rock 'n' Roller Coaster Starring Aerosmith! Hollywood Studios is a favorite of those looking for rides that make you scream!

Disney's Animal Kingdom
With popular rides like Expedition Everest, stunning shows, and beautiful exotic animals, Animal Kingdom is the third most popular destination (but nearly tied with Hollywood Studios). The newest expansion, Pandora—The World of Avatar, cost $400 million to build and is one of the most popular areas in all of Walt Disney World! Animal Kingdom is perfect all ages—especially animal lovers!

The Waterparks
Disney also offers two world-class water parks at its Walt Disney World Resort. Typhoon Lagoon is a thrilling shipwreck-themed oasis

where islands filled with waterslides bring the fun! Meanwhile, Blizzard Beach brings a frosty look to Florida's warm weather. Built like a ski lodge, Blizzard Beach offers loads of fun down slopes of waterslides and wave pools.

Universal Orlando
Separate from Disney World are three stunning theme parks in the heart of Orlando. Universal Studios, Islands of Adventure, and Volcano Bay are theme parks based around the cinema magic from *Harry Potter* and *Despicable Me* to *Transformers* and *Jurassic Park*. We cover these parks with tips, tricks, and travel plans near the end of this guide.

THE DISNEY WAY

The Walt Disney World Resort prides itself for being "show ready" — meaning that the attractions and experiences are all part of a believable, functioning show. Every piece of Disney World is treated like an on-going theatrical production and run like a well-oiled machine. The idea is that the storytelling is convincing and surprising to all guests. After all, you're paying a ticket price to visit a place that feels like magic.

Another facet of Disney's "show ready" concept is a spotless stage. The Walt Disney World Resort is immaculately clean. This means that you're never too far from a trash or recycle bin (they're practically everywhere). These receptacles are decorated to fit within the lands and are frequently emptied by custodial staff. The janitors in the theme parks are also part of the show. You might catch them greeting guests and painting Disney characters on sidewalks with their brooms and a bucket of water!

In the event that an attraction doesn't feel show ready, Disney will pull the plug. A single, flickering lightbulb on a ride could force the attraction to close until it's show ready again. If you've ever visited another theme park and spotted dirty restrooms, piles of trash, and graffiti, Walt Disney World will feel like a breath of fresh air.

WHY DO I NEED A GUIDE?

While you can visit the Walt Disney World Resort any time and attempt to experience it on your own, having invaluable tips from insiders will make all the difference. This guide will save you time waiting in lines, money, and give you the best options to fit your mood.

Truthfully, you'd need to stay an entire month (or more) to do everything in Walt Disney World—it's *that* massive. Think of it as a playground for the whole family, where you'll feel safe, accommodated, and in awe as you make your adventure through the Magic Kingdom and beyond. As there is so much to do in Disney World, people often wonder: where do I start? Where should I stay? How long should I stay? Is this going to cost me an arm and a leg? That's where we come in! At Magic Guidebooks, we absolutely love the Disney theme parks. We visit all of the time and know the ins and outs of theme park travel. Not only can our insider know-how help make your vacation more enjoyable, but we can also save you time waiting in lines and money on travel, tickets, and hotels. We also recommend the best of where to eat, how to get from place to place, and where to stay.

So, how do we do it? Why is this guide important? We're glad that you asked! As you read this guidebook, we'll show you all of the tips, tricks, and secrets to maximize your vacation! We've done Disney World on the cheap and never felt like we were uncomfortably frugal. With careful planning and our help, you can have the time of your life with your family and build everlasting memories!

WHAT TO EXPECT

Orlando, Florida is an ideal location for the Walt Disney World Resort because of its year-long sunshine. Likely, as your plane lands or car or bus arrives, you'll see the sun shining with white tufts of cottony clouds. Many times, especially in the late afternoon, it'll be cloudy and gray for an hour or so. Thunderstorms, especially in the summer months, will sweep by and leave as quickly as they came. It's not uncommon for it to rain each day at the Walt Disney World Resort, but, fortunately, it doesn't last for long. Meanwhile, half of the year in Florida, the humidity is high—sometimes 100% saturating the air. It can feel a bit stifling, but the resorts and parks know this. Air conditioning pumps in every car, hotel, and indoor ride to help you enjoy your stay.

Walt Disney World uses mobile device technology to enhance guest experience. The Walt Disney World mobile app makes purchases, acts as a room key, and accesses reservations, including Virtual Queues. If you've checked in ahead of time, you can continue directly to your room without stopping at the front desk. Soon you'll be at the parks or the pool, enjoying your stay.

The parks are massive and filled with people ready to enjoy Walt Disney World. You'll see visitors from all over the world. The magic of Disney overtakes them, and they instantly act happier. Walt Disney World is a different place, and while it's not cheap, it gives you countless memories for your dollar!

The employees of Walt Disney World are also generally friendly and have been properly coached to show you a good time. They keep the parks and hotels especially clean, setting the Walt Disney World Resort apart from the typical feel of a carnival or other theme parks. You and your family or group will feel safe and welcome everywhere you go. There are several delicious items to eat throughout the resort, as well as picturesque scenes that come to life before your eyes.

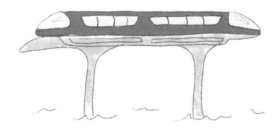

WHY IS DISNEY WORLD SO EXPENSIVE?

It's no secret that Walt Disney World tickets, hotel rooms, dining, and merchandise cost a pretty penny. Alright, it's more than a pretty penny; Disney World is expensive! A bottle of soda costs around $4-$5 and one meal for a family of four can easily exceed $100. Disney claims that it raises prices to help with guest flow. Popular dates, like weekends, have higher prices than a Tuesday or Wednesday. We've been a little skeptical of this claim in the past (is Disney just being greedy?), but recently the crowds have thinned on typically popular days. Even traditionally busy summer months like June, July, and August have dwindled in attendance. Instead, guests are visiting during the fall and spring to save money on vacation. Families can often save *hundreds* of dollars just by booking on a less expensive date versus a holiday weekend.

Parents who want to experience Disney magic with their kids often save for years before booking. We understand the worry that your trip could break the bank—or become a total bust with a high price tag. Thus, we've created this guide to plan your Disney World trip with ease—and save some money along the way. Keep in mind that Walt Disney World isn't just any set of amusement parks. This is a world-class, premium resort. Yet, there are several tricks, discounts, and tips you'll learn from this guide before you go.

GUIDEBOOK LINGO

If you are new to the Disney theme parks or just haven't been in some time, you'll instantly notice the vibrant lingo that arises at the resort. Most of the time these come from well-seasoned guests and Disney employees—known as Cast Members. Sometimes they will say something like "Snow White is a classic dark ride" and if you're not up on the knowledge, you might feel lost at the start. Whether you're talking to a fellow guest, Cast Member, or reading signs by the rides, it helps to know the terms first.

We also have our own terms that we frequently use throughout this book. They are fairly intuitive, but just so that we are all on the same page (yay book puns!), we invite you to familiarize yourself with this section to help with reading this guide.

DISNEY LINGO

The Walt Disney World Resort – The area that encompasses all of Disney's theme parks (Magic Kingdom, Epcot, Disney's Hollywood Studios, Disney's Animal Kingdom, and the water parks), the Walt Disney World hotels, the Disney Springs shopping area, parking lots, and more. We may also shorten Walt Disney World to, simply, Disney or Disney World.

Cast Member – A term for all Disney employees. They often wear themed costumes when they work in the resort, but the behind-the-scenes employees will typically wear business casual clothing or engineering jumpers.

MagicBand – This amazing (and stylish) piece of technology allows guests to do it all with a simple bracelet. The MagicBand allows you to unlock the door of your hotel room, it's your ticket into the theme parks, and you can make purchases with it! MagicBands are an extra cost (around $20-$30) for those who don't already have one. Guests staying at a Disney Resort may receive discounts when they order MagicBands.

Park Hopper – A ticket that allows you to visit multiple parks, as many times as you'd like throughout that day. Park Hopper tickets allow you to hop between the four theme parks—with add-on options for the water parks.

Virtual Queue - A virtual line where a guest is called back to the attraction once their "boarding group" time is called. Guests often use the Disney World app to secure a boarding group within the virtual queue to select attractions.

Lightning Lane – Skip the lines through a dedicated queue at dozens of attractions. Lightning Lane is accessible as an extra-paid feature that guests can access using the Disney World mobile app.

Disney Genie – An in-app planning tool for building your daily itinerary. Guests can manage their plans day-of and get forecasts about lower wait times. An upgradeable feature called Disney Genie+ allows guests to pay in bulk for access to most Lightning Lanes.

Single Rider Line – A fast way to get on the rides as long as you don't mind riding by yourself.

Passholders – A nickname for those who purchased Annual Passes.

PhotoPass and Memory Maker – A paid Disney service to have professional photographers take your picture around the Walt Disney World Resort. We *highly* recommend adding this feature so that you can download quality photos on your mobile device or home computer!

My Disney Experience (Walt Disney World Mobile App) – Walt Disney World's stunning app that works with your phone or tablet. You can manage and book reservation times, schedule and check dining reservations, see line wait times, use the Disney Genie, and much more!

Early Theme Park Entry – Special extended hours for Disney Resort hotel guests. Early Theme Park Entry typically gives guests about 30 minutes early entry into the parks each day before standard visitors. However, Deluxe Resort hotel guests may take advantage of extended park hours after closing on select dates. Early Theme Park Entry hours are visible on the Walt Disney World app.

"Dark Ride" – An indoor ride where the vehicle is guided along a track. Typically, these are family-friendly rides like "it's a small world," and they also have air conditioning to escape the heat on hot days!

Disney Dining Plan – Pre-purchased meal plans to select eateries around the Walt Disney World Resort.

Animatronic – Robotics brought to life for music and narration, typically used in stage shows and rides.

Closed for Refurbishment – No one likes seeing this sign as it means that the ride is closed for restoration. Some refurbishments can last a couple of days, while others have lasted years. Refurbishment scheduling occurs most often in the off-season months like January through March. You can view a list of closed attractions in the calendar portion of the Walt Disney World app.

OUR LINGO

Magic Tips – These are special tips and secrets to enhance your vacation! Magic Tips are designed to save time waiting in lines, get the best viewing areas for shows and parades, save you money, and *a lot* more!

RIDE LEVELS

+ **Everyone** – Perfect for anyone of all ages.
+ **Thrill Riders** – Those looking for the maximum thrill from attractions. Whether it's a ride with loops like the Rock 'n' Rollercoaster or the high-dropping Tower of Terror, we guide you to the biggest thrills of the Walt Disney World Resort!
+ **Family** – Suited for anyone of all ages, both kids and adults. However, these rides may not interest Thrill Riders.
+ **Young Kids** – Children ages 2-5.
+ **Kids** – Children ages 6-9.
+ **Tweens** – Children ages 10-12.
+ **Teens** – Young people ages 13-17.
+ **Adults** – People ages 18 and older.

RESOURCES

CONTACT

The following are official contact channels for the Walt Disney World Resort. We recommend booking online or using the app as phone wait times can be long.

> **· Magic Tips ·**
> The Walt Disney World mobile app is an excellent tool for getting your questions answered by a Cast Member. Just log into the app, click the menu button, and tap "Chat with Us."

RESOURCE	CONTACT
General information	**Web:** www.waltdisneyworld.com
Hotel Reservations	**Phone:** (407) 939-1936 **Web:** https://disneyworld.disney.go.com/resorts
Disney Dining	**Book/Manage:** Disney World app **Phone:** (714) 781-DINE **Web:** https://disneyworld.disney.go.com/dining
Tickets	**Purchase:** Disney World app **Web:** https://disneyworld.disney.go.com/tickets **New Purchases:** (407) 939-7679 **Existing Tickets:** (407) 939-7523 **Group Reservations (10 or more):** (407) 939-1942
Annual Passholders	**Purchase:** Disney World app **Phone:** (407) 560-7277 **Web:** https://disneyworld.disney.go.com/passes **Manage Reservations:** https://disneyworld.disney.go.com/experience-updates/park-reservations/
Disney App help	**Phone:** (407) 939-4357

DISCOUNT BOOKING WEBSITES

DisneyRewards.com
If you have a Disney Visa® Card, earn points and claim special rewards.

Orbitz.com/deals
For special promotions (look for codes up to 15% off hotels).

Amextravel.com
If you have an American Express® Card, this can save you, plus earn more rewards.

CHAPTER ONE

PLANNING YOUR WALT DISNEY WORLD VACATION

PLANNING WHEN TO VISIT

Wanting to go to Walt Disney World is easy—planning *when* to go can be a whole other animal! As we've said before, there's *so* much to do at Walt Disney World that it can feel impossible to wrap your mind around the seemingly limitless possibilities. We completely understand your headache! Depending on the dates you choose, whether it's seasonal events like Halloween or the holidays, there are several unique attractions in store. In short, whether you have a set of dates in mind or you're looking for the best times to go—we're here to help.

We've picked up TONS of useful tips for you during our vacations, our friends' vacations, and by talking to the Cast Members. In this chapter, we will walk you through the choices of travel and our recommendations for saving time and money. Choosing a time for your vacation may not be entirely up to you. It could depend on your work schedule, your travel schedule, or your children's vacation days from school. Whether you have flexible travel days or not, we have laid out a month-by-month breakdown of what to expect when you visit Walt Disney World. We also give you tips on how to avoid the long lines and save time to make your stay a magical one!

MOST-RECOMMENDED MONTHS

1. **September**
   Summer continues throughout September in Central Florida. Expect hot days and far less crowds than in June, July, and August. Halloween decorations will spread throughout the Magic Kingdom most of the month. Mickey's Not-So-Scary Halloween Party also premieres. While the weekends can get a bit packed, the weekdays have the thinnest crowds.

2. **February**
   The Walt Disney World Resort typically has fewer crowds at this time, though weekends can be busier. Still, we find that this is one of the better months if you are looking for cooler weather and thinner crowds. However, Presidents' Day week is often very busy.

3. **October**
   Though Halloween has become one of the busier times to visit, the experiences and weather still make it a great bet. The Disney parks continue to come alive during Halloween with typically perfect weather. Decorations, desserts, special rides, and Mickey's Not-So-Scary Halloween Party await you!

> **· Magic Tips ·**
> Walt Disney World's 50th Anniversary began in 2021 and runs through all of 2022. We expect new attractions to debut throughout the year. During these times, crowd levels are expected to be much higher than normal. We plan to post updates and tips for visiting during the anniversary on our website, MagicGuidebooks.com.

LEAST-RECOMMENDED MONTHS

1. **December**
   While park guests are treated to the holiday decorations, treats, and special rides, the crowds are some of the most massive. If you must go in December, we recommend the first week.

2. **July**
   Massive crowds from all over the world flood the Walt Disney World Resort. Expect long lines, and the hottest, most humid weather of the year.

3. **August**
   Similar to July, summer crowds and hot weather make this month one of the most miserable times to visit. August crowds die down in the last two weeks of the month when children go back to school.

Note: Are you planning your visit during one of our least recommended travel dates? Don't worry! This guide will help you avoid those long lines. Be sure to follow one of our pre-planned attraction lists. We use them ourselves and they can save you hours of time waiting in lines—or help you avoid them altogether. Tips for beating the crowds are at the end of this chapter.

MORE DATES TO CONSIDER

Holidays
Holidays can feel quite bustling when throngs of people escape the cold and head to the warmth of Florida. Here is a list of days you may want to avoid:

+ Christmas (all week)
+ New Year's (all week)
+ Thanksgiving (all week)
+ Easter (all week)
+ The 4th of July (all week)
+ Memorial Day weekend
+ Labor Day weekend
+ Martin Luther King Jr. weekend
+ Presidents' Day (all week)
+ Columbus Day
+ Veterans Day weekend
+ Mother's Day
+ Father's Day (even more crowed than Mother's Day)

Weekdays
This might not seem like much of a secret, but weekdays are the best times to plan trips to the more popular parks like the Magic Kingdom and Disney's Animal Kingdom. If you must go on a weekend date, we would recommend saving Hollywood Studios and Epcot for those dates, since those parks don't attract as many visitors.

Marathons
Many vacation planners wouldn't normally consider running a marathon as part of their vacation. However, *run*Disney is an awesome event (with an extra fee) for runners to marathon around the resort. Though these take place in the early hours on the weekend, the crowds flock to the parks afterward. Sometimes guests will stay for a few days after the run, making it extra crowded on dates you might not otherwise think would be packed.

RunDisney.com has released the dates for 2022:
✦   Jan 5-9, 2022: Walt Disney World Marathon Weekend
✦   Feb 24-27, 2022: Disney Princess Half Marathon Weekend
✦   Mar 31 - Apr 3, 2022: Springtime Surprise Marathon Weekend
✦   TBA November 2022: Wine & Dine Half Marathon

Considering running?
Visit **www.runDisney.com** for more details.

> · **Magic Tips** ·
> The runDisney events can be extremely crowded. Typically, families stay after the running event and pack the parks.

DAILY CROWDS

Monday
Often these can be just as crowded as Sundays because people take off extra days to avoid weekend traffic. On Monday holidays, expect very large crowds.

Tuesday
Typically has the fewest crowds during the week.

Wednesday
Typically has the second fewest crowds.

Thursday
Third most recommended day for thinner crowds.

Friday
Less busy in the morning, but busiest in the evening after school is out for the Annual Passholders.

Saturday
The busiest day at the resort.

Sunday
Weekend crowds, but far less than Saturday. Sundays are especially busy on holiday weekends.

Holidays
It's best to avoid the busy holidays and three-day weekends (Friday through Tuesday) as they get very busy.

· Magic Tips ·

We gathered our crowd information from inside sources and our own observations and calculations. Some crowd measurements can be seen via the Walt Disney World mobile app when looking at ride wait times. Keep in mind that this data can be faulty as the app isn't always accurate.

A better way to check for crowds is via Walt Disney World's website ticket price calendar. Ticket costs will be higher during more crowded weeks.

MOST CROWDED DAYS

1. Christmas Day (and week)
2. New Year's Eve/Day
3. Thanksgiving week
4. Veterans Day
5. Memorial Day weekend
6. Fourth of July
7. Labor Day weekend

MONTH BREAKDOWN

JANUARY

Overview: January is busy in the first week—when holiday attractions still run—and gets generally less crowded after that. However, you may still see a spike during the marathon weekend.

Weather: Mid-70°F (mid-20°C) during the day and chilly at night (sometimes in the 40's F / 4-9°C). The humidity is low.

Least Crowded Days: The last week in January.

Most Crowded Days: The first two weeks (especially around New Year's) and Martin Luther King Jr. Weekend (Friday through Monday). January 5-9, 2022 for the Walt Disney World Marathon Weekend.

SPECIAL EVENT: NEW YEAR'S EVE
December 31st

New Year's is a popular—and crowded—event widely celebrated around Walt Disney World. The Magic Kingdom and Epcot display fireworks at midnight. Hollywood Studios keeps a dance party going until 1am. Animal Kingdom hosts a New Year's Eve countdown around the Tree of Life. If you wish to escape the crowds, head to the Beach Club Resort or Polynesian Resort and watch the fireworks from the beach area. These spots become crowded, but getting in and out of the hotels is much easier from there than at the theme parks.

For those looking for an upscale event, Disney's Contemporary Resort hosts an annual New Year's Eve party in their Fantasia ballroom. There's live music, gourmet food, and champagne. Just before midnight, guests head outside to watch the fireworks from the Magic Kingdom. Tickets are around $300 each and adults must be 21 years or older to drink with a valid ID. While adults attend the party, kids can enjoy the Pixar Play Zone on NYE. Reservations should be made in advance for both. Book online at **www.waltdisneyworld.com**.

FEBRUARY

Overview: Possibly the least crowded month to visit Walt Disney World. Like January, the weather is cooler, and some of the rides may be closed for refurbishment.

Weather: Mid-70°F (mid-20°C) during the day and chilly at night (low 50's F / 10-12°C). Also expect far less humidity than in the summer and fall. The humidity is low.

Least Crowded Days: Any week except near Presidents' Day Weekend (Friday through Monday).

Most Crowded Days: Presidents' Day Weekend and the following week for the Disney Princess Half Marathon (February 24-27, 2022).

Mardi Gras: Disney World often holds brief Mardi Gras events in late February and early March. Expect to see celebrations and delicious New Orleans food at the Magic Kingdom, Disney Springs, and Disney's Port Orleans hotel.

SPECIAL EVENT:
Epcot INTERNATIONAL FESTIVAL OF THE ARTS
Select dates January - February, 2022
From music to specialty dishes, Epcot's Festival of the Arts takes you on a virtual journey around the world to celebrate a variety of cultures. Look for fantastic chalk drawings on the streets, living statues (street performers dressed as metal statues), nighttime concerts, delicious treats, and more! Festival of the Arts is highly rated by guests and we recommend checking it out!

· Magic Tips ·
The Disney water parks typically close for refurbishment in the winter. Expect one or both parks to close sometime in January through March.

MARCH

Overview: March's popularity has increased recently as spring breaks spread throughout the month. If you visit in March, be sure to do so during the week, Tuesday through Thursday.

Weather: mid-70°F (21°C) during the day and chilly at night. March has been known to have occasional heatwaves, bringing the weather above 90°F (32°C). The humidity is medium.

Least Crowded Days: the first Tuesday, Wednesday, and Thursday of March.
Most Crowded Days: Last two weeks of the month.
St. Patrick's Day – Wear green on March 17th to celebrate the holiday! There are also some St. Patrick's Day treats found around the resort. Raglan Road in Disney Springs is typical busy while offering live music, Irish beer, and traditional food.

SPECIAL EVENT:
Epcot FLOWER AND GARDEN FESTIVAL
Select dates March - June, 2022
Every spring, Epcot hosts the unforgettable International Flower and Garden Festival. Sample delicious treats from around the world while you walk the park and spot floral topiaries made into classic and new Disney characters. Also feed butterflies, walk fields of flowers, and break near pop-up play areas for the kids! This festival comes with your Epcot ticket cost, however, sampling most of the food and drink costs extra.

APRIL

Overview: With spring breaks continuing through April, the end of the month tends to be the least crowded. We love visiting in April because the weather feels a lot more manageable (though it may not be very ideal for the water parks). Also there usually isn't very much humidity in the air. Lately, Walt Disney World has been more crowded in April. We believe that this is because of schools changing their spring break schedules.
Weather: Low-80°F (25-28°C) during the day and cooler at night (mid-60°F / 15-19°C). The humidity is medium.
Least Crowded Days: The last two weeks of the month.
Most Crowded Days: First two weeks of the month, and March 31 - April 3, 2022 for the Springtime Surprise Marathon Weekend.

SPECIAL EVENT: EASTER
Sunday, April 17, 2022
See a special Easter parade at the Magic Kingdom. Rare characters and the Easter bunny make appearances in this colorful daytime parade.

MAY

Overview: Spring at Disney World is beautiful and it will feel like the Floridian summer has begun. Storms tend to pick up during this time and it might rain during the day for an hour or so. The rain consists of short showers, so it shouldn't put a damper on your vacation.

Weather: Mid-70°F (21°C) during the day and sometimes chilly at night. The humidity is medium/high.

Least Crowded Days: The first two weeks of the month.

Most Crowded Days: Memorial Day weekend (Friday through Tuesday).

JUNE

Overview: The warm June weather perfectly suits the Walt Disney World Resort. The first two weeks of June are the least crowded until schools release mid-June and the summer crowds begin.

Weather: Mid-80°F (27°C) during the day. Typically keeps warm at night. The humidity is medium/high.

Least Crowded Days: Tuesdays, Wednesdays, and Thursdays, and the first week of the month.

Most Crowded Days: The last week of the month.

Events: Sounds Like Summer Concert Series – Bands and musicians take over Epcot's World Showcase as they perform covers of your favorite songs and tributes to your favorite artists.

JULY

Overview: The weather heats up (often unbearably so) and crowds from all over the world venture into the Walt Disney World Resort during July. Though July is crowded, it does make a great opportunity to visit the water parks and ride the many water-themed attractions, like Splash Mountain, throughout the parks.

Weather: Low-90°F (32-34°C) during the day, but the humidity can make July feel even warmer. The weather typically stays warm and humid at night. The humidity is high.

Least Crowded Days: Tuesday, Wednesdays, and Thursdays (unless one is July 4th).

Most Crowded Days: July 4th

Events: Sounds Like Summer Concert Series continues and a special **Fourth of July "Concert in the Sky"** displays on Independence Day.

AUGUST

Overview: Just when you think Florida couldn't get any hotter than in July, August comes around. This is most likely the hottest month all year round. The weather continues to blaze in August as crowds continue to pour in until school begins around the middle of the month. August rarely feels as crowded to us as July does, so if you want to get away during the summer, this is the month to pick.

Weather: Mid-90°F (32°C) during the day with usually near 100% humidity. Nights are sometimes just as warm and balmy. Showers typically occur once a day for an hour or two, but the queues for most rides have coverings. The humidity is very high.

Least Crowded Days: Tuesdays, Wednesdays, and Thursdays and the last two weeks of the month.

Most Crowded Days: The first two weeks of the month.

Early Halloween: The Magic Kingdom begins its Halloween events in mid-August. Expect to see pumpkins and other fall decor line Main Street, U.S.A. during this time. It's a bit strange to see a jack-o-lantern during August, but many guests love seeing Disney's spooky season before schools resume. We cover more about Halloween events in the October section.

SPECIAL EVENT:
Epcot INTERNATIONAL FOOD AND WINE FESTIVAL
End of August through Mid-November
Every fall, Epcot hosts the wildly popular International Food and Wine Festival. Taste foreign delights from around the world while you walk the park. With dozens of kiosks of food and drink to fill your curiosity, adults will especially love Epcot's Food & Wine Festival!

Eat to the Beat is another great seasonal attraction that takes place during Epcot's Food & Wine Festival. See popular singers and bands perform their hits in World Showcase. Best of all, these concerts are free! Concert lineups are usually announced in the spring. For the best seats, book an Eat to the Beat dining package at select restaurants.

More information and booking: www.EpcotFoodandWine.com

SEPTEMBER

Overview: The balmy summer weather typically lasts through September. Expect Halloween decorations all month in the Magic Kingdom and great deals on rooms due to the dip in tourism. If September wasn't so humid, it might be the best time to visit!

Weather: High-90°F (32°C) during the day. Typically keeps very warm at night. The humidity is very high.

Least Crowded Days: Tuesdays, Wednesdays, Thursdays, and Fridays (except for Halloween event nights—more on that next).

Most Crowded Days: Labor Day weekend.

OCTOBER

Overview: October is a fan-favorite month at the Walt Disney World Resort! The weather cools down (though many days can still feel like summer) and Halloween celebrations kick into full gear. Guests can dress up in costume during special events held at Magic Kingdom.

Weather: High-80°F (29-31°C) during the day, cools a bit at night. The later you go in October, the more likely tropical storms can come into play. If you are planning a visit, we recommend somewhere in the first couple of weeks. The humidity is very high.

Least Crowded Days: Tuesday, Wednesdays, and Thursdays

Most Crowded Days: Halloween party on select dates and Halloween day, October 31st.

SPECIAL EVENT:
HALLOWEEN AT MAGIC KINGDOM
Mid-August - October 31st

The Magic Kingdom's popular Halloween parties are a real treat! Running on select nights from mid-August through Halloween Day, guests can expect to see their favorite Disney Villains, a spooky parade, and plenty of decor around the park. Guests who attends these separately ticketed events also have access to complimentary candy at treat spots.

Many adults love visiting as much as the kids because they can finally wear their costumes into the park (Disney has a ban on anyone over 13 from entering the park dressed as a character for safety reasons). Event access is not included with standard daytime admission. Halloween parties usually start around $130 each for anyone age 3 or older. Event tickets usually go on sale in the spring at WaltDisneyWorld.com.

HALLOWEEN PARTY REVIEW

Join Mickey, Minnie, Donald, Goofy, and the rest of their friends as you trick or treat around the park, see a Halloween parade, meet rare costumed characters, and scoop up complimentary candy. The Halloween parties aren't necessarily scary, but there is some fun spookiness to them.

Disney may host one of two Halloween events: Mickey's Not-So-Scary Halloween Party or Disney After Hours Boo Bash. We're not sure which event will run in 2022 but both parties have similar theming, characters, and experiences. However, Mickey's Not-So-Scary Halloween Party usually has an amazing fireworks show but the After Hours events have far fewer guests. Ride wait times are typically short for both events.

The Halloween parties are lot of fun—and *very* popular. Expect tickets to sell out early for dates in October. Whether or not the event reaches capacity, you'll likely face heavy crowds for the Halloween parade and fireworks (though attraction wait times tend to remain low). Buy in advance because Disney limits the tickets.

> **· Magic Tips ·**
> Most families opt to see the early Halloween parades and shows. To avoid crowds, watch the later showings.

MICKEY'S NOT-SO-SCARY HALLOWEEN ATTRACTIONS

- **Hocus Pocus, Parade, and Fireworks** – During Mickey's Not-So-Scary Halloween Party, Disney Villains—including Maleficent, the Sanderson Sisters from *Hocus Pocus*, and more—take over the Magic Kingdom. You'll also see Mickey's Boo-to-You Halloween Parade led by the Headless Horseman! The night concludes with stunning Halloween-themed Not-So-Spooky Spectacular fireworks!
- **Halloween Décor** – See Mickey-shaped pumpkins, try delicious treats, and see your favorite characters dressed in their Halloween costumes!
- **Halloween Dining** – The Be Our Guest restaurant, Cinderella's Royal Table, and Crystal Palace, host special dining events for

Halloween. Enter one of these dining areas for a Halloween-themed dining experience.

- **Halloween Attraction Overlays** – During the Halloween Party, ride Space Mountain in complete darkness, see live actors on Pirates of the Caribbean, and hear an eerie new tune on the Mad Tea Party.
- **Cruella's Hide-a-Way** – An extra-paid event at Tony's Town Square Restaurant with treats, wine and beer (for guests 21+), and the chance to hang with Cruella De Vil! You'll also have exclusive viewing of Mickey's Boo-to-You Halloween Parade and the fireworks.

NOVEMBER

Overview: The holidays begin mid-November at the Walt Disney World Resort. Expect larger crowds beginning Veterans Day and onward.

Weather: High-70°F during the day, cools at night to High-50°F. The humidity is medium.

Least Crowded Days: The first week of the month.

Most Crowded Days: Veterans Day weekend and Thanksgiving week. The first weekend of the month for the marathon.

SPECIAL EVENT: THANKSGIVING AT WALT DISNEY WORLD
November 24, 2022

Thanksgiving is a busy day at Disney, but there are plenty of places to enjoy a delicious turkey dinner—and many other Thanksgiving favorites! Restaurants all over the resort offer fine meals, including most of the hotels and these spots in the parks:

- **Magic Kingdom** – Liberty Tree Tavern
- **Epcot** – Akershus Royal Banquet Hall, Biergarten, Coral Reef, Le Cellier Steakhouse, Rose & Crown
- **Disney's Hollywood Studios** – 50's Prime Time Café
- **Disney's Animal Kingdom** – Tusker House

DECEMBER

Overview: The holidays are in full gear at the Walt Disney World Resort. See decorations all around with special treats, fun holiday-themed rides, and a chance to meet Santa Claus!

Weather: Low-70°F (21-23°C) during the day, cools at night to Low-50°F (10-12°C). The humidity is low.
Least Crowded Days: The first week of the month.
Most Crowded Days: The last two weeks, especially Christmas Day and New Year's Eve.

HOLIDAY

Holiday attractions at Walt Disney World mostly focus on the Christmas holiday. See glittering lights dazzling Cinderella Castle, Toy Story Land, and the Hollywood Tower Hotel! From magnificent Christmas trees to endless strings of ornaments, you'll be in awe of the holiday transformation around the resort.

Note: The holiday events at Walt Disney World run from mid-November through the first week of January.

HOLIDAYS IN THE THEME PARKS

Magic Kingdom – The park comes alive with stunning seasonal decorations. Nightly, Cinderella Castle dazzles with white and blue holiday lights! There are also themed attractions, shows, and plenty of holiday treats to enjoy around the park.

✦ **Jingle Cruise** – A special Christmas layover of the classic ride with holiday humor and decorations.
✦ **A Christmas Fantasy Parade** – Mickey, Santa, and Disney Princesses celebrate Christmas aboard stunning floats.
✦ **Santa Claus** – Meet Santa on Main Street!
✦ **Be Our Guest** – The restaurant dazzles with Christmas decor!

> · **Magic Tips** ·
> Santa Claus also shows up at Disney Springs for photo opportunities with guests!

Magic Kingdom Holiday Parties (*select dates in November and December*) – Mickey and his friends (including Santa Claus) bring Christmas spirit to the Magic Kingdom with special costumes, shows, fireworks, and even snow! Similar to the Halloween parties, this is a nighttime event with a separate admission cost.

Though Disney specifically uses the word "holiday" to describe many of its attractions, the Magic Kingdom holiday parties are mostly centered around Christmas traditions. Disney could host one of two holiday parties: Mickey's Very Merry Christmas Party or Disney's Very Merriest After Hours. Both usually have limited tickets, characters in their holiday best, short ride wait times, complimentary snacks, and special attractions.

· **Magic Tips** ·

There are fewer guests during the Magic Kingdom holiday parties compared to the daytime crowds. If you're visiting during the busier dates closer to Thanksgiving or Christmas, you may want to purchase a ticket to this party to save on wait times. However, popular rides like Peter Pan and the Seven Dwarfs Mine Train often still have long waits.

Several exclusive holiday-themed attractions are designated for the parties. The Once Upon a Christmastime Parade, Minnie's Wonderful Christmastime Fireworks Show, and more dazzle the night with winter magic. Best of all, you only need to show up 5-10 minutes early for a great spot. Other attractions like Space Mountain, the Mad Tea Party, and the Tomorrowland Speedway often have Christmas overlays with music and added lighting. These attraction overlays cannot be experienced during normal park hours.

Tony's Merriest Town Square Party – This event is an add-on ticket for the Magic Kingdom holiday parties. Tony's Town Square Restaurant serves appetizers, sweets, and drinks for all guests (including alcoholic beverages for adults 21 and older). These are gourmet treats including meat and cheese boards and hand-decorated Christmas sweets. Guests also have premium views of the parade. However, at about $100 a ticket (on top of your Christmas Party admission), you'd have to eat a lot of cheese to make up for the cost.

Epcot Holidays – From stunning fireworks displays at night to the holiday traditions of Epcot's eleven countries, you'll feel the magic of the holidays! There is also a Candlelight Processional with a massive orchestra and choir. Holidays Around the World celebrates global winter traditions at each of the World Showcase pavilions. Tour around to taste the delicious holiday cuisine of nearly a dozen countries!

Disney's Hollywood Studios Holiday – If you're visiting Disney World during the holiday season, you'll want to add a night at Hollywood Studios to your list! With a nighttime show, "Jingle Bell, Jingle BAM!" and the new "Sunset Seasons Greetings," there is plenty of Christmas spirit at the park! Toy Story Land also lights up with special decorations and picturesque moments that look fantastic at night.

✦ **Jingle Bell, Jingle BAM!** – See a stunning Christmas fireworks and projection show on the Chinese Theatre. Show times are usually around 8pm, so get there 20-30 minutes early for a better spot!
✦ **Sunset Seasons Greetings** – Mickey, Minnie, Olaf, and their friends celebrate Christmas on Sunset Blvd. See a wonderland of decorations and holiday projections on the Tower of Terror!
✦ **Toy Story Land Holiday** – Andy's toys come to life to bring Christmas cheer! Expect unique decorations and a jolly song on Alien Swirling Saucers.

Disney's Animal Kingdom Holiday – Animal Kingdom celebrates holidays from around the world with artisan crafts, live music, and a puppet menagerie on Discovery Isle. At night, the lanterns around the park glow with festive colors. Projections on the Tree of Life also star illuminated animals with wintery magic. In Pandora, the humans have lightly decorated areas with tinsel and small ornaments from their worldly celebrations.

Holiday Dining Events – Nearly every resort hotel's dining features holiday treats from Mickey caramel apples to holiday macaroons. With Christmas décor all around, the holidays are a treat for your sights and your taste! Epcot's Promenade Refreshments hosts annual Christmas quick-service savory and sweet treats like turkey-inspired bites, holiday teas, hot chocolates, and ciders.

TIPS TO BEAT CROWDS

1.   **Be Early** – Get to the park at opening before the crowds. If you are staying at a Walt Disney World Resort hotel you can get "Early Theme Park Entry" which will allow you to enter 30 minutes early. Check the Walt Disney World app for hours.

> **· Magic Tips ·**
> Some non-Disney hotels can take advantage of Early Theme Park Entry. We list these in our hotels chapter.

2.   **Plan Your Day** – Follow one of our pre-set day plans (or make your own). We use these planners ourselves and it will save you hours of time waiting in lines (many times you'll miss the long lines altogether).

3.   **Book Dining Reservations Early** – We can't stress this enough. Many of the more popular restaurants will be booked full, like the Beauty and the Beast Be Our Guest dining experience in the Magic Kingdom.
Book Early: https://disneyworld.disney.go.com/dining or call (407) 939-3463

4.   **Avoid Typical Meal Times** – If you don't have a restaurant reservation, the times to go would be:
      Lunch: Dine before 11.30am and after 2.30pm
      Dinner: Dine before 5.00pm and after 7.30pm

5.   **Plan Your Parks** – We recommend avoiding the Magic Kingdom and Epcot on the weekends as they often pull the most crowds. Instead, head over to Animal Kingdom or Hollywood Studios. If you can, it's best to save the Magic Kingdom and Epcot for the weekdays. Watch out for Mondays at the Magic Kingdom as these can often be busier than the weekends. Since so many people know to avoid the weekends at this park, they tend to save it for a weekday when it's believed that no one will be there. Magic Kingdom is less busy usually Tuesday through Thursday.

6. **Book an After Hours Party** – Disney's After Hours parties are a great way to enjoy the parks with far less crowds. These extra-paid evening events cost a little less than a typical daytime ticket and have limited late-night hours. However, the sparse crowds, unique entertainment, and sometimes complimentary snacks are well worth the cost!

7. **You Might Have to Wait** – Waiting in line isn't the end of the world. Sometimes we all have to do it for the best attractions. The trick is to wait the *shortest* amount of time for the *fewest* rides possible. You can avoid the longest lines by following our planned-out ride lists.

8. **Stay Late** – Disney Deluxe Resort hotels can take advantage of extended park hours after closing on select dates. These hours are posted on the Walt Disney World mobile app.

9. **Take a Break –** If you are feeling worn out, take a break at your hotel or visit Disney Springs for some shopping. If you're not near your resort hotel, head to the nearest one for dinner or to look around. The Walt Disney World Resort offers so many surprises that you might have a blast drinking a cup of coffee while you listen to music near Starbucks rather than surrounded by a swarm of people. After you and your group have recharged, take a free bus back into the parks.

DISNEY MOBILE APPS

WALT DISNEY WORLD APP

We highly recommend downloading the Walt Disney World application on your phone or tablet (also known as My Disney Experience). Walt Disney World's official mobile application works on most Apple and Android devices and can save you a lot of hassle while planning your visit.

You can do the following with the application:

1. Purchase park tickets and use them while at the resort
2. View wait times for attractions at every park
3. Book and manage your Disney Genie+ selections and Virtual Queues for your entire group
4. Reserve Disney Dining around the resort
5. Mobile Order food at several locations
6. Resort hotel details and check-in
7. Unlock hotel room door
8. View your reservations, park hours, show schedules, and more
9. Use Mobile Merchandise Checkout to purchase for products in select stores. Retail locations are listed under "Shop In Store" in the Disney World app.
10. View and download PhotoPass images

> **· Magic Tips ·**
> Keep in mind that this app may drain your battery and does need a cellular or Wi-Fi connection to work. We recommend bringing a pocket phone charger and having a data plan to support your needs. Disney also offers free Wi-Fi throughout the theme parks and resort hotels.

MAGIC MOBILE

Part of the My Disney Experience app, MagicMobile allows guests to access digital theme park tickets, park reservations, make contactless payments, and more. MagicMobile essentially works like the MagicBand but is free and on your phone. Most devices including iPhones, Androids, and Apple Watches, can use MagicMobile's contactless features. Find it in the Disney World app!

PLAY DISNEY APP

Play Disney is a free mobile application to play games around the theme park. This app is available to download on the Apple and Android mobile market places as a complimentary entertainment piece. Simply download, create an account, and start playing! The app works especially well with features in Star Wars: Galaxy's Edge.

It was inevitable that guests would stare at their phones while waiting in lines, so Disney designed a free mobile app to use for this specific purpose. Play Disney immerses visitors in games and other added magic designed for all ages. Some of these fun experiences include trivia, music, and collectables!

Overall, Play Disney will score better with kids and tweens as the cartoonish appearance of the app seems catered to them. Teens and adults might enjoy the trivia which can be challenging at times. Play Disney is also better in small groups as the competition can heat up to see who scores the highest.

If you're planning on trying Play Disney, we recommend downloading the app before you leave home, that way you don't have to worry about poor connectivity or waiting to download a large file. The application is also a bit of a battery drainer, so make sure to pack a portable charger!

Some of the experiences can only be played while physically in the queue for a ride. For example, Space Mountain Rocket Race is a competitive mini game designed for 2-5 players, and will only open once your phone recognizes that you are near Space Mountain in Tomorrowland. However, some other experiences, like listening to music from around the park and Disney Parks Trivia, can be played anywhere—including home! Getting acquainted with the application and its features before you arrive will help with the fun of using it at the theme parks.

· **Magic Tips** ·
The Play Disney app also accesses special digital experiences at Disney's Art of Animation Resort. If you're interested in exploring these, you'll need to be at the hotel. We recommend taking a Disney Skyliner gondola to Art of Animation to play!

HEALTH AND SAFETY

In 2020, the COVID-19 pandemic shook the world. As international borders closed and statewide lockdowns were enforced, Disney had to follow suit. By mid-March 2020, all of the Disney Resorts closed worldwide. This included all of the theme parks, hotels, and shopping districts in Walt Disney World. For months these typically crowded spaces sat dormant, just waiting to see how the pandemic would play out.

About three months after Walt Disney World's closing, the resort began a phased reopening. The Disney Spring shopping district welcomed guests again on May 20, 2020. Its safety precautions included limited indoor capacity, physical distancing markers, temperature screenings, and required face coverings for all guests ages 2 and older. In July,  the four Disney World theme parks reopened to all guests. Over the course of a year and a half, Disney worked to open attractions, restaurants, and its hotels as interest in tourism grew.

Though the Walt Disney World Resort has since pretty much fully reopened, unforeseen events could see more resort-wide closures. While we don't expect the parks to shut down, it's possible that limited capacity, social distancing measures, and required masks will be used again. For example, guests may be required to wear face coverings inside indoor public spaces. Markers for physical distancing may also be placed in the queues. Furthermore, some attractions, dining experiences, and accommodations may limit their availability.

Since preparation is key—especially when planning a vacation, it's important to consider what health and safety measures might look like during your visit in 2022. Overall, we felt that Disney did an excellent job enforcing physical distancing, cleaning, and mask compliance. For the first several months, we only noticed a few guests not properly wearing their masks from time to time. However, by spring 2021, physical distancing was pretty much ignored and many more guests stopped properly wearing their masks.

Once vaccines became widely available, Disney dropped its physical distancing rules. However, the resort also changed its mask policies several times, so anything is possible in the new year.

LIMITED EXPERIENCES

Some rides, restaurants, menu options, and Resort hotels may be unavailable during limited capacity. Disney rolls out experiences based on demand, so if larger crowds are not present, restaurants and Resort hotels may not be available to accommodate guests. Disney updates the availability on their website and mobile application.

For the most part, character experiences, playgrounds, and live shows have the biggest setback during limited crowds. To maintain social distancing, large crowds cannot gather for parades, shows, and fireworks. Furthermore, guests should not come in close contact with Cast Members, including costumed characters. Instead, each theme park rolls out special cavalcades throughout the day. These are lively mini-parades with Mickey & Minnie, Disney Princesses, and other favorite characters. Expect music, dancing, and plenty of photo opportunities with characters as they drive by on floats. Though it's not the same as getting a hug from Mickey, Disney restores some of the lost magic with these special cavalcades.

> **· Magic Tips ·**
> Since we don't know which attractions, dining options, and hotels will be unavailable in 2022, we've included all of our reviews and recommendations in this guide. Just know that some experiences could be limited. Disney will likely inform you by e-mail if one of your experiences is cancelled.

EXPERIENCES THAT MAY HAVE LIMITATIONS OR CLOSURES:
1. Shows including fireworks and parades.
2. Character meet and greets, including dining events.
3. Disney Resort hotel perks including Early Theme Park Entry.
4. Special Events including Magic Mornings, After Hours, and Mickey's Not-So-Scary Halloween Party.
5. Restaurant availability.
6. Hotel amenities including kid club houses.
7. Parking lot trams to and from the theme parks.
8. Interactive touch features within the ride queues.

9. Physical ticket sales may be discontinued.
10. Cash payments may not be allowed.

DISNEY PARK PASS

To keep crowds limited, Walt Disney World requires a reservation for visiting the theme parks. The Disney Park Pass allows guests to reserve their chosen theme park dates. Reservation slots are broken into three categories: Annual Passholders, existing ticket holders, and Disney Resort guests. It appears that Disney gives priority to Disney Resort guests staying on property, as they often have the most availability.

If you're staying off property, your category would be "existing ticket holders." However, if you have a ticket or an annual pass but are staying on property, you're considered a Disney Resort guest. In some instances, you may find that your choice of theme park is booked up for the day.

Keep in mind that Disney may also limit when you can park hop. In the past, guests with park hopper tickets could visit all four theme parks whenever they'd like. However, new park hopping guidelines may make it so guests can only hop after 2pm.

· **Magic Tips** ·

Disney's Hollywood Studios and Magic Kingdom reservations book up faster than Epcot and Disney's Animal Kingdom.

CHAPTER TWO

WALT DISNEY WORLD'S 50TH ANNIVERSARY

50 YEARS OF MAGIC

On October 1, 2021, the Walt Disney World Resort celebrated its 50th anniversary. To commemorate this amazing milestone, Disney launched an 18-month long event called "The World's Most Magical Celebration." Guests are invited to celebrate at all four theme parks with new attractions, special merchandise, and shimmering "EARidescent décor."

We believe that Disney had bigger plans for this event, including the opening of new attractions in a much more timely manner. However, it appears that the closures due to the Covid-19 pandemic watered down the celebration. Nonetheless, we expect to see several surprises roll out in 2022.

MAGIC KINGDOM

Cinderella Castle comes to life with sparkling new additions. Gold ribbons swirl around the castle's spires along with a massive medallion commemorating 50 incredible years of magic. In addition, fifty golden statues of popular Disney characters dazzle guests near the castle!

New attractions include an all-new *Coco*-inspired scene added to the Mickey's PhilharMagic show in Fantasyland. At night, guests can view the breathtaking Disney Enchantment fireworks show with iconic music, characters, and incredible projections on Main Street, U.S.A.! We also expect that the highly anticipated Tron Lightcycle Run roller coaster will debut in Tomorrowland sometime in 2022.

CELEBRATION AT THE OTHER PARKS

Epcot, Disney's Hollywood Studios, and Disney's Animal Kingdom will all host special attractions for the 50th Anniversary. See EARidescent décor shimmer on park landmarks including Epcot's Spaceship Earth, Hollywood Studios' Tower of Terror, and Animal Kingdom's Tree of Life.

Epcot debuts its new lagoon show, Harmonious, a music-filled celebration of Disney with amazing special effects—including pyrotechnics! Disney's Animal Kingdom hosts a daytime attraction called Disney KiteTails. Performing multiple times throughout the day, guests can see kites and wind catchers bring to life iconic Disney animal characters.

OTHER NEW ATTRACTIONS

For guests who haven't visited the Walt Disney World Resort in over five years, you are in for a treat. Since 2017, Disney launched several amazing experiences all around the resort. Pandora — The World of Avatar takes guests into an immersive, 12-acre land based on the record-breaking *Avatar* film. Here, guests can fly over an alien world and travel by boat into a bioluminescent forest.

At Disney's Hollywood Studios park, Star Wars expands into a massive, 14-acre land! Star Wars: Galaxy's Edge brings guests into the fictional planet of Batuu. With amazing attractions, exotic shopping, delicious dining, and even an alien cantina, guests will spend hours exploring this adventurous new area.

New family-friendly rides like Mickey and Minnie's Runaway Railway and Remy's Ratatouille Adventure send guests through pure Disney magic. Each year, Epcot revamps its annual festivals with new dining experiences that adults love.

Finally, the Star Wars: Galactic Starcruiser experience flies fans into a galaxy far, far away. With immersive storytelling like no other, this two-day, two-night experience allows guests to become part of the Star Wars universe.

In addition, the classic Electrical Water Pageant received a special 50th anniversary float (more on this attraction later). We're incredibly excited that you're making a trip to the Walt Disney World Resort in 2022. There's so much to encounter and experience in this celebratory year. If you plan things right, this could be the best vacation ever!

CHAPTER THREE

BOOKING YOUR TRIP

INTRODUCTION

If you've never been to Walt Disney World, booking a vacation to the resort can feel overwhelming. While booking websites are extremely helpful, they don't give you a feel for what it's like to stay there or visit the parks firsthand. There are dozens of choices in and out of the resort, and they all seem to be fun and full of magic. The earlier you can begin planning your Walt Disney World vacation, the better. We recommend at least 6-8 months ahead of your trip in order to book the hotel and dining reservations.

If you're planning last-minute, there are several ways that you can save on booking a hotel. Depending on your plans, personality, and needs, some of the resort hotels will fit you better than others—that's where this chapter comes into play. Here, we outline how to save yourself money when booking so that you can pick your favorite hotel with ease (Chapter 13 covers hotels). You also might be wondering which park to check out and which ones you could afford to skip. If you are planning a week-long visit, we highly recommend getting a park hopper ticket so that you can visit any location when you want (more on that later).

DISNEY WORLD THEME PARKS

MAGIC KINGDOM
This park was designed as an alternate version of the original Disneyland Park. However, the Magic Kingdom is the most visited theme park in the world, so its walkways and attractions often hold more guests than Disneyland. Popular attractions like Space Mountain, Jungle Cruise, Big Thunder Mountain, and Peter Pan bring millions of guests in each year. Magic Kingdom has more attractions than anyone can experience in a single day, and is the ideal park for anyone looking for a day of pure Disney magic.

EPCOT
A unique theme park about innovation, the world, and the human experience! As the second park to open in Walt Disney World, Epcot can feel a little dated. Luckily, as it approaches its 40th anniversary in 2022, Disney is updating many of Epcot's attractions and walking areas. A foodie's park, Epcot is great for those looking to eat and drink around the world at the eleven represented countries. Stroll around a massive lagoon to pavilions designed like Mexico, Norway, France, and more! At night, stay for the awesome spectacular, Harmonious!

DISNEY'S HOLLYWOOD STUDIOS
With the addition of Star Wars: Galaxy's Edge and Toy Story Land, Hollywood Studios has become a prime destination at Walt Disney World. There are dozens of attractions, from stunning shows starring the characters from *Beauty and the Beast* to thrilling rides like The Twilight Zone Tower of Terror and the Rock 'n' Rollercoaster. Nothing will blow your mind more than the immersive galaxy of *Star Wars* brought to life in this epic, real-life adventure!

DISNEY'S ANIMAL KINGDOM
Perhaps the best themed park in the world, Disney's Animal Kingdom pulls guests into real-life tropical environments with live animals. In some ways, this park is like the Magic Kingdom meets a zoo—but each enclosure feels more like the wilderness than anything else. Animal Kingdom has over 500 acres of rides, lush foliage, and exotic animals.

Water Parks – Disney also has two distinct water parks, Typhoon Lagoon and Blizzard Beach. These well-designed parks are respectively themed after a post-storm beach and a snowed-over ski resort. If you are deciding which of the two water parks to visit, we recommend Typhoon Lagoon since the attractions are generally in more variety.

TIPS BEFORE YOU BOOK

PRE-BOOK YOUR HOTEL
The further out you book your vacation, the less expensive it tends to be. This is almost always true with flights, but the car rentals and hotels sometimes have better deals that fluctuate. If you are booking with the Walt Disney World Resort, they give you lots of wiggle room. You can change your bookings to add more dates or completely change your hotel just days before your travel dates. If the price changes or you cancel, you may have to pay a fee (usually around $50 for each package).

> **· Magic Tips ·**
> View theme park hours using the Walt Disney World app or by visiting WaltDisneyWorld.com. We recommend checking again before your visit as times often change.

FLY INTO ORLANDO INTERNATIONAL AIRPORT
If you are planning to fly, we recommend Orlando International because it tends to be the least expensive and easiest to travel from. The airport is located right next to highways that will take you to Walt Disney World. We review more of that in the next chapter.

BUNDLE FOR BIGGER SAVINGS
Sometimes purchasing a flight/hotel/car package from WaltDisneyWorld.com or a third party travel website can save you a lot of money. If you collect points with airlines like Southwest or Alaska, you can get even better points with the bundle.

DISCOUNTED TICKET OFFERS
Walt Disney World occasionally offers multi-day tickets at a discounted price. These deals occur seasonally when crowd levels and vacation package booking are at a low.
To get updated on these discounted offers, subscribe to our free e-mail newsletter: **www.magicguidebooks.com/list**

KNOW THE TICKET PRICE STRUCTURE

Park tickets vary in pricing for each day, sort of like a hotel or airline. If you book on a crowded day like a holiday weekend, the price will be more than if you book on a Tuesday or Wednesday outside of the busy season. Tickets are typically less expensive Monday through Thursday outside of summer and holidays.

GETTING THE BEST TICKET PRICE

Ticket prices decrease per day the more dates you visit. For example, a 2-day ticket could cost about $110 per day, but a 5-day ticket could cost about $90 per day. For this reason, sometimes it could save to book an extra day. It's best to play with ticket prices on WaltDisneyWorld.com before purchasing to score the best deal.

Tickets also have expiration dates depending on your number of days. This means that if your vacation lasts a week, but you only purchase a 4-Day ticket, you can space out your theme park visits over the course of a week.

FLEXIBLE DATE TICKETS

If you need more flexibility, the Flexible Dates add-on is about $20-$30 a day and allows tickets to be used any day before the end of the year (though they do expire 14 days after the first use). Ticket terms may change, so always check the fine print.

PARK HOPPER TICKETS

If you want to visit two or more theme parks in a single day, a Park Hopper ticket is the ideal upgrade. Park Hoppers are an extra $65 for a single day (the pricing goes down with multi-day purchases).

In previous years, when the theme parks had fewer attractions, we've highly recommended Park Hoppers. However, if you're looking to save money, there's now enough to do at each park for a one-park-per-day ticket. Conversely, if you're staying just a couple of days and want to see all of the parks in a short time, we recommend a Hopper ticket. Furthermore, if you're staying much longer (say, 10-14 days), and want flexibility for your vacation, a Hopper is also a great choice.

· **Magic Tips** ·
Park Hopping may have time restrictions. For example, you may have to reserve your first park in the day and will be allowed to hop at 2pm. However, after 2pm, you can visit as many parks as you'd like. In the event that a theme park is booked up for the day, you may not be allowed to hop to it. To check park capacity, call Disney's hotline: 407-560-500. It's possible that Disney will update these rules in 2022, so check DisneyWorld.com and any e-mail correspondence from Disney before your visit.

UK TICKET OFFERS
Disney has special offers for guests visiting from the United Kingdom. From a dedicated website, UK residents can book flight, hotel, and ticket bundles as well as access exclusive deals! The 14-Day Ultimate Ticket allows for park hopping at a heavily discounted price. Each year, Disney rolls out early free dining bundles for residents of the UK: **https://www.disneyholidays.co.uk/**

PHOTOPASS & MEMORY MAKER

Disney PhotoPass is a fantastic way to save digital versions of your vacation photos taken by resort-wide photographers. Several key spots are located around the resort including in front of the Cinderella Castle at Magic Kingdom, in Star Wars: Galaxy's Edge, and at character meets!

Some rides like Tower of Terror and Seven Dwarfs Mine Train have special videos that automatically sync to your Memory Maker when you have a MagicBand! Saving photos and videos onto your device is easily done through the Walt Disney World app. You'll only need one Memory Maker for your party and buying ahead saves about $30 ($169 total—typical price is $199).

Guests who purchase Memory Maker can access digital photos or purchase a USB. If you'd like to set up a photography session at a theme park, Disney will provide you a photographer for your time and location. Capture Your Moment is a commemorative product that allows 20-minute sessions are $50 each, or $100 for 40 minutes (comes with two locations). Theme parks may be limited to Magic Kingdom and Disney's Animal Kingdom.

DISCOUNT HOTELS

There are many ways to save on booking your stay. Some are better than others depending on the offer. Here are our most recommended choices based on how much they can save you:

WALTDISNEYWORLD.COM (407-939-1936)

Disney's home website is the only place to get a "Magic Your Way" package where you can bundle a resort hotel, park tickets, and a Disney Dining Package. When WaltDisneyWorld.com has hotel sales, usually the third-party websites will as well—but not always. WaltDisneyWorld.com often has the most variety of room choices, but rarely discounts tickets. At times, there may be a one-park-per-day discounted deal for multi-day tickets. These promotions aren't guaranteed and are often for off-season booking only.

Since discounted one-day theme park tickets are nearly impossible to find (sometimes you can save a few bucks a ticket through discounted sites), we recommend booking a hotel room with a third party website and your tickets through WaltDisneyWorld.com.

Walt Disney World will offer discounts even for spring and winter getaways. Check the website for discounts on hotels and more. Here, you can book any of the resort hotels, purchase theme park tickets, and add features like Disney Memory Maker.

SPECIAL DISCOUNTS
Always check this link before booking to see if you're getting the best deal. This link provides discounts for Military, Groups, and more: https://disneyworld.disney.go.com/special-offers

---

· **Magic Tips** ·
Sometimes the best deals come from using multiple sites. Try booking your hotel with Orbitz and your flight with an airline like Southwest or Alaska.

THE BEST WALTDISNEYWORLD.COM DEAL
The best promotion for Walt Disney World's website is the Free Dining Offer. The deal usually arrives in the spring (typically mid-April) and is available for dates August through December. To qualify for this discount, you often must book a select, full-price Walt Disney World Resort hotel and Park Hopper ticket package for each traveling member. In turn, you'll receive Disney Dining for free for each night of your stay per person. We've done the math and this deal can save you hundreds of dollars—if not thousands—during your stay! This deal is popular and reservations go quickly for the more popular resort hotels like Disney's Beach Club and Disney's Yacht Club.

PROS
1. For most packages, only $200 down is required to book. The balance is due around 30 days before your trip.
2. Larger selection of rooms that are not available on third-party sites (though the other way around can happen, too).
3. Bundle park tickets, dining packages, and features like Memory Maker.
4. You can add flights, transportation, character dining, and tickets to theme parks and water parks.
5. Often has flexible cancellation policies for full refunds.

CONS
1. The travel insurance is a lot pricier than most other sites.
2. Third party sites can generally save you more money.

ORBITZ.COM
Highly recommended!
Get discounts on rooms for your vacation at hotels in and around Walt Disney World. We love Orbitz because you can often use their promo code to get a discount on many hotel rooms and earn points that work like cash toward future bookings.

PROS
1. Option to pay in full upfront or at check-in.
2. Big discounts on flights when you book a vacation package that includes a rental car.
3. Easy to use website with rewards program.
4. Promotional discount codes routinely available.

CONS
1. Some of the better deals cannot be cancelled.
2. Orbitz usually has limited availability of hotel rooms within Walt Disney World, so they often run out quickly.

PRICELINE.COM
Great hotel selections and vacation packages on an easy to use site. It's hard to find promotional codes for Priceline, but they have great prices. If you're okay with any nearby resort, but wish to get a big discount, Priceline's Express deals might fit your needs. On their website, fill out your hotel preferences and you could save big on a hotel room. Sometimes you can even get a heavily discounted Disney-owned hotel!

AAA, AMEX TRAVEL, ETC.:
If you're an AAA member or American Express® card holder you may have access to another set of discounts. We highly recommend checking out your affiliated companies for exclusive deals.

BOOKING MULTIPLE HOTELS
If you'd like to stay in multiple Disney-owned hotels during your vacation, it's very possible! We recommend visiting a theme park on the day of your transfer. Just ask bell services to bring your luggage to the new resort and they'll be happy to deliver!

MAGICGUIDEBOOKS.COM
Check out our website for the latest discounts and deals for visiting Walt Disney World! We keep an updated list for both Disney-owned properties and other accommodations nearby.

ANNUAL PASSES

The Walt Disney World Resort offers several annual passes for its theme parks. One of these passes is available to anyone, while the others are reserved for Florida residents or Disney Vacation Club members. All passes are for ages 3 and up and include admission to all four theme parks, up to 20% off merchandise and dining, and complimentary parking. Passholders also get early access to special events, discounted event tickets, hotel deals, and more!

RESERVATIONS
Each pass type is limited to a certain number of reservations. Once you use a reservation, a new one will become available for booking via the Disney World app. Annual Passholders have a separate allotment of reservations than hotel guests and standard ticket holders. However, if you stay on a Disney property, you will likely have the allotment given to hotel guests. Generally there is more availability for hotel guests so this is usually a good thing!

DISNEY INCREDI-PASS – $1299 / $1,104 (renewal price), plus tax
Availability: All guests
Visit any of the four Walt Disney World Resort theme parks without blockout dates! This pass can hold up to 5 reservations at a time.

DISNEY SORCERER PASS – $899 / $764 (renewal price), plus tax
Availability: Florida residents and Disney Vacation Club members
Visit most days with very limited blockouts around Thanksgiving, Christmas, and New Year's Eve. Hold up to 5 reservations at a time with this pass.

DISNEY PIRATE PASS – $699 / $594 (renewal price), plus tax
Availability: Florida residents
Blockout days apply, mostly around popular holidays and spring break. The Pirate Pass allows for 4 theme park reservations at a time.

DISNEY PIXIE DUST PASS – $399 / $339 (renewal price), plus tax
Availability: Florida residents
Valid most weekdays outside of major holidays and spring break. Guests can hold 3 park reservations at a time with this pass.

MONTHLY PAYMENTS

Florida residents may be eligible to make payments on their Walt Disney World annual passes. A required $205 down payment is taken before 12 interest-free monthly payments. Disney usually does not require a credit check for these payments and guests can apply for this monthly program when signing up online.

· Magic Tips ·

If you're not a Florida resident, a Disney annual pass likely won't save you much money. Since out-of-state residents only have access to the expensive Incredi-Pass, you're usually better off purchasing a multi-day ticket, unless you plan to visit multiple times in a year.

ADD-ONS

Get a year of Disney PhotoPass added to your AP for $99 annually (plus tax). Disney Water Parks and Sports (including golf courses, ESPN Sports Complex access, and Disney miniature golf) can also be added for an additional $99 a year (plus tax).

For more AP information, details, and purchasing, visit:
https://disneyworld.disney.go.com/passes

· Magic Tips ·

You may be able to upgrade your ticket to an annual pass! Before the final day of its use, check for the upgrade button in your Walt Disney World app to see if your ticket is eligible.

SPECIAL EVENTS

DISNEY AFTER HOURS EVENTS

If you want to visit Walt Disney World without the crowds, the After Hours events are your best bet. Imagine being at the park with limited crowds, free snacks, and incredibly short wait times! This is exactly what you get with Disney's After Hours events.

Magic Kingdom, Hollywood Studios, and Animal Kingdom throw these 3-hour events on select nights. Since space is limited, popular attractions like Toy Story Land and Pandora rides have very short wait times (usually 15 minutes or less). Tickets start at $139 (plus tax) per guest and come with complimentary ice cream, popcorn, and some beverages.

EARLY MORNING MAGIC
Similar to the After Hours events, Early Magic Morning is an exclusive early event taking place before the parks open. These often are just 90 minutes, but come with breakfast. Prices start at $79 (plus tax) per guest. Overall, Early Morning Magic is for guests wanting to spend time in the parks without the crowds. So, if you're an early riser and don't mind the extra cost, this event is for you! It's also a great time to take photos around the parks without large amounts of other guests. This option may not be available in 2022.
Here are some tips for visiting during Early Morning Magic:
• <u>Buy Ahead</u> – This event is limited, so tickets could sell out.
• <u>Get There Early</u> – Guests who come early have been able to experience the attractions more frequently in the first 15 minutes.
• <u>Wait to Eat</u> – Everyone tends to eat at the start, but we recommend bringing a snack and eating after you've experienced the rides.

GO VIP

Walt Disney World offers several VIP tours to cut the lines, go behind the scenes, and see how some of the best dining experiences come to life. The 7-Hour Ultimate Day of Thrills VIP Tour starts at $349 per person and is offered on Mondays, Tuesdays, Fridays, and Saturdays starting at 8:30am. You'll need a park hopper ticket for this amazing and unforgettable experience.

Want more exclusiveness and luxury? If you're visiting Walt Disney World—with $12,000 to spare—book the World of Dreams Ultimate VIP Tour. Essentially, Walt Disney World will grant you as many wishes as you want during this time. Cut the lines to the ride, enter Cinderella Castle's secret chambers, go behind the scenes in Star Wars: Galaxy's Edge and more! Disney VIP services are top-notch experiences with the best hosts in the world—so don't forget to tip!

DISNEY VACATION CLUB

For those wishing to visit Disney properties year after year, Disney Vacation Club (DVC) may be a right fit. We only briefly overview DVC because we feel that an entirely new book can be created based on the ins and outs of this membership program. In short, Disney Vacation Club is a non-traditional timeshare. Members purchase points to use annually for stays at the Walt Disney World Resort, Disneyland Resort, Aulani in Hawaii, Disney Cruise Line, and many other exciting destinations around the world.

THINGS TO CONSIDER BEFORE BUYING DVC

1. **It's Not Cheap** – Disney is a premium company with premium prices, meaning that you will get the quality experiences for the money that you pay. DVC points can cost over $200 each, and the lowest nightly hotel rates for 2022 are around 10 points. In addition, you'll pay annual dues per point. These fees increase annually.

2. **Best for Frequent Guests** – How often do you plan to vacation at Walt Disney World? If you said every year or every other year, the DVC may be a great option that can save you money. It's more ideal if you can travel during the off-season (February or September) when hotels cost fewer points. The points also have a "use year" for the month that they expire. You can bank your points up to one year and borrow from the next. For example, if your use year is in September, your new points will be available then. If you want your trip in July, you can borrow from the points that will be available in September and combine them with your current points.

3. **Home Resort** – Points have home resorts, but they can be used at any DVC property. The benefit of a home resort is that you can book up to 11 months in advance there. For non-home resorts, you can book up to 7 months in advance.

4. **Early Bird Gets the Worm** – Those who can plan 11 months ahead usually come out on top. They snag all of the best properties right away and leave everyone else with the scraps. Resorts like Old Key West and Saratoga Springs often have plenty of availability for last-minute decision makers—as long as those resorts fulfill their needs.

5. **Financing** – Making payments on your DVC may be more affordable but it won't likely save you any money. Since DVC financing charges interest, it won't be a good deal in the end. The best way to purchase is upfront and in full.

6. **Some Benefits Aren't Guaranteed** – While Disney has amazing perks for members like discounted annual passes and free park nights like Moonlight Magic—where DVC members have exclusive access to a Disney theme park at no additional cost— these options don't always stick around. At one time, DVC offered discounted resort tickets—but not anymore. The only thing guaranteed is that your points won't lose value. Meaning, that if one hotel room price goes up a point, another one must go down a point.

7. **Limited Membership** – To keep the real estate at a specific value, only so many points can be sold per property. However, there may be a waitlist for a resort property of your choosing.

8. **Right to Refusal** – Disney has a first right of refusal for those selling their points. Since demand is so high, Disney may pay you for your points instead and resell them back to other members.

9. **More to Come** – Disney Vacation Club continues to add more resorts in the future as demand increases!

BUYING RESALE

If you want access to the membership perks of DVC, you'll need to buy your first 175 points through Disney directly. As of now, this is the only way to get the extra benefits. Those who buy resale aren't privileged to a digital membership card that accesses the special events, discounts, and more. You can always purchase more points at a cheaper price through resale after your initial 175 and still keep your benefits. There are several websites that offer Disney Vacation Club resale where buyers can add points.

· **Magic Tips** ·
Many of the food and merchandise discounts offered to Disney Vacation Club members are also available when you have a Disney Visa® card.

More Information About DVC:
https://disneyvacationclub.disney.go.com

CHAPTER FOUR

TRAVELING TO WALT DISNEY WORLD

INTRODUCTION

Contrary to what many believe, Walt Disney World is not exactly the heart of Orlando, Florida. The resort is located in Lake Buena Vista, Florida, which is about 20 miles southeast of the Orlando International Airport. It appears that most people who visit Disney World either drive or fly into Orlando International. If you have a family of three or more and live within a comfortable driving distance, then going by car might be your best bet. If you live on the other coast or the Midwest, driving might be a bit taxing. Thankfully, Walt Disney World has you covered no matter your form of transport. In fact, you can arrive at the resort via bus, train, shuttle, or a taxi!

When we visit Walt Disney World, we typically fly into Orlando International (though we have driven there before). Flying is great because as soon as you arrive, there are plenty of options to get to your hotel.

> **· Magic Tips ·**
> If you're looking for the complimentary Magical Express bus service provided for Disney hotel guests, it is unfortunately no more. Disney concluded this before 2022.

Many guests opt for a private car or rideshare apps (like Uber) to get to the Walt Disney World Resort. These are nice because the drivers tend to know the areas very well and they get you to your hotel quickly without stopping anywhere else. Typically, we've saved about 10-15 minutes in travel time. Expect to be charged anywhere from $30 or more each way. This is a standard price for these rideshare apps, and the private cars can cost up to $100. Whichever way you choose, we highly recommend planning ahead and having a back-up plan just in case. Taxis are always available in front of the airport to help get you to your destination. Just make sure to ask the driver if he or she has a flat fee. If you are driving yourself, the coastal routes are extremely scenic. We love driving up the middle of the state and seeing Florida's flat, lush landscapes, many lakes, and wildlife along the route. By the time you get to the resort, you'll be ready to hit the pool for relaxing—or the bed for some much-needed sleep.

In this chapter, we review the several different methods of getting to the resort. How you get there is entirely up to you, but if you're feeling indecisive (or just need more information in order to choose), read the next section thoroughly to get the best choices.

BY AIRLINE

If you aren't planning a road trip and live far away from the Walt Disney World Resort, flying will likely be your best option. While airlines can be expensive at times, there are several ways to save money:

+ Compare airlines to see the best pricing.
+ Check baggage fees and allowed carry-on items (we like Southwest because they give you 2 free checked bags). If you live on the East Coast, Spirit Airline is an à la carte option that can save you hundreds of dollars, especially on last-minute flights.
+ Book early to get the best discounts.

OUR TOP-CHOICE AIRLINES

SOUTHWEST
We love Southwest Airlines! If you grab their "Wanna Get Away" deals, you can score some great rates. Southwest works perfectly if you book ahead. If you are late to the game, they can get pretty pricey. Southwest's staff is friendly, the aircrafts are generally comfortable for long flights, they include snacks and soft drinks for free, and each passenger gets 2 free checked bags of luggage. This can be a *very* sweet deal if you plan on your Disney World vacation being longer than 5 days. This airline also does not charge for change fees, meaning, if you have to reschedule your flight for whatever reason, you can do so without charge during an allotted time period. Because Southwest offers first-come-first-served seating, we highly recommend paying the extra money to get the "Early Bird" option. This will allow everyone in your party to pick seats together for your flight. You can also ask any of their helpful flight attendants to assist with seating your family together, though it can't be guaranteed. Family boarding is called after the "A-list" section finds their seat (which is about one-third of the customers).

ALASKA
We also love Alaska! This is a friendly airline is well-know for great customer service and wide variety of flights. Book early enough and their rates are very affordable. Alaska gives you the free option to select your seat, but checked bags are often a moderately priced additional charge. They also offer free soft drinks and snacks for the flights. If you've never flown Alaska, we invite you to give them a try!

DELTA
Delta is a premium airline that excels in what it does. While it's not as innovative with its deals as Southwest, it does deliver fantastic flights and aircrafts. This is usually our third choice above other airlines like United or American because of its quality. Delta is often more expensive than Southwest or Alaska.

BUDGET AIRLINE OPTIONS

SPIRIT
This airline is *à la carte*, so the general price you see is just for a seat on the plane—everything else is an extra cost. The extra costs

include: picking your own seat, checking a bag or putting a bag in the overhead compartment, and drinks and snacks. If you don't mind where you sit and only need to bring a personal item, Spirit can save you some big bucks. Once you pick a seat and opt to bring another bag (carry-on bags are also extra), the prices begin to stack. Also, Spirit Airlines doesn't have much of a customer service department in our opinion. We've had an issue with a delayed flight and no one was there to assist at the gate. But we've had a good experience with them as well. Just understand that you usually get what you pay for and Spirit is no exception to that rule.

FRONTIER
Works similarly to Spirit and can get to be very pricey. We find that Spirit tends to have more comfortable seats than Frontier. If you're only on a two-hour flight or less, you may not mind.

FLYING INTO ORLANDO INTERNATIONAL
We recommend Orlando International because it tends to be the least expensive and easiest to travel from. The airport is located right next to the highways that will take you to the Walt Disney World Resort.

BY CAR

Whether you're on a road trip, staying in a neighboring city, or you live close enough to drive to the resort, this can be a great method to take in the beautiful sights of Florida's wetlands before you head to the Walt Disney World Resort. If you're flying, then renting a car might be the best option. You won't have much of a need for a car if you are staying on the property, however, a trip to Universal Orlando or other attractions outside of Walt Disney World might be more cost effective if you do have your own car.

CAR RENTAL
We recommend Enterprise.com or Dollar.com for car rental as they typically have a great selection and the best pricing. Pre-booking before you arrive at the airport is advised.

- www.Enterprise.com – You can visit the company's website or see typically better deals on Priceline.com (or bundle with your airfare and hotel booking).
- www.Dollar.com – Click the "specials" tab for deals.
- www.Budget.com – Click the "deals" tab for offers.

PARKING

- **Theme Parks** – Standard theme park parking costs $25 per day for a car or motorcycle and $30 per day for an oversized vehicle like an RV. Closer preferred parking can save up to 15 minutes in travel time into the parks and is $45-$50 per day (higher during summer, spring break, and holidays).
- **Water Parks** – Typhoon Lagoon and Blizzard Beach offer complimentary parking.
- **Resort Hotels** – Value resorts charge $15 per night; Moderate, $20 per night; and Deluxe, $25 per night.
- **Disability Parking** – Closer parking spaces are available for those with disability parking permits all across the resort. Parking attendants will guide guests to disability parking spots.

· Magic Tips ·

If you're staying at a Walt Disney World Resort hotel, you likely won't need a rental car. The bus transport around the resort is free and will save you money on rental costs as well as parking charges.

BY TRAIN

Taking the train can be a relaxing and beautiful way to travel to the Walt Disney World Resort. The trains let out at the Orlando Station (or Kissimmee) and you will need to have a second transport from the train station to the Resort which is roughly 20 minutes away by car. We recommend renting a car for the best value. Taxis work great, too.

AMTRAK

www.Amtrak.com

Perfect for longer distances on a budget (and if you have the time to travel). Check the "Deals" tab for discounts on Amtrak's website.

There are a few great reasons to take the train to the Walt Disney World Resort:

1. **Saves Money** – This is usually the top reason you might want to go with the train. Airfare and the train can cost ten times the amount.
2. **It's Relaxing** – The train can be a calming, easy way to travel from your home to Walt Disney World.

3. **A Discount** – Seniors and students can receive discounted rates with Amtrak.

BY BUS

We recommend Greyhound as our top pick for busses. They have a great reputation and are often the fastest way with the most options to get to Orlando. Keep in mind that the Orlando Bus Station is not near Orlando International or the Walt Disney World Resort. You'll need to take a private car into the resort or to your hotel—and that might cost you a lot of money.

BY RIDESHARE APP

Ridesharing apps like Uber and Lyft make great choices for traveling during your vacation. Both of these services offer private drivers in clean cars (these are not cabs). Here are a few ways you can book:

UBER / LYFT MOBILE DEVICE APPS
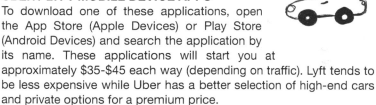
To download one of these applications, open the App Store (Apple Devices) or Play Store (Android Devices) and search the application by its name. These applications will start you at approximately $35-$45 each way (depending on traffic). Lyft tends to be less expensive while Uber has a better selection of high-end cars and private options for a premium price.

The estimated ride-sharing costs are just that—estimations. The time of day and traffic does matter. In these apps, you can select an estimated fare by entering your destination. You don't have to tip on these apps and the drivers won't ask for one. However, you may leave an additional tip once the ride has completed.

BY TAXI & SHUTTLE

Hail a taxi in front of the airport and ask for a flat rate. The typical price is usually around $45 each way. We recommend tipping your cab driver 15-20%, depending on your experience with the drive.

For a shuttle, we recommend Mears Connect. This service takes guests roundtrip from the airport to their resort hotel. Mears also promises short wait times once you've checked in and limited stops before connecting to your Disney Resort hotel. Prices start at $16 each way for adults and $13.50 for kids (ages 3-9). When compared to a standard Uber car, this isn't a great deal. However, guests with several bags may want to have a larger bus or van from Mears.

Booking: http://www.mearstransportation.com

DISNEY TRANSPORT

If you are staying off of the resort property and haven't elected to rent your own car, many hotels will offer a free or paid shuttle to the Walt Disney World Resort. Once inside of the resort, Disney offers a free bus transport to the hotels, parks, and parking lots. These are clean, standard busses that run day and night. After 1am, they will only run to the Disney World hotels. Look for the Bus Stop signs outside of each hotel, theme park, and Disney Springs. There are usually multiple locations outside of the gates of the parks. The bus line you desire will have your location marked on the display in front of the bus. Sometimes you may have a stop or two before your destination.

We have a love/hate relationship with the Walt Disney World bus system. On one hand, it's free and has excellent air conditioning. On the other, it can feel crowded at times and slow to arrive. Sometimes you have to do a bit of walking to get to your stop. We much prefer using the boats and the monorail system when they are available because they are much more enjoyable to ride. Walt Disney World also offers free ferries between some of the parks and Disney Springs as well as a monorail system around the Magic Kingdom Park and Epcot, each with separate loops that connect near Disney's Polynesian Resort. The monorail takes you to Disney's Contemporary Resort, Disney's Grand Floridian, and Disney's Polynesian. The ferries travel to all of those locations with trips to many other resort hotels and to Disney Springs.

DISNEY SKYLINER GONDOLAS

This new gondola system connects several resort hotels to Disney theme parks. These gondolas work very similarly to those at high-end ski resorts. A Disney feel with painted characters and music will play as you ride. This system connects Disney's Art of Animation, Pop Century, Caribbean Beach Resort, and the new Riviera to Epcot and Hollywood Studios, emptying in front of both theme parks. The gondolas move at a moderate speed over land and water. While they aren't air conditioned, the cabins are designed with ventilation systems to keep them cool. Each gondola holds about ten guests and has benches for seating.

MINNIE VANS (POSSIBLY DISCONTINUED)

Lyft and Disney teamed up to create a unique on-demand transport within the Walt Disney World Resort! These polka dot vans look like Minnie Mouse's dress and operate using the Lyft mobile app. The driver can also answer any questions you have about Walt Disney World during your ride. Rides range from about $25-$35 each way and the cars hold up to six passengers. Minnie Vans also drop off guests right in front of the theme parks, so if you're running late, this might be a great option instead of the bussing system. Minnie Vans also take guests to and from Orlando International Airport (you can pre-book this with your Disney vacation package, when available).

CHAPTER FIVE

WHAT TO WEAR AND BRING

INTRODUCTION

Now that you've planned your vacation, it's time to figure out what to wear! Luckily, this part is easy (and to experienced theme park travelers, it's common knowledge). Walt Disney World is filled with people from all walks of life, style, and attitude. But everyone is there for the same reason: *to have fun*! The important thing is to be yourself! Here we explain how to maximize your fun through comfortable clothing and bringing the right items. Did you know that a bottle of water at the Walt Disney World theme parks can cost $4 or more? Be aware that security will inspect your bags before you enter the parks. There also may be a metal detector. In this section, we review tips and tricks for a comfortable and cost-effective stay at the resort.

WHAT TO WEAR AND BRING

1. **Comfortable Clothing** – Shorts, T-shirts, sneakers (trainers), and tank tops are seen all around the resort for a good reason: they are comfortable. You'll be standing in the hot (and often humid) Florida sun all day, so we recommend that you dress comfortably.

2. **Hats and Sunglasses** – Again, the Floridian sun! It's a wonderful thing, but you don't want to get burned. Be careful of hats and sunglasses on rides (most high-speed attractions will have a compartment on the ride for you to store your items).

3. **Sunscreen** – Even on a cloudy day the ultraviolet rays from the sun can give you an uncomfortable burn. Be careful and stay protected—you don't want to ruin your vacation by looking and feeling like a boiled lobster.

4. **Stroller** – Kids can get tired and Walt Disney World has zones to park these with attendants that watch them while you ride. You can bring your own or rent one at one of the parks. If you're worried that your child may be too tired to walk around all day, it's best to use caution and set aside extra cash for a stroller rental. For longer stays, the Walt Disney World Resort gives a bit of a discount.

    Stroller Rental Cost:
    - Single – $15 per day / $13 for multi-day
    - Double Stroller – $31 per day / $27 for multi-day
    Note: Disney Springs requires a $100 credit card deposit in addition to the daily cost. This is done for theft prevention reasons since anyone can walk in and out of Disney Springs and take the strollers they've rented.

5. **Jacket or Sweater** – Hot days at the Walt Disney World Resort can become chilly nights. Therefore, we highly recommend bringing a jacket or sweater just in case.

6. **Water Bottles and Snacks** – You can save money (or help any picky eaters in your party) by bringing your own snacks. Walt Disney World will allow you to bring sealed bottles of water into the parks. Save yourself money and bring your own. If you don't mind fountain water, you can refill them at water fountains near any restroom for free.

7. **Hand Sanitizer** – Though we know that science tells us not to use hand sanitizer on a daily basis, it's virtually a must-have at the parks. You'll likely touch handrails, seat cushions, and many other things that will require you to disinfect before eating.

8. **Face Covering** – Guests may be required to wear a face covering during their stay. Bring one that fits Disney's current guidelines listed on WaltDisneyWorld.com. Disney also sells branded masks at the stores within the parks, hotels, and Disney Springs. You will likely need one that fits over your mouth and nose, is made of breathable material, has loops or ties, and doesn't have mesh or holes.

9. **Extra Phone Charger and Waterproof Cellphone Bag** – If you have a smartphone, we highly recommend an extra portable charger. We also recommend becoming familiar enough with your smartphone so that you can turn on the battery-saver mode in the settings. This will prevent you from running out of juice too early while you take pictures and use the Walt Disney World app. Also, if you plan on riding the water attractions like Splash Mountain or Kali River Rapids, you're likely to get soaked. The last thing you want is to accidentally drench your cellphone! We *highly* recommend bringing a plastic sandwich baggie to safely store your cellphone.

10. **A Standard Backpack** – Carry your items in one of these. Make sure it's not too large to fit on the rides. Also keep in mind that your bag will be checked by security before entering the park area. If you don't feel like lugging it around all day, rent a locker and store it in there.

11. **Money** – The Walt Disney World Resort accepts all major credit cards. If you are staying at a Walt Disney World Resort hotel, you can link  your MagicBand to your credit card for easy paying. The Walt Disney World Resort accepts the following credit cards: Visa®, MasterCard®, American Express®, Discover®, Diners Club®, and the Japan Credit Bureau.

12. **Identification** – For adults, make sure you plan on bringing your government-issued ID if you plan to drink alcoholic beverages. At times, you may be asked to present ID when purchasing at shops in Disney Springs.

13. **Water Resistant Clothing** – Rainstorms in Orlando are highly unpredictable. In the summer, the rain will last under an hour, but you don't want to wear something that can't get wet. Leave the suede shoes and stick to cotton shirts. Just in case you don't want to deal with the rain, this is what we recommend bringing with you:
   • Compact Umbrella – On rainy days, this is very handy. Don't bring a full-sized umbrella, as it won't fit on rides and will be difficult to carry around.

- Poncho – It might be a bit of a fashion *faux pas* to some, but a poncho could keep you and your belongings dry. Many visitors love wearing these on the water rides.

> **· Magic Tips ·**
> If you forget any of these items, Disney World sells them. Check the shops near the entrances to any of the parks for some of these items.

WHAT NOT TO WEAR AND BRING

1. **Ice** – Loose ice isn't permitted as it is a safety hazard, though ice packs are allowed. If you need ice, ask quick-service restaurants for a cupful.

2. **Selfie Sticks** – It seems like it would be so much fun to take photos with one of these, but Walt Disney World bans them for the safety of other guests.

3. **Adult Costumes and Masks** – Children under 14 are allowed to wear costumes; but as not to trick people into thinking a non-Cast Member is a character, Walt Disney World bans these for adults. During Mickey's Not-So-Scary Halloween Party, adults may dress in costume. For safety reasons, adults are not allowed to wear masks to the park.

4. **Skateboards, Rollerblades, Bikes, Roller Skates** – Walt Disney World bans these for safety reasons. Even those skates that slide out from kids' shoes are banned. If you need a vehicle, you may rent a scooter or wheelchair from Guest Services to the right of the Walt Disney World entrance gates.

5. **Remote Control Toys and Drones** – Sorry, but not allowed— even in Tomorrowland.

6. **Your Pet** – Animals are not permitted in any of the six parks, Disney Springs, most of the hotels, or any of the transportation at the Walt Disney World Resort. Although, some of the campsites at Fort Wilderness do allow dogs. If you need a place for your pet during your stay, the resort offers pet boarding and kennels at Best Friends Pet Care, located near Disney Springs and the Port Orleans Resort hotels. The facility is huge, air conditioned, and a premium resort for your pet. They offer dozens of trained pet caregivers to accommodate your family's furry member while you enjoy the resort.

Accommodations include play and grooming services for both dogs and cats. Your length of stay will determine the pricing. For more information, please visit:
www.bestfriendspetcare.com (advanced reservations required along with proof of certain vaccines).

7. **Alcoholic Beverages** – These are not allowed in the parks (though adults 21 and over with a valid ID may purchase alcoholic drinks at all theme parks).

8. **Lawn Chairs** – You might be tempted to bring these to watch a parade, but Walt Disney World bans them. We assume it's to keep the resort's aesthetics from looking like a 4th of July picnic.

9. **Glass Bottles** – Another safety precaution. However, small glass containers of baby food are allowed.

10. **Cigarettes** – Walt Disney World has banned smoking inside its theme parks. Designated smoking areas are located outside of each theme park and water park entrance. Disney Springs and Walt Disney World Resort hotels have several smoking spots around their properties. Use the search tool on the Walt Disney World app to find a list of designated smoking areas around the resort.

11. **Bags with Wheels and Hiking Backpacks** – It's okay to bring these into the hotels, but you'll need to leave them out of the parks.

12. **Wrapped Gifts** – For inspection reasons, you cannot bring wrapped gifts into the parks. If you plan on giving someone a present, use a gift bag.

BACKUP PLANS

Rent a Locker

There's no need to tire yourself out with a hefty backpack when a locker that fits your belongings starts at just $8/day plus a $5 key deposit. Larger lockers are $10/day with a $5 key deposit. You get the deposit back when you return the key. The water parks have a different cost at $10/day for regular-sized lockers and $15/day for large-sized lockers. The water park lockers work with a 4-digit pin that you create in order to keep your belongings safe and secure. Most theme parks have locker storage inside and outside of the entry gates.

Locker Locations

- Magic Kingdom – Just before Main Street, U.S.A. outside of the gates.
- Epcot – Bus Stop outside of the park, International Gateway at the entrance, and near the Camera Center.
- Hollywood Studios – at the entrance and near the bus stop.
- Animal Kingdom – Expedition Everest and Kali River Rapids.
- Typhoon Lagoon – There are two: at the entrance and just after the entrance.
- Blizzard Beach – There are two: at the entrance, and to the right after you enter.

Plan a Midday Return to Your Hotel – If you don't want to rent a locker, make a plan to return to your hotel midday. There you can eat, refill on drinks, and maybe take a power nap. When you're refreshed, head back to the parks for more fun!

Get Park Hoppers – Sometimes you don't get everything done in one day and if the extra cost works with your budget, the Park Hopper is the way to go. This pass allows you to visit any of the four main theme parks in a single day (though there is a water park option as well).

CHAPTER SIX

SKIPPING THE LINES

NO MORE WAITING

On average, our readers worry the most about waiting in long lines during their Walt Disney World trip. Over the decades, guests have complained about spending hours in a queue for a ride that only lasts a couple of minutes. Disney is super conscious of this common guest complaint. As millions flock to the Walt Disney World Resort each year, the company wants to give the best impression for its visitors—after all, a glowing word-of-mouth review is the best marketing!

To combat the long lines, Disney has implemented features like Virtual Queues to keep guests out of the lines. For Disney, having guests roaming the parks is a big win because they'll often spend money when they're not waiting in line. With so much fun food and immersive shopping experiences, it only makes sense that guests would rather shop and dine than wait in a one-hour line for Space Mountain.

In the past, Disney used FastPass+ to help guests skip long lines. However, this product was replaced by the updated Disney Genie, an in-app tool for avoiding long wait times. When Star Wars: Rise of the Resistance opened in 2019, Disney World implemented a new Virtual Queue option. Using Disney's mobile app, guests can snag a virtual place in line and return to the attraction when called.

Disney says that it plans to keep Virtual Queues well into the future. However, both Genie and Virtual Queues have a number of flaws that can make them not-so-user-friendly. In this chapter, we give you the best tips for using these products to skip the lines.

DISNEY VIRTUAL QUEUE

INTRODUCTION

When Disney first introduced the epic Star Wars: Rise of the Resistance, they ran into a giant issue: more guests wanted to ride the attraction than there were available seats in a day. To keep up with the demand, Disney developed a virtual "boarding pass" for this attraction. This new system works separately from products like the Disney Genie and allows guests to reserve their spot in line for a specific attraction.

HOW THE VIRTUAL QUEUE WORKS

To obtain a ride "boarding pass" in the Virtual Queue, guests need the My Disney Experience mobile app on their phone and park tickets linked to their account. Boarding passes "drop" at pre-determined times throughout the day, typically before the park opens and again later in the afternoon. During these drops, guests should move quickly to reserve spots for their party. On an average day, boarding groups are often gone in *seconds*!

Once a guest joins a boarding group, they will see an estimated wait time on the app, and will be notified via a pop-up message when it is their time to return to the attraction. Typically, guests have an hour to return to the ride (the pop-up message sends an alert from the app). The app issues each member of your party a code that is scanned by the Cast Member at the start of the attraction's queue.

However, rules often change for how Virtual Queues work. For example, when Rise of the Resistance first opened, guests could only join the Virtual Queue from *inside* Disney's Hollywood Studios. When the parks reopened, new rules allowed guests access to the Virtual Queue beginning at 7am each day from anywhere—including their home or hotel room. A second time slot was added at 1pm for guests once they scanned into Disney's Hollywood Studios. Only guests with a reservation for Hollywood Studios could ride Rise of the Resistance that day.

Since Virtual Queue rules change often, we recommend reviewing them in the Disney World app before your visit. You can also get updates about the Virtual Queue via our free e-mail newsletter: **www.magicguidebooks.com/list**.

VIRTUAL QUEUE TIPS

One or more attractions may use a Virtual Queue during your visit. Disney may also change which attractions use boarding passes with this queue. Whatever the case, here are some tips for grabbing one:

Link Your Party – Before you head to the parks, you'll need to link all of your party's theme park tickets to Disney World's My Disney Experience app. This can be done by scanning the barcodes or entering them manually under "Tickets and Passes" in the app's menu. Each person must also have a theme park reservation for that day. You can also confirm your party in the app one hour before each Virtual Queue release time.

Designate Someone – Though multiple people in your party can try for a boarding pass at the same time, we don't recommend it. Disney Cast Members have warned us that having multiple people access the queue with the same tickets could confuse the system. We've tried both methods and have found that having one person on one device is the most reliable.

A Refreshing Start – Before you try for the Virtual Queue, look for the tab under the Disney World app's menu (it's also usually on the main screen). When you enter the "Join Boarding Group" screen, it will refresh. The page will not show a "Join" button until the time has dropped. You may also be able to drag down the screen and let go to refresh the page right when the time comes.

Full Bars – We highly recommend that you have a reliable signal on your phone before trying for a boarding pass. So give yourself a few minutes before the time drops to find a nice spot. We also recommend against using Disney's Wi-Fi as it is often much slower than cellphone carriers.

> · **Magic Tips** ·
> Need a reliable connection? The Animation Courtyard in Disney's Hollywood Studios often has strong cellular signal for joining the Virtual Queue!

Right on Time – Since boarding groups book up in seconds, time is of the essence. Disney apparently syncs its clock with the official one on www.time.gov. We recommend having one person in your party holding their phone to show the Eastern Daylight Time on this website. As soon as the time strikes, the boarding group portion of the app should be refreshed. If successful, a "Join" button will appear. Tap to join as quickly as possible!

Keep Moving – There may be a few screens to move through before securing boarding passes. Keep moving through the screens until you've seen that you are successful!

DISNEY GENIE

INTRODUCTION

As you may have realized by now, planning a trip to the Walt Disney World Resort can feel overwhelming. Even if you're a meticulous planner, it still can be very tricky to get everything lined up in the right way during your stay. After all, unpredictable things like attraction closures, weather, and other factors can literally put a damper on your plans. We've noticed that, over the years, organizing a trip to Disney World has required more and more pre-planning. Almost to the point where it could feel like a chore.

So to overcome all of these planning issues, Disney introduced a new product to help guests manage their visit. Disney Genie is supposed to work like "magic" by giving suggestions, forecasts, and recommendations to plan their day. Using the Walt Disney World app, guests tell Genie which attractions, dining, and other experiences they would like to enjoy. Genie goes to work by building daily itineraries for the visit.

While all of that sounds amazing on paper, there are some major flaws. For example, everything Genie tells guests is through Disney's filter. Meaning, you won't hear that a suggested restaurant actually has lackluster food. Nevertheless, Disney Genie does update with suggestions for the shortest wait times. While it's nice to get up-to-date alerts, you may find yourself feeling a bit lost with Genie's suggestions. But if you're up for some spontaneity, this feature could work very well for you.

· **Magic Tips** ·
Disney Genie and Genie+ have completely replaced the now retired FastPass+. You will no longer be able to book FastPass+ reservations for any attractions in the parks.

HOW TO USE DISNEY GENIE

1. Sign in to the Walt Disney World app and make sure that your park tickets are linked to your account.
2. Before your visit, you can start creating your itinerary by punching in your requests in Disney World's app. Find the Genie button in the app's menu.
3. If you have dining reservations, Genie will automatically plug them into your itinerary.
4. When you're ready to visit the parks, Genie will give you suggested times to experience your choice of attractions. Like we said earlier, these suggestions may also update throughout the day to improve your experience.

DISNEY GENIE+

Though Disney Genie is free, it does have paid options for guests wishing to skip the lines on their own. Disney Genie+ costs $15 per person, per day, and allows guests to use a "Lightning Lane" to skip the lines at all four theme parks. You may have already guessed but the Lightning Lanes are just the former FastPass+ lines renamed. These dedicated lines form separately from the standard queues to skip the bulk of the wait. Lightning Lanes can save you hours of waiting in long lines in one day.

ABOUT LIGHTNING LANES

Dozens of attractions at the Walt Disney World Resort have access to the Lightning Lanes. Most of these are accessible with the Disney Genie+ paid feature. You will not be able to use a Lightning Lane without paying for it.

Guests are able to book one attraction at a time. Lightning Lanes are restricted to once per ride per day. Meaning, you cannot use Lightning Lane for the same attraction in one day. Once you've used a Lightning Lane, you'll be able to book another with Genie+.

The $15 per day fee works at all four parks in a single day. Just keep in mind that park hopping restrictions may prevent you from using Genie+ at other parks.

However, some attractions have Lightning Lanes that do not work with Genie+. Popular rides including Star Wars: Rise of the Resistance and Avatar Flight of Passage require guests to pay an *à la carte* fee for these Individual Lightning Lanes. Prices range from about $7-$15 and can vary depending on how busy the parks are during your visit. Guests are also limited to two Individual Lightning Lane reservations per day.

> **· Magic Tips ·**
> You can mix and match paying for Disney Genie+ and Individual Lightning Lanes. However, you do not have to pay for Genie+ to buy an Individual Lightning Lane and vice versa. Furthermore, no attraction requires that you pay for the Lightning Lane to experience it. You'll just need to wait in the regular standby line instead.

WHO SHOULD GET DISNEY GENIE+

1. **Love to Ride** – Guests who want to experience as many rides as they can in one day should certainly consider Disney Genie+. You may be able to experience twice as many rides in a single day with Lightning Lane.
2. **Sleeping In** – If you like to sleep in, Genie+ is a great feature. You won't need to get to the parks at opening to have shorter wait times. However, we still recommend getting to the parks by late morning to maximize your Disney Genie+ benefits.
3. **Magic Kingdom** – The Magic Kingdom has by far the best deal for using the Lightning Lane. Over 15 attractions here use Disney Genie+, far more than the other parks but for the same price.
4. **Park Hopping** – Since Genie+ works at all of the parks, you'll be able to book your next attraction before you leave. Since other parks can become busy midday as guests hop, we think Disney Genie+ can be well worth your money to skip the lines.

5. **Breakfast with Characters** – Some of the best times to meet characters is at one of the breakfast spots. If you've booked a character breakfast and want to enjoy the parks after, you may see that lines increase once you arrive. You'll be able to book your Lightning Lane reservations while dining and then head to the attraction once you've finished.

WHEN NOT TO GET DISNEY GENIE+

1. **Slow Days** – We don't recommend getting Disney Genie+ on very slow days. If you're seeing Big Thunder Mountain at a 15-minute wait and Jungle Cruise at 10 minutes, it may be a waste of money to upgrade.

2. **Very Busy Days** – Though Disney Genie+ is limited in quantity per day, guests may find using it on very busy dates difficult. For example, you may only get to use the Lightning Lane a few times on a very busy day. Even worse, you'll still have to wait in very long lines for rides not covered by Disney Genie+. In this instance, it may be better to pay *à la carte* to skip the lines for rides like Seven Dwarfs Mine Train and Avatar Flight of Passage.

3. **Epcot Day** – If you're only planning to visit Epcot for the day, Disney Genie+ may not be worth the money. There simply aren't enough rides here to make sense for the money. Worst of all, two of the most popular rides in the park—Remy's Ratatouille Adventure and Frozen Ever After—don't work with Genie+. However, if you're planning a day with Epcot and another theme park, then Genie+ becomes much more valuable.

4. **Long Vacation** – If you're planning for a long vacation, you may not need the Genie+ upgrade for each day of your trip. Instead, you may wish to put the money toward extra days on your park tickets to visit more often.

5. **For Moral Reasons** – It's clear that we live in a world of "haves and have-nots," but are products like Disney Genie+ digging that line even deeper? After all, Lightning Lanes used to be free when they were part of FastPass+. So arguably, Genie+ is just a product that only gives FastPass+ to families with money.

DISNEY GENIE+ TIPS

1. **Be Dedicated** – Dedicate one person in your party to be in control of booking the Lightning Lanes. This will make it much easier to get the same time slot as the rest of your guests.

2. **Don't Be Drained** – Carry a portable battery to charge the phone in case your battery drains.

3. **Get Ready** – Genie+ reservations may be redeemed by scanning the barcode on your phone, MagicBand, or individual park ticket.
4. **Time for Seconds** – If your Lightning Lane reservation is later in the day, you can book a second reservation two hours after booking the first. For example, if your Lightning Lane reservation is for 5pm but you reserved it at 12pm, you'll be allowed to book a second reservation two hours later at 2pm.

GENIE+ RECOMMENDATIONS

We've listed the Genie+ reservations by their demand and wait time length. High and Very High attractions book the quickest while Low and Very Low attractions may not need Lightning Lane purchases:

$\sum$ = Individual Lightning Lane attractions that do not work with Disney Genie+

MAGIC KINGDOM

The Barnstormer	Very Low
Big Thunder Mountain Railroad	Medium
Buzz Lightyear's Space Ranger Spin	Medium
Dumbo the Flying Elephant	Low
Haunted Mansion	Medium
"it's a small world"	Low
Jungle Cruise	Medium
Mad Tea Party	Low
The Magic Carpets of Aladdin	Low
The Many Adventures of Winnie the Pooh	Low
Mickey's PhilharMagic	Low
Monsters, Inc. Laugh Floor	Very Low
Peter Pan's Flight	High
Pirates of the Caribbean	Medium
Seven Dwarfs Mine Train $\sum$	Very High
Space Mountain $\sum$	Very High
Splash Mountain	High
Tomorrowland Speedway	Medium
Under the Sea – Journey of The Little Mermaid	Low

EPCOT

Disney & Pixar Short Film Festival	Very Low
Frozen Ever After $\sum$	High
Journey Into Imagination With Figment	Very Low

Living with the Land	Low
Mission: SPACE (Green and Orange)	Medium
Remy's Ratatouille Adventure ∑	Very High
Soarin'	Medium
Spaceship Earth	Medium
Test Track	High
The Seas with Nemo & Friends	Low
Turtle Talk With Crush	Low

> **· Magic Tips ·**
>
> We expect that the Disney Genie+ list will update in the future to include more attractions. For example, we expect TRON: Lightcycle Run and Guardians of the Galaxy: Cosmic Rewind to use both a Virtual Queue and Lightning Lane without Genie+. Space Mountain and Frozen Ever After could then join the list of Disney Genie+ attractions once this happens. Get updates on Genie+: subscribe to our free e-mail newsletter at www.magicguidebooks.com/list

DISNEY'S HOLLYWOOD STUDIOS

Alien Swirling Saucers	Medium
Beauty & The Beast Live on Stage	Low
Disney Jr. Dance Party	Low
For the First Time in Forever: A Frozen Sing-Along Celebration	Low
Indiana Jones Epic Stunt Spectacular	Medium
Mickey & Minnie's Runaway Railway ∑	Very High
Millennium Falcon: Smugglers Run	High
Muppet*Vision 3D	Very Low
Rock 'n' Roller Coaster	High
Slinky Dog Dash	Very High
Star Tours – The Adventures Continue	Medium
Star Wars: Rise of the Resistance ∑	Very High
Toy Story Mania!	Medium
The Twilight Zone Tower of Terror	High

DISNEY'S ANIMAL KINGDOM

The Animation Experience at Conservation Station	Low
Avatar Flight of Passage ∑	Very High
Celebration of the Festival of the Lion King	Medium
DINOSAUR	Medium
Expedition Everest ∑	Medium

Feathered Friends in Flight!	Very Low
It's Tough to be a Bug!	Very Low
Kali River Rapids	Low
Kilimanjaro Safaris	High
Na'vi River Journey	Medium

> **· Magic Tips ·**
> See our Genie+ booking recommendations by interest and age group in our Pre-Planned Attraction Lists chapter.

OTHER DISNEY GENIE+ FEATURES

Your purchase of Disney Genie+ also comes with augmented reality lenses to capture very cool snaps around the park. See Cinderella Castle with retro overlays and other effects at Walt Disney World. These filters can usually be used even after you're home from vacation! You'll also get a tour with Audio Tales that gives you secrets about the theme parks as you travel through them.

NOT USING THE DISNEY GENIE

Though the Disney Genie is interesting technology, you may not have much use for it. Perhaps you're not that tech savvy or you just don't want to bother using your phone all day. That's totally fine! In fact, we've designed our tips so that you don't have to rely on the Genie at all to have fun in the parks.

With that said, it's still pretty difficult to get away from technology in Walt Disney World. As Disney sees more and more guests staring at their phone screens around the parks, it makes sense to use these devices around the Resort. However, there could be instances when the technology fails. For example, if you're unable to install an application or connect to the internet, things could get sticky. Even worse, something might happen to your device, rendering it useless during your vacation. If this were to happen, we recommend talking with a Cast Member during your visit. There are often several around the parks at various information desks waiting to assist guests. If plans aren't working out, don't give up before talking to one of them. From our experience, Disney can work wonders to make good when things go wrong!

CHAPTER SEVEN

THE MAGIC KINGDOM

INTRODUCTION

The Magic Kingdom is Walt Disney World's epicenter and most beloved theme park. Designed after the original Disneyland concept, the Magic Kingdom offers a world-class experience into the heart of Disney. With 20 million annual visitors, the Magic Kingdom is the most-visited theme park in the world! It opened in 1971 and has over 100 square acres of classic rides, roller coasters, themed lands, delicious food, beautiful scenery, a massive lake, and, of course, the iconic Cinderella Castle.

The six sizable lands are all differently themed and have their own set of rides. Main Street, U.S.A. is the gateway into the stunning park. Though Main Street feels like a tempting beginning, the allure of the distant castle will have your feet moving toward Fantasyland with rides designed for families with young kids. Adventureland is like walking into a dense jungle, and Frontierland places you in the heart of the Wild West! Liberty Square rounds out the classic experiences with its unique, American attractions, and Tomorrowland pulls guests into the future where anything is possible!

There are nearly countless things to do in the lands of the Magic Kingdom, but we've reviewed every single one of them to give you

the best planning opportunity. In this section, we explore everything from the rides to the spectacular shows that bring the magic of Walt Disney's Kingdom!

MAGIC KINGDOM WELCOME SHOW

The Let the Magic Begin welcome show takes place in front of Cinderella Castle on most mornings. Guests are greeted by Mickey Mouse and several other characters. The 5-minute show has music, special effects, and can be very popular. We recommend arriving at least 30 minutes before park opening to catch this event.

"THE KISS GOODNIGHT"

Guests who stay until the closing of the Magic Kingdom are treated to a special, somewhat unofficial show. Cinderella Castle dazzles as an announcement plays over the speakers. Disney worked carefully on this special announcement, making certain that you'll feel the last bit of magic it has to offer before you leave. While the Kiss Goodnight isn't as spectacular as the Welcome Show, it still leaves you with some good feelings.

MAIN STREET, U.S.A.

The Magic Kingdom's iconic grand entrance is filled with shops, dining, and a magnificent view of the castle. The first thing you'll notice is the train station, beautiful flower arrangements, and smiling faces. Choose the left or the right side of the entrance to find yourself in a hub of horse-drawn street cars and Disney characters waiting to greet you.

Theme: Turn-of-the-century American town—specifically, Walt Disney's hometown of Marceline, Missouri in the early 20th century

RIDES

WALT DISNEY WORLD RAILROAD
Best for: Young Kids, Adults 50+

Description: This iconic, relaxing steam train moves around the perimeter of the park. It's a 20-minute ride over a mile and a half of track. Other stops include Frontierland and Fantasyland.
Level: Everyone
Recommendation: Best if you are looking for a way to stay out of the sun and appreciate a leisurely experience. Tweens, Teens, and Thrill Riders may not enjoy this experience as much.
Line Length: Short / **Lightning Lane:** No
Refurbishment: This attraction may be closed for part of the year as construction begins on the *Tron* roller coaster (set to open in 2022).

SHOWS AND ATTRACTIONS

TOWN SQUARE THEATRE
Best for: Young Kids, Kids, Family
Description: Meet Mickey Mouse in this stunning theatre.
Level: Family
Recommendation: This is your best opportunity for a photo with Mickey Mouse. Other characters like Tinker Bell and Disney Princesses show up throughout the day. Check the Walt Disney World app for character times on the day of your visit.
Lightning Lane: No

DISNEY ENCHANTMENT FIREWORKS
Best for: Everyone of all ages!
Description: An epic new fireworks and image projection show around Cinderella Castle!
Level: Everyone
Recommendation: Conclude your day with this stunning fireworks display that dazzles the sky while projecting magical displays on Cinderella Castle and Main Street, U.S.A. We recommend standing in the middle of Main Street to get the best view of the projections and the Castle as fireworks burst from above. Get there 30-60 minutes before showtime to secure your spot. Most crowds will gather closer to Cinderella Castle and may wait hours before showtime.

Outside Viewing: Disney hotels like the Grand Floridian, Contemporary, and Polynesian have excellent viewing of the fireworks. However, you may not be able to see the projections very well. We also recommend making a dining reservation at the California Grill for fantastic viewing around showtime. The restaurant also plays the fireworks theme music and dims the lights when the show starts!

· Magic Tips ·
Reserve your seat for the Disney Enchantment fireworks by booking one of the exclusive dessert parties. These are very pricey ($114 per adult and $69 for kids) but offer prime viewing from Tomorrowland Terrace and a variety of tasty desserts (like chocolate-covered strawberries, pudding, cheese, and more). Beer and wine are also included for adults 21 and older. We think that the viewing is fantastic but the price is pretty steep, even when you consider the included drinks. Booking: DisneyWorld.com.

MORE ATTRACTIONS

Main Street Vehicles – Ride a horse-drawn streetcar, horseless carriage, or a double-decker bus that will take you down to Cinderella's Castle.

Move It! Shake It! MousekeDance It! Street Party – A lively midday dance party with Disney and Pixar characters on parade floats! The route goes from Main Street and loops around the hub in front of Cinderella Castle. As with most parades, we recommend finding a spot about 20-30 minutes ahead of time for the best viewing.

Browse Main Street – You can also discover the many shops, City Hall, and the Main Street Chamber of Commerce.

· Magic Tips ·
Instead of shopping early and carrying bags around all day, head to the stores right before you leave! The Main Street shops typically stay open an hour after park closing.

Cinderella's Wishing Well – A beautiful wishing well near Cinderella Castle. Toss a coin in and make a wish! All change is donated to Give Kids the World, an organization that helps bring families with a very ill child on a Walt Disney World vacation. To find the wishing well, go to the right of the castle and head slightly toward Tomorrowland.

Harmony Barber Shop – Get a haircut in this charming barbershop. Look for the famous barbershop quartet, the Dapper Dans, singing in four-part harmony! Haircuts start at $19 for adults and $18 for kids. Harmony isn't a salon, so those with long, stylized hair may prefer not to visit this location.
Reservations: (407) 939-7529

FANTASYLAND

Disney animated films come to life in this colorful and kid-friendly land located behind Cinderella Castle. The Magic Kingdom's Fantasyland is divided into three sections: the Castle Courtyard, the Enchanted Forest, and the Storybook Circus. In Fantasyland, you can ride classic attractions and meet your favorite Disney Princesses.

Theme: Land of Fairytales

RIDES

SEVEN DWARFS MINE TRAIN
Best for: Kids, Tweens, Teens, Adults, some Thrill Riders
Description: A family-friendly rollercoaster through the mines of the Seven Dwarfs. The carts move side to side, creating a unique experience like no other rollercoaster.
Level: Family (must be 38" / 97cm or taller)
Recommendation: The Seven Dwarfs Mine Train is one of the park's most popular attractions. If you purchase the Memory Maker, you'll receive a video of your party on the ride—which makes this a great first-time roller coaster for a kid!
Line Length: Very Long / **Lightning Lane:** Individual

PETER PAN'S FLIGHT
Best for: Young Kids, Kids, Tweens, Adults 50+
Description: Fly along Peter Pan through London and Neverland on a pirate ship!
Level: Young Kids / Everyone
Recommendation: Peter Pan is a ride for all ages! We even recommend this attraction for Thrill Riders looking for a fun, classic Walt Disney World attraction.
Line Length: Long / **Lightning Lane:** Yes, Disney Genie+

· **Magic Tips** ·
Popular rides like Seven Dwarfs Mine Train and Peter Pan's Flight often have shorter wait times at park opening and closing.

THE MANY ADVENTURES OF WINNIE THE POOH
Best for: Young Kids and Kids
Description: A slow-paced ride through the brightly-colored world of Winnie the Pooh.
Level: Young Kids / Family
Recommendation: Great for Kids of all ages, but Tweens, Teens and Thrill Riders will likely want to skip it.
Line Length: Short / **Lightning Lane:** Yes, Disney Genie+

DUMBO THE FLYING ELEPHANT
Best for: Young Kids and Kids
Description: Soar high while boarding Dumbo! You control how high or low Dumbo goes.
Level: Young Kids / Family
Recommendation: Perfect for families with Young Kids. Dumbo may use a "queue-less" experience for guests to be paged when it's their time to ride. While they wait, kids can play in the big-top tent playground.
Line Length: Short / **Lightning Lane:** Yes,
Disney Genie+

MAD TEA PARTY
Best for: Everyone
Description: Disney's famous tea cups inspired by *Alice in Wonderland*! Spin with your friends (up to 3-4 adults per tea cup).

Level: Kids / Everyone
Recommendation: Perfect for all ages and a Disney classic that we also recommend to Thrill Riders (the tea cups can spin fast or slow, depending on how hard you turn them). If you get motion sickness easily, you might want to skip this spinning attraction.
Line Length: Short / **Lightning Lane:** Yes, Disney Genie+

PRINCE CHARMING REGAL CARROUSEL
Best for: Young Kids and Kids
Description: A classic carrousel with horses from Cinderella.
Level: Family
Recommendation: Perfect for families with Young Kids.
Line Length: Short / **Lightning Lane:** No

"it's a small world"
Best for: Young Kids, Kids, Families, Adults 50+
Description: A boat floats through several countries with children singing the "It's A Small World" theme song in different languages.
Level: Young Kids / Family
Recommendation: Perfect for families with young children. Adults may enjoy the ride as they beat the heat in this air-conditioned boat ride. Some may find this ride horribly annoying because of the endless singing children—we're not kidding!
Line Length: Short / **Lightning Lane:** Yes, Disney Genie+

THE BARNSTORMER
Best for: Kids and Tweens
Description: A kid-friendly outdoor rollercoaster starring Goofy as the Great Goofini.
Level: Family
Recommendation: Like the Seven Dwarfs Mine Train, this is a great introductory rollercoaster.
Line Length: Very Short / **Lightning Lane:** Yes, Disney Genie+

UNDER THE SEA ~ JOURNEY OF THE LITTLE MERMAID
Best for: Young Kids, Kids, and Tweens
Description: Board shell-shaped chairs as you travel "underwater" to see Ariel and her friends. There's music, special effects, fish, and the wicked Ursula!
Level: Family
Recommendation: Perfect for fans of *The Little Mermaid*.
Line Length: Medium / **Lightning Lane:** Yes, Disney Genie+

SHOWS AND ATTRACTIONS

CINDERELLA CASTLE WALKTHROUGH
Best for: Everyone
Description: Walk through the famous Castle! There's also a dining area called Cinderella's Royal Table.
Level: Everyone
Recommendation: Take a picture outside of the castle! If you don't have someone to snap your photo, there is often a Disney photographer outside of the castle. He or she will take your picture for free (though you have to pay for the prints, unless you have PhotoPass/Memory Maker).
Lightning Lane: No

MICKEY'S PHILHARMAGIC
Best for: Young Kids, Kids, Tweens, Families
Description: A 4-D film show starring Mickey Mouse and his friends. Though, to be honest, it should be called Donald's PhilharMagic because most of the show stars him and Mickey just seems to make a cameo.
Level: Family
Recommendation: Great for show lovers of all ages. Awesome special effects and music. We recommend sitting in the center of the theater. Seats further up can cause blurring in the 3D glasses.
Line Length: Short / **Lightning Lane:** Yes, Disney Genie+

CASEY JR. SPLASH 'N' SOAK STATION
Best for: Young Kids and Kids
Description: A Dumbo-themed water playground for kids.
Level: Everyone
Recommendation: On the hottest days when your kids don't feel like waiting in lines, this can be a memorable attraction. It's best to plan to head back to the hotel afterward or bring a change of clothes. Though, many times, the Florida sun may be enough to dry them off.
Lightning Lane: No

FESTIVAL OF FANTASY PARADE
Best for: Young Kids, Kids, Tweens, Families
Description: An afternoon parade set to Disney music with impressive floats, singing, and dancing.
Level: Family
Recommendation: Great for parade lovers of all ages. Get there early for the best seating! We recommend being near the Cinderella

Castle (on the Main Street side) at least 30 minutes before the parade begins. The park map will list showtimes as they can change from day to day.
Lightning Lane: No

· **Magic Tips** ·
Typical daytime parades won't run when it's raining. Instead, the Magic Kingdom sometimes rolls out the Rainy Day Cavalcade, a set of costumed characters singing and marching in the rain!

BIBBIDI BOBBIDI BOUTIQUE
(inside the Cinderella Castle)
Best for: Young Kids and Kids
Description: Dress up in princess clothing and makeup.
Level: Kids and Young Kids
Recommendation: Perfect for children who are inspired by Disney Princesses (for pricing starting around $60, kids can get their makeup and hair done—and even a gown from their favorite Disney princess). There are more packages, including a "Knight Package" and a "Frozen Package."
Lightning Lane: No

CHARACTER MEETING SPOTS

ARIEL'S GROTTO
Best for: Young Kids, Kids, and Tweens
Description: Take photos with Ariel from Disney's *The Little Mermaid*.
Level: Family
Recommendation: Perfect for fans of *The Little Mermaid*.
Lightning Lane: No

PETE'S SILLY SIDESHOW
Best for: Young Kids, Kids, and Tweens
Description: Take photos with Daisy and Minnie or Donald and Goofy in this circus-themed meet-and-greet attraction. The characters are dressed in circus attire.
Level: Family

Recommendation: Perfect for those looking for any of these characters.
Lightning Lane: No

PRINCESS FAIRYTALE HALL
Best for: Young Kids, Kids, and Tweens
Description: Take photos with Cinderella and other Princesses in this royal hall.
Level: Family
Recommendation: Perfect for fans of Disney Princesses.
Lightning Lane: No

> **· Magic Tips ·**
> Fantasyland has a *Tangled*-themed rest area on the way to Liberty Square and the Haunted Mansion. This well-designed space has stroller parking, cellphone charging stations, and some of the best public restrooms in Walt Disney World. To charge your phone, look for the tree stumps across from the restroom. You'll need to bring your own cord but there are several plugs to use.

ENCHANTED TALES WITH BELLE
Best for: Young Kids, Kids, and Tweens
Description: Take photos with Belle from *Beauty and the Beast*.
Level: Family
Recommendation: Perfect for fans of Disney Princesses.
Lightning Lane: No

MEET MERIDA AT FAIRYTALE GARDEN
Best for: Young Kids, Kids, and Tweens
Description: Take photos with Merida at the Fairytale Garden.
Level: Family
Recommendation: Perfect for fans of *Brave*.
Lightning Lane: No

ADVENTURELAND

Discover adventure brought to life with some of Disney's best storylines and attractions set in a dense jungle. Brave seas ruled by pirates and fly high on a magic carpet!

Theme: The jungles of South America, Asia, and Africa

RIDES

JUNGLE CRUISE
Best for: Young Kids, Kids, Families, Tweens, Adults 30+
Description: Venture down a massive river on a boat with your comedic tour guide. See animatronic Amazonian and African animals from monkeys and crocodiles to elephants and lions on this 7-minute long ride.
Level: Everyone
Recommendation: A classic, humorous Disney ride that most guests will enjoy. Teens, Young Adults, and Thrill Riders may want to skip it.
Line Length: Medium / **Lightning Lane:** Yes, Disney Genie+
Holiday Overlay: Jingle Cruise (the holiday version of the Jungle Cruise) offers Christmas lights, a different script, and animals wearing Christmas hats. This attraction runs mid-November through the first week of January.

PIRATES OF THE CARIBBEAN
Best for: Everyone!
Description: Pirate-themed boat ride in the dark. Also a great air-conditioned ride to cool off on hot days.
Level: Everyone, though some young kids may be frightened by the drop, loud sounds, and darkness.
Recommendation: A must-see Disney classic for all! Both thrill riders and families will love Pirates of the Caribbean for its stunning scenery, animatronics, and pirate humor. The boats load quickly, but

this is one of the Magic Kingdom's most popular rides, so the line can be quite long.

Line Length: Medium / **Lightning Lane:** Yes, Disney Genie+

Staying Dry: To avoid getting wet, sit near the center of the boat. If you are in the fourth or fifth row, and on the right side, a cannon blast can send a mighty splash of water your way. Avoid these seats if you want to stay dry.

THE MAGIC CARPETS OF ALADDIN

Best for: Young Kids, Kids, Families

Description: Spinning flying carpets similar to the Dumbo the Flying Elephant ride. However, the Magic Carpets can also tilt!

Level: Families

Recommendation: Kids under ten enjoy this ride the most as they control the flying carpets to go high or low.

Line Length: Short / **Lightning Lane:** Yes, Disney Genie+

SWISS FAMILY TREEHOUSE

Best for: Young Kids, Kids, Tweens, Families

Description: A climbable treehouse themed after the 1960 *Swiss Family Robinson* film.

Level: Young Kids / Everyone

Recommendation: Kids ages 10 and under will enjoy this attraction that typically has a very short line (or no wait at all). There are also great photo opportunities from the top!

Line Length: Very short / **Lightning Lane:** No

SHOWS AND ATTRACTIONS

WALT DISNEY'S ENCHANTED TIKI ROOM

Best for: Kids, Adults 60+

Description: An animatronic show starring birds and Tikis in a tropical island setting.

Level: Family / Everyone

Recommendation: Have a Dole Whip while you watch the 15-minute long show. Tweens, Teens, Young Adults, and Thrill Riders will want to skip this one, as it's a classic attraction that can feel a bit dated.

Line Length: Short / **Lightning Lane:** No

PIRATE'S ADVENTURE ~ TREASURES OF THE SEVEN SEAS

Best for: Kids, Tweens

Description: Pirates of the Caribbean-themed walkthrough attraction. Help Captain Jack Sparrow discover treasures in this fun ,explorative mini-adventure!
Level: Kids and Tweens
Recommendation: Perfect for Kids and Tweens, but it may be too complex for Young Kids, and it's not aimed for Adults.
Line Length: Short / **Lightning Lane:** No

FRONTIERLAND

Immerse yourself in the wild west near the Rivers of America. Ride the high-speed Big Thunder Mountain Railroad or catch a lighthearted show at the Diamond Horseshoe.

Theme: North America's Wild West

RIDES

BIG THUNDER MOUNTAIN RAILROAD
Best for: Kids, Tweens, Teens, Adults, Thrill Riders
Description: A fast rollercoaster with a few dips called "The Wildest Ride in the Wilderness!"
Level: Thrill Ride (must be 40" /102cm or taller)
Recommendation: Many families and thrill riders will love this fast rollercoaster with short dips and great special effects. If you're unsure whether to take your child on this rollercoaster, have them ride the family-friendly Seven Dwarfs Mine Train first in Fantasyland.

Line Length: Medium / **Lightning Lane:** Yes, Disney Genie+

SPLASH MOUNTAIN
Best for: Tweens, Teens, Adults, Thrill Riders

Description: Water-based log ride starring the singing critters from Disney's *Song of the South.*

Level: Thrill Ride (must be 40" /102cm or taller)

Recommendation: If you love drops and getting wet, this is the ride for you! There are several drops in this ride, including a 50-foot drop at 45 degrees at the end. This ride typically has the longest lines in Frontierland, especially during the hotter days and can be well over an hour wait.

Line Length: Long / **Lightning Lane:** Yes, Disney Genie+

Staying Dry: Sit near the back to avoid getting as wet (though you will still likely get wet). Tell a Cast Member at the end of the queue that you'd like to sit in the back and they will help accommodate you. If it's a cold day or you just don't feel like getting your clothes wet, either buy or bring a poncho—or skip this attraction altogether.

> **· Magic Tips ·**
>
> In June of 2020, Disney announced that it would reimagine its Splash Mountain ride to *The Princess and the Frog.* Though we expect the attraction to remain open through 2022, it's possible that Disney could close it before then.

TOM SAWYER ISLAND

Best for: Kids, Tweens

Description: Explore a remote island in the center of the Magic Kingdom's famous river. You must get there by raft!

Level: Family

Recommendation: We recommend this island playground for kids. There are hideaways and trinkets for them to play with, though teens, adults, and Thrill Riders will likely want to skip this one. Tom Sawyer's Island closes before sunset, so make sure that you get this attraction done earlier in the day if it's on your list.

Line Length: Short / **Lightning Lane:** No

SHOWS AND ATTRACTIONS

COUNTRY BEAR JAMBOREE

Best for: Young Kids, Kids, Adults 50+

Description: A country music-filled jamboree featuring the classic animatronic Country Bears. There are over twelve songs in this nearly 16-minute long show.

Level: Everyone
Recommendation: Perfect for nostalgic Disney World-goers, but the theme may feel lost on others. The Country Bear Jamboree might be a classic, but the crowds have thinned over the years and the show doesn't have the same excitement as from its previous fans.
Line Length: Short / **Lightning Lane:** No

MORE ATTRACTIONS

Walt Disney World Railroad – A station for the park's iconic train. Guests may board the train here or get off from another station.

Frontierland Shootin' Arcade – A paid experience where guests can shoot targets with laser-guided toy rifles.

LIBERTY SQUARE

A colonial America-themed land filed with shops, treats, and one of the park's most popular rides, the Haunted Mansion.

Theme: 18th-Century New England

RIDES

HAUNTED MANSION
Best for: Kids, Tweens, Teens, Adults
Description: A slow-paced ride through a haunted house filled with spooky special effects, animatronics, and creepy sounds!
Level: Everyone – though young children may become frightened
Recommendation: It's a Disney classic that many thrill-riders may want to skip for it's slow movement and effects that are only scary enough to terrify young kids. You can fit 2-3 people per "Doom Buggy" chair. We've sat 3 adults together, but it's not very comfortable.
Line Length: Medium / **Lightning Lane:** Yes, Disney Genie+

SHOWS AND ATTRACTIONS

HALL OF PRESIDENTS
Best for: Young Kids, Adults 50+
Description: Animatronics show with a patriotic story.
Level: Everyone
Recommendation: A well-told, 25-minute show hosted by animatronic versions of the United States Presidents. Every U.S. President in history has an animatronic featured within this show. The current President also has a speech recited during the show. Thrill riders may want to skip this one but the space is very well air conditioned for anyone looking to escape the heat.
Line Length: Short / **Lightning Lane:** No

LIBERTY BELLE RIVERBOAT
Best for: Young Kids, Adults 50+
Description: Explore a beautiful American-style riverboat over the Rivers of America.
Level: Everyone
Recommendation: For those looking to cool off and ride on a large river boat.
Line Length: Short / **Lightning Lane:** No

TOMORROWLAND

A futuristic land filled with rides for thrill seekers and sci-fi fans. Tomorrowland is also home to Space Mountain and Buzz Lightyear!

Theme: The land of the future

RIDES

SPACE MOUNTAIN
Best for: Thrill Riders
Description: A rollercoaster in the dark.
Level: Thrill Riders (must be 40" / 102cm or taller)
Recommendation: A must for Thrill Riders! Space Mountain at the Magic Kingdom feels a little bit dated with its worn carpet in the

queue and '70s-style exterior. However, the ride hasn't lost its unique charm as you blast through outer space! We highly recommend this unique experience for Thrill Riders.

Line Length: Very Long / **Lightning Lane:** Yes, Individual

TOMORROWLAND SPEEDWAY
Best for: Kids and Tweens
Description: Where kids can drive cars around a track.
Level: Kids / Family (must be 32" / 81cm or taller to ride; must be 54" / 137cm to drive alone).
Recommendation: Designed for kids and tweens to drive motorized go-kart style vehicles.
Line Length: Medium / **Lightning Lane:** Yes, Disney Genie+

TOMORROWLAND TRANSIT AUTHORITY PEOPLEMOVER
Best for: Young Kids, Kids, Adults 50+
Description: A futuristic, slow-moving vehicle through Tomorrowland.
Level: Kids / Family
Recommendation: Perfect for those looking for a break. The PeopleMover is a 10-minute-long ride and a great way to beat the heat as the ride travels through air-conditioned spaces.
Line Length: Short / **Lightning Lane:** No

BUZZ LIGHTYEAR'S SPACE RANGER SPIN
Best for: Everyone
Description: Compete against others in this fun *Toy Story*-themed ride. It's fun for everyone to blast the laser guns and try to rack up the points.
Level: Everyone (including most Thrill Riders)
Recommendation: A crowd favorite for everyone to enjoy.
Line Length: Medium / **Lightning Lane:** Yes, Disney Genie+
Scoring Big: There are special targets on the robot and alien enemies that give different points. It's not clear how much these are worth unless you know these tips.
1. You can hit the targets as many times as you'd like, including the ones worth the most.
2. Orange Robot (first room) – Shoot the inside of its glowing hands for 100,000 points.
3. Volcano (second room) – Aim for the volcano with green lava in the back of the room and get 25,000 points.
4. Alien Ant – There's an ant with a target on its rear worth 50,000 points.
5. Zurg's Ship – There's a difficult target at the bottom of the crab-like ship that's worth 100,000 points.

6. Hyperspace Warp – There's a huge spaceship at the end with a target worth 100,000 points.

ASTRO ORBITER
Best for: Young Kids and Kids
Description: Orbit a solar system model on rocket ships (similar to Dumbo but much higher).
Level: Kids / Family
Recommendation: Fun for Young Kids
Line Length: Short / **Lightning Lane:** No

TRON LIGHTCYCLE RUN
Likely opens in 2022
Best for: Tweens, Teens, Adults, and Thrill Riders
Description: A thrilling launch coaster that simulates riding on motorbikes through a video game.
Level: Thrill Riders (height TBA)
Recommendation: Perfect for Thrill Riders
Line Length: Very Long / **Lightning Lane:** Likely Individual

SHOWS AND ATTRACTIONS

MONSTERS, INC. LAUGH FLOOR
Best for: Young Kids and Kids
Description: A comedy club-style show with digital puppetry that allows characters from Pixar's *Monsters, Inc.* to interact with the audience.
Level: Kids / Family
Recommendation: Fun for Families with Kids
Line Length: Short / **Lightning Lane:** Yes, Disney Genie+

WALT DISNEY'S CAROUSEL OF PROGRESS
Best for: Young Kids and Adults Ages 50+
Description: Watch as animatronic characters bring you the future of gadgets in a turning carousel-like building.
Level: Everyone
Recommendation: Overall, this roughly 20-minute show gets mixed reviews. Some find it to be a wonderfully nostalgic American story. Others feel that the Carousel of Progress is dated in both ideology and innovation. Other guests just use the building for a short cool-down in its air conditioning.
Line Length: Very Short / **Lightning Lane:** No

EPCOT

INTRODUCTION

Since its opening in 1982, Epcot has been a staple of the Walt Disney World experience. Its name is an acronym for Experimental Prototype Community of Tomorrow. It's a place where "joy, hope, and friendship" are launched into a space of creativity, exploration, and innovation.

We are asked a lot: "Is Epcot worth visiting?" For us, the answer is a clear *yes*. Epcot is like the Magic Kingdom's Tomorrowland, fully expanded over 300 acres. It's a world of tomorrow and today where guests can ride futuristic attractions, try delicious food from all over the world, and play into the night. However, those looking just for thrills may feel disappointed by Epcot's lack of rideable attractions. Disney aimed to fix this with the addition of Remy's Ratatouille Adventure and Guardians of the Galaxy: Cosmic Rewind debuting later in 2022. However, there are still only a handful of rides within this park.

We love the immersive feel of Epcot matched with its hopeful message about the future. With exciting rides like Soarin' and Test Track, delicious food festivals, and countless amazing sights, Epcot is a must-do!

THE NEIGHBORHOODS

Epcot is divided into four neighborhoods: World Celebration, World Discovery, World Nature, and World Showcase, which consists of eleven represented countries. The neighborhoods are designed to appropriately place attractions in well-themed areas.

The entrance neighborhood, World Celebration, invites guests into the park near Spaceship Earth. From there, guests can go left to World Discovery to experience thrilling attractions like Test Track, Mission: Space, and Guardians of the Galaxy: Cosmic Rewind. To the right is World Nature where the land and sea meet with family-friendly experiences.

Finally, World Showcase is the largest of the neighborhoods. Guests can shop, dine, and explore eleven different countries including Mexico, Norway, China, Germany, Italy, America, Japan, Morocco, France, United Kingdom, and Canada! These countries surround the giant World Showcase Lagoon, and allow for guests to easily move from one to another like fast world travel! At night, the lagoon comes to life with the dazzling Harmonious spectacular!

· Magic Tips ·
Epcot is undergoing a multi-year transformation that won't conclude until its 40th anniversary later in 2022. Because of this, some of the neighborhoods and attractions may not be open until later in the year.

BACK ENTRANCE

Epcot has two entrances: one at the Main Entrance near Spaceship Earth, the second between the United Kingdom and France sections in the World Showcase on the other side of the park. The second entrance is known as "The International Gateway." The two entrances may also have different opening times, with the World Showcase entry often opening later.

· Magic Tips ·
Epcot is often open late, allowing for locals to wine and dine around its beautiful, massive lake in the center of World Showcase. Because of this, it's sometimes best to avoid visiting on Friday and Saturday nights.

RIDES

FROZEN EVER AFTER
Neighborhood: World Showcase (Norway)
Location: Norway
Best for: Everyone
Description: Explore the culture of Norway and the magic of Disney's *Frozen* in this unique boat ride.
Level: Everyone / Family
Recommendation: The World Showcase's most "daring" ride, though it's fun for the whole family. There are some small dips and senses of danger, but the *Frozen* characters keep young kids happy.
Line Length: Long / **Lightning Lane:** Yes, Individual

THE GRAN FIESTA TOUR STARRING THE THREE CABALLEROS
Neighborhood: World Showcase (Mexico)
Best for: Everyone
Description: Explore the culture of Mexico in a boat ride with music.
Level: Everyone
Recommendation: We recommend experiencing the ride for its fun with Donald Duck and his pals.
Line Length: Very Short / **Lightning Lane:** No

GUARDIANS OF THE GALAXY: COSMIC REWIND
Opens sometime in 2022
Neighborhood: World Discovery
Best for: Kids, Tweens, Teens, Adults, and Thrill Riders
Description: A family-friendly launch coaster with epic scenes starring the Guardians of the Galaxy!
Level: Kids to Adult
Recommendation: Perfect for Marvel fans! Those who do not enjoy roller coasters may wlsh to sit this one out.
Line Length: Very Long / **Disney Genie+:** Likely Yes, with Virtual Queue and paid Lightning Lane only

JOURNEY INTO IMAGINATION WITH FIGMENT
Neighborhood: World Celebration
Best for: Young Kids, Kids, and Tweens
Description: The Imagination pavilion explores the creative mind for its fun and importance to the human experience. Its main attraction

is Journey Into the Imagination with Figment, a classic dark ride with a scientific twist that explores our senses!
Level: Everyone
Recommendation: Great for families with Kids.
Line Length: Very Short / **Lightning Lane:** Yes, Disney Genie+

LIVING WITH THE LAND
Neighborhood: World Nature
Best for: Everyone
Description: A slow-paced, informative ride that beautifully describes how we harvest the land for food.
Level: Everyone
Recommendation: Perfectly informative and fun. Thrill Riders may want to skip this slow-paced ride and head straight for Soarin'.
Line Length: Very Short / **Lightning Lane:** Yes, Disney Genie+

MISSION: SPACE
Neighborhood: World Discovery
Best for: Tweens, Teens, Adults, and Thrill Riders
Description: A dizzying astronaut training excursion into outer space with a new mission!
Level: Everyone
Recommendation: Thrill Riders should choose the more intense "orange" mission while those who experience motion sickness should choose a stationary "green" mission—or skip this ride altogether.
Line Length: Medium / **Lightning Lane:** Yes, Disney Genie+

REMY'S RATATOUILLE ADVENTURE
Neighborhood: World Showcase (France)
Best for: Everyone
Description: A trackless dark ride fit for the entire family! Journey along Remy the rat from Pixar's *Ratatouille* as you dash through a kitchen.
Level: Everyone / Family
Recommendation: This exciting dark ride uses physical sets and 3D elements. We recommend it for kids and adults!
Line Length: Very Long / **Lightning Lane:** Yes, Individual and a Virtual Queue

THE SEAS WITH NEMO & FRIENDS
Neighborhood: World Nature
Best for: Everyone
Description: Learn about the oceans in this *Finding Nemo*-themed

attraction. The ride loads quickly with seats similar to the "doom buggies" in the Haunted Mansion. There are also massive aquariums with live fish, manatees, and more!

Level: Everyone
Recommendation: A spectacular ride with plenty to see and experience. Thrill Riders may want to skip out unless they are interested in seeing the aquariums.
Line Length: Very Short / **Lightning Lane:** Yes, Disney Genie+

SOARIN' AROUND THE WORLD
Neighborhood: World Nature
Best for: Kids, Tweens, Teens, Adults, and Thrill Riders
Description: Fly over some of the world's most famous landmarks in this unique hang glider simulation.
Level: Kids to Adult
Recommendation: Small children and those with a fear of heights may want to skip this one, though the ride feels very relaxing.
Line Length: Medium-Long / **Lightning Lane:** Yes, Disney Genie+

SPACESHIP EARTH
Neighborhood: World Celebration
Best for: Everyone
Description: A slow-moving dark ride set inside of the Epcot sphere. The ride has animatronics and more as it discusses humans' ability to communicate on Earth throughout time.
Level: Everyone
Recommendation: Spaceship Earth might be a slow-paced ride, but it's a Walt Disney World favorite. Even Thrill Riders will want to experience this iconic attraction inside of the "golf ball."
Line Length: Short / **Lightning Lane:** Yes, Disney Genie+

TEST TRACK
Neighborhood: World Discovery
Best for: Tweens, Teens, Adults, Thrill Riders
Description: Zoom along a simulated test track in a futuristic car. The vehicle races at over 60 miles per hour with turns and movement inside and outside of a building.
Level: Thrill Ride
Recommendation: Perfect for Thrill Riders. If you don't want to pay for Lightning Lane, use the Single Rider Line.
Line Length: Very Long / **Lightning Lane:** Yes, Disney Genie+

TURTLE TALK WITH CRUSH
Neighborhood: World Nature
Best for: Young Kids and Kids
Description: Interact with Crush the turtle from *Finding Nemo* in this unique and hilarious theatre-like event designed for Young Kids.
Level: Everyone
Recommendation: Young Kids
Line Length: Short / **Lightning Lane:** Yes, Disney Genie+

FIREWORKS

HARMONIOUS
Best for: Everyone
Description: Dazzling nightly fireworks around the World Showcase Lagoon in the center of Epcot.
Level: Everyone
Recommendation: Conclude your day with this epic show told with fireworks and massive screens with water features on the lagoon.
Best Seating: We recommend snagging a spot 30-60 minutes before showtime by Mexico or the Mitsukoshi Store in Japan. On busier days, you'll want to claim your spot about 90 minutes ahead of time. If you don't get there early, find standing room where you can. You can also request a patio or window seat at any of these restaurants for firework viewing: Rose and Crown Pub (United Kingdom), Bistro de Paris (France), Cantina de San Angel (Mexico), La Hacienda de San Angel (Mexico), Nine Dragons (China), and Tokyo Dining (Japan). Some of these restaurants may also offer dining packages with exclusive viewing of the fireworks.

> **· Magic Tips ·**
> The crowds pour out from Epcot after the show. Most of the time, the International Gateway, between Great Britain and France, is the best exit. There are a few ways out of the park after the fireworks: bus, monorail, boat, or your own car. The first three are much easier as Disney has this system down for getting guests back to their hotels. If you don't have a hotel and you drove, it's sort of a mad rush to the parking lot. To avoid this, we recommend being one of the first to leave through the International Gateway.

SHOWS & ATTRACTIONS

The American Adventure (World Showcase) – A stunning 30-minute show with dozens of audio-animatronics, special effects, and more that tell the tales of several iconic American events.

Awesome Planet (World Nature) – A breathtaking film showcasing the most magnificent places on Earth.

Beauty and the Beast Sing-Along (World Showcase, France) – What if LaFou was really behind all of the magic of the *Beauty and the Beast* animated film? That's the story behind this 15-minute singalong movie that uses the same theater as "Impressions de France." It sounds like an interesting concept but the overall execution is boring and confusing. We recommend skipping this attraction.

> **· Magic Tips ·**
> Disney worked with several countries to create these unique pavilions. In fact, many of the Cast Members are from the country represented in each pavilion! Unfortunately, due to travel restrictions in 2022, Epcot may not host its international Cast Members.

Canada Far and Wide (World Showcase, Canada) – A humorous short film told in Circle-Vision 360 with screens that encircle the theater! For most of the show, guests will stand in the center of the room as they watch the 12-minute story narrated by Eugene Levy and Catherine O'Hara.

Disney & Pixar Short Film Festival (World Celebration) – The creative geniuses behind the Academy Award winning Pixar films bring an 18-minute show. Experience Pixar shorts like never before with 4-D effects! We recommend this attraction for kids ages 3-8.

DuckTales World Showcase Adventure (World Showcase) – A scavenger hunt around the showcases. DuckTales is a fun game for kids and tweens!

Impressions de France (World Showcase, France) – An 18-minute cinematic film showcasing the wonders of France. The film is pretty dated but entertaining nonetheless. This film switches daily with the "Beauty and the Beast Sing-Along" show.

> **· Magic Tips ·**
> Make some time in each pavilion to explore all of the unique gift shops! We highly recommend the immersive **Plaza de los Amigos** (Mexico) which feels like you're shopping at night in a Mexican village. The **Mitsukoshi Department Store** (Japan) is filled with imported Japanese collectables, and the **Karamell-Küche** (Germany) is a caramel fan's dream!

Moana Journey of Water (World Nature) – A beautiful walkthrough attraction with themes from Disney's *Moana*.

Play! Pavilion (World Discovery) – A vibrant, interactive indoor pavilion centering on play! Guests learn to draw popular Disney characters, play high-tech games, and meet several characters.

Walt Disney Imagineering Presents The Epcot Experience – A stunning 360-degree display of upcoming Epcot attractions!

Wondrous China (World Showcase, China) – A film that explores the cultures, land, and beauty of China. This film is told in Circle-Vision 360 and guests will stand during it.

CHAPTER NINE

DISNEY'S HOLLYWOOD STUDIOS

INTRODUCTION

Previously known as MGM Studios—until it was revamped in 2008—Disney's Hollywood Studios is a park dedicated to Hollywood's Golden Age in the 1930s. Disney felt inspired to bring a movie-themed park to its Resort as Universal Studios eyed Orlando for its next project. With thrilling rides like The Twilight Zone Tower of Terror and stunning shows like *Fantasmic!*, Hollywood Studios brings famous films and characters to life in a spectacular way!

Hollywood Studios is also home to immersive themed areas like Toy Story Land—where guests shrink down to the size of a toy—and Star Wars: Galaxy's Edge—where guests begin their own *Star Wars* adventure! This theme park heavily focuses on Pixar, Star Wars, and Disney Junior attractions designed with the entire family in mind.

Disney's Hollywood Studios has many shows. So if you are just looking for rides, you might want to consider doing Hollywood Studios and Epcot on the same day. They are a 15-minute walk (or 10-minute boat ride) from one another. We recommend starting at Hollywood Studios and then heading to Epcot in the late afternoon.

Note: We cover the Star Wars: Galaxy's Edge attractions in the next chapter.

HOLLYWOOD BOULEVARD

The grand, golden age-themed entrance of the park. You'll feel like you're walking down a glamorized version of the real Hollywood Boulevard in the same way that Walt Disney experienced it when he first moved to Los Angeles. There are shops, a coffee joint, and loads of Hollywood golden-age glamour!

Theme: Golden Age Hollywood entrance

RIDES

MICKEY & MINNIE'S RUNAWAY RAILWAY
Best for: Everyone
Description: A family-friendly trackless dark ride with projection mapping, animatronics, and cartoonish action! Starring Mickey, Minnie, Goofy, and Donald, this attraction can be enjoyed by most guests as it doesn't have frightening moments or a height restriction. Some segments use motion simulation.
Level: Everyone (no height restriction)
Recommendation: Due to the newness of this attraction and the rising popularity of Hollywood Studios, lines are long for Mickey and Minnie's Runaway Railway in the morning and afternoon.
Line Length: Long / **Lightning Lane:** Yes, Individual

SHOWS AND ATTRACTIONS

Mickey Shorts Theater – A zany cartoon compilation starring Mickey and Minnie Mouse. The seats here even look like Mickey's iconic red shorts! Kids 3-12 will love this show, and it's a great way to escape the heat—or rain—during the day. Afterward, pose for snaps in several Mickey Mouse-themed photo ops.

Wonderful World of Animation – A 12-minute stunning nighttime projection show with displays of Disney animation on the iconic Chinese Theatre. See the magic of Disney movies come to life with special effects and projections!

Star Wars: A Galactic Spectacular – The music and images from the Star Wars films come to life on the Chinese Theatre with an epic fireworks display. This show may run ten minutes after Wonderful World of Animation in the same location.

ECHO LAKE

This land is a bit of a hodgepodge of themes from George Lucas films like *Star Wars* and *Indiana Jones*, with the addition of theaters that recreate the palm-tree crowded Southern California feel from just outside of Hollywood.

Theme: Mock studios around a central lake

RIDES

STAR TOURS – THE ADVENTURES CONTINUE
Best for: Kids, Tweens, Teens, Young Adults, Thrill Riders
Description: A Star Wars themed 3D motion simulator hosted by C-3PO. During the ride, you visit two of nine planets from the films, but they mix them up. Ride multiple times and get a different experience each time!
Level: Thrill Riders (must be 40" / 102cm or taller)
Recommendation: A perfect ride for *Star Wars* fans. If you get motion sickness, you may want to skip this ride.
Line Length: Medium / **Lightning Lane:** Yes, Disney Genie+

SHOWS AND ATTRACTIONS

FOR THE FIRST TIME IN FOREVER: A FROZEN SING-ALONG CELEBRATION
Best for: Young Kids, Kids, Tweens, Adults 50+
Description: A 30-minute theatre show at the Hyperion Theatre starring Elsa, Anna, and their Frozen friends with music and more from the massively popular film.
Level: Family
Recommendation: Bring every *Frozen* fan that you know.
Line Length: Short / **Lightning Lane:** Yes, Disney Genie+

INDIANA JONES EPIC STUNT SPECTACULAR!
Best for: Everyone
Description: A 25-minute live stunt show starring Indiana Jones. See the action of *Raiders of the Lost Ark* in this epic attraction.
Level: Everyone
Recommendation: Great for everyone, though Young Kids who have a hard time sitting still for long or don't enjoy loud noises may want to skip this attraction.
Line Length: Short / **Lightning Lane:** Yes, Disney Genie+

GRAND AVENUE

Grand Avenue is home to LA-style shops, dining, and fun attractions starring the Muppets!

Theme: Present-day Downtown Los Angeles

SHOWS AND ATTRACTIONS

MUPPET*VISION 3D
Best for: Young Kids, Kids, Tweens, Adults 50+
Description: A hilarious 15-minute 4D show with special effects and

silly surprises starring Kermit the Frog and nearly every other character from *The Muppet Show*.
Level: Family
Recommendation: Perfect for families with Kids and fans of *The Muppet Show*.
Line Length: Very Short / **Lightning Lane:** Yes, Disney Genie+

> **· Magic Tips ·**
> Muppet*Vision was one of director and creator Jim Henson's final films. Unfortunately, he passed away before its debut in 1991, but it's exciting to know that his legendary work is still entertaining audiences today.

ANIMATION COURTYARD

Venture into a studio lot dedicated to the art of Walt Disney Animation Studios. See live shows as well as meet characters in this unique land.

Theme: Walt Disney Animation Studios

SHOWS AND ATTRACTIONS

DISNEY JUNIOR DANCE PARTY!
Best for: Young Kids
Description: A live-action dance show starring Disney Junior characters designed for preschool-aged children.
Level: Young Kids
Recommendation: Families with young children.
Line Length: Short / **Lightning Lane:** Yes, Disney Genie+

VOYAGE OF THE LITTLE MERMAID
Best for: Young Kids, Kids, Tweens
Description: A family-friendly live show that brings to life the characters, adventure, and music of Disney's *The Little Mermaid*. The entire show is 17 minutes in length.

Level: Family
Recommendation: Great for families with Young Kids and fans of Disney's *The Little Mermaid*. Others might want to check out the Indiana Jones show or Beauty and the Beast.
Line Length: Short / **Lightning Lane:** No

WALT DISNEY PRESENTS – See sneak peeks of upcoming attractions as well as exhibits detailing how Disney brings its theme parks to life.

SUNSET BOULEVARD

A fictionalized version of the famous Sunset Boulevard with the harrowing Hollywood Hotel in the distance. There are also iconic shows and fantastic shops in this area.

Theme: Hollywood Street

RIDES

THE TWILIGHT ZONE TOWER OF TERROR
Best for: Tweens, Teens, Adults, Thrill Riders
Description: Plummet down thirteen treacherous stories in this *Twilight Zone*-themed thrill ride.
Level: Thrill Riders (must be 40" / 102cm or taller)
Recommendation: Tower of Terror is an extreme thrill ride with several drops that can plunge up to thirteen stories! There are also several different combinations of drops, so each ride feels different.
Line Length: Long / **Lightning Lane:** Yes, Disney Genie+

> **· Magic Tips ·**
> The library room (with the black and white TV) shuffles guests around. If you want to be the first group to ride, move to the back of the room where you'll see a closed door. That's the quickest way to the final line once the preshow finishes.

ROCK 'N' ROLLER COASTER STARRING AEROSMITH
Best for: Teens, Adults, Thrill Riders
Description: Similar to Space Mountain, this coaster is indoors and fairly dark. You are launched into loops, corkscrews, and inversions to get your blood flowing! Aerosmith sets the tone and music to this epic attraction.
Level: Thrill Riders (must be 48" / 122cm or taller)
Recommendation: We notice that the lines can be quite long for this ride as there aren't many options for Thrill Riders in Hollywood Studios. However, purchasing Disney Genie+ may be worth it alone for guests who love extreme coasters like this. You'll likely be able to ride multiple times during the day.
Line Length: Long / **Lightning Lane:** Yes, Disney Genie+

SHOWS AND ATTRACTIONS

LIGHTNING MCQUEEN'S RACING ACADEMY
Best for: Young Kids, Kids, Tweens
Description: An animated theater racing show with characters from Pixar's *Cars*.
Level: Family
Recommendation: Great for kids ages 3 and up! Stay afterward to meet Cruz Ramirez near the attraction's entrance.
Line Length: Short / **Lightning Lane:** No

BEAUTY AND THE BEAST – LIVE ON STAGE
Best for: Young Kids, Kids, Tweens, Adults 50+
Description: A 25-minute live Broadway-style musical starring the cast of Disney's animated film *Beauty and the Beast*.
Level: Everyone
Recommendation: Perfect for fans of Broadway-style musicals
Line Length: Short / **Lightning Lane:** Yes, Disney Genie+

FANTASMIC!
Best for: Everyone
Description: The stunning Hollywood Hills Amphitheater brings to life the 26-minute Disney spectacular, *Fantasmic!* See Mickey and more in this epic show of lights, music, and special effects all on the water. But be careful, because the Disney Villains are on the loose!
Level: Everyone

Recommendation: Everyone should see this show at least once. After *Fantasmic!* you'll either want to leave or head to the Star Wars Fireworks show. Either way, head near the entrance to watch the fireworks.
Line Length: Medium / **Lightning Lane:** No (may be added later)
Reserved Seating with Dining: Reserve a Dining Package and receive a voucher for seating in the center. We recommend the Hollywood & Vine or Brown Derby dinner packages.

STAR WARS LAUNCH BAY – Meet Star Wars characters like Darth Vader and Jawas, who are not found in Galaxy's Edge.

TOY STORY LAND

A colorful land based on Pixar's *Toy Story* film series. Shrink down as you enter Andy's backyard to experience life the size of a toy!

Theme: Pixar's *Toy Story*

RIDES

SLINKY DOG DASH
Best for: Everyone
Description: A family-friendly launch rollercoaster through Andy's backyard. Andy has placed his slinky dog on the RC racer track!
Level: Kids, Tweens, Teens, Adults, Thrill Riders (must be 38" / 97cm or taller)
Recommendation: Great for rollercoaster lovers of all ages.
Line Length: Very Long / **Lightning Lane:** Yes, Disney Genie+
Holiday Overlay: The same attraction changes with sleigh bells and seasonal decorations beginning in November.

ALIEN SWIRLING SAUCERS
Best for: Everyone
Description: Get flicked and whirled around on flying saucers while escaping the ominous claw!
Level: Family (must be 32" / 82cm or taller)

Recommendation: Perfect for families with kids looking for a fun and thrilling ride. Thrill riders might also enjoy this unpredictable attraction!

Line Length: Long / **Lightning Lane:** Yes, Disney Genie+

Holiday Overlay: The same attraction changes with holiday music beginning in November.

TOY STORY MANIA!

Best for: Everyone

Description: A 4D game where riders attempt to score the most points by shooting at animated targets with a plunger canon.

Level: Everyone

Recommendation: All ages will enjoy this ride from Young Kids to Thrill Riders. Not recommended if you have trouble seeing with 3D glasses.

Line Length: Very Long / **Lightning Lane:** Yes, Disney Genie+

Scoring Big:

1. Many "pro" riders hold the plunger between two fingers with their palm facing them.
2. Higher-point targets are at the bottom of the screens.
3. Scene #1 (Hamm and Eggs) – Hitting the pigs on the fence will make a cat appear that can be hit multiple times for big points.
4. Scene #2 (Rex and Trixie) – Pop the lava balloons on the volcano to make it erupt with 500-point balloons.
5. Scene #3 (Green Army Men) – Look for the yellow-tinted plates that are worth 2,000 points.
6. Scene #4 (Alien Ring Game) – On the far sides are rocket ships and aliens worth big points.
7. Scene #5 (Woody's Western Theme) – Aim for the doors of the saloon to reveal higher point targets. At the end of this scene there are mine carts that roll toward you. Look for the bats above the mine carts that are worth some major points.

· Magic Tips ·

Even though Toy Story Land connects to Star Wars: Galaxy's Edge, during busier mornings, guests may be required to enter Galaxy's Edge from Grand Avenue on the opposite side of the park.

MORE LANDS

PIXAR PLACE

A small area dedicated to the storytelling of Pixar characters. There aren't any rides or major attractions in this area. However, you can often meet popular Pixar characters like the Incredibles. There's also some themed snacks and merchandise available.

STAR WARS: GALAXY'S EDGE

Start a new adventure in a galaxy far, far away! Galaxy's Edge is an immersive *Star Wars*-themed land with recognizable characters, amazing set pieces, an alien shopping district, distinct dining, and two signature rides. We cover everything you need to know about Star Wars: Galaxy's Edge in the next chapter.

CHAPTER TEN

STAR WARS: GALAXY'S EDGE GUIDE

INTRODUCTION

For decades Disney theme parks have gone virtually unmatched by competitors. Not only are they the most popular theme parks in the world, but the Disney brand is practically synonymous with themed entertainment. All of that changed when The Wizarding World of Harry Potter opened in Universal's Islands of Adventure in Orlando. Suddenly, there was a theme park experience so stunningly immersive it became a central tourist destination.

To Disney, it was abundantly clear that they needed a realist world of their own. Star Wars felt like the perfect answer to Harry Potter. In its 40-year history, the franchise has earned an estimated $65 billion in merchandise, box office sales, home videos, and more. Its fandom is also wide-reaching and multigenerational, making the storylines familiar to millions of potential park guests.

Disney's impressive plan was to transport visitors to a galaxy far, far away, have them become Jedis, fly the Millennium Falcon, and even meet Chewbacca. With Star Wars: Galaxy's Edge, Disney pulls all of this off and more in its largest, most riveting expansion to date. There are Stormtroopers marching down ancient walkways, a secret hideaway where guests can build a lightsaber, and even a danger-filled cantina. Disney even went as far as omitting signage in Galaxy's Edge and uses alien language to make the land feel as authentic as possible.

Galaxy's Edge stretches across 14 acres, which is roughly the same size as 2-3 lands in a typical Disney theme park. The magic is in the details; it took Imagineers about two years just to complete the rock work and paint needed to bring Galaxy's Edge to life. One half of the land is crowded with shops, dining, and the Millennium Falcon! This is where guests can explore and also fly the famous ship on the flight simulator, Millennium Falcon: Smugglers Run.

The other half is the hiding spot of the Resistance. This area isn't as populated, but there are some iconic ships and characters to take photos with. The Resistance side is supposed to look unassuming as it holds a hidden path to the land's signature attraction, Star Wars: Rise of the Resistance. This jaw-dropping dark ride has guests join the Resistance to battle the First Order in an epic intergalactic confrontation!

In this chapter, we review the story, attractions, and tips for exploring Star Wars: Galaxy's Edge. It's like visiting a theme park within another theme park—and is like nothing you've ever seen before!

THE STORY

Star Wars: Galaxy's Edge is an entirely immersive land with a vibrant backstory. Set on the fictional planet of Batuu at the edge of the Star Wars galaxy, this ancient destination is home to a variety of creatures. Black Spire Outpost is the main area guests explore in Batuu. It's an old trading town once used as a ship refueling station before hyperspace was invented. Black Spire gets its name from an enormous dark, petrified tree at its center. At night, all of the petrified spires around the outpost glow with vibrant hues!

Today, Black Spire Outpost is the home of rogues looking to escape the clutch of the First Order. In this timeline—set shortly after the events of *Star Wars: The Last Jedi (Episode VIII)* but before *Star Wars: The Rise of Skywalker (Episode IX)*—the wicked First Order has indeed arrived. Kylo Ren and his fleet of Stormtroopers scour Black Spire Outpost for "rebel scum." Meanwhile, Resistance members like Rey and Chewbacca hide on the outskirts of town.

Now, if Batuu doesn't sound familiar, it's because Disney invented the planet for its theme parks. They wanted a new yet familiar land for Galaxy's Edge. Nearly every major element from across  *Star Wars* films and animated TV series can be found on Batuu. The round-top buildings of Black Spire Outpost are reminiscent of Naboo, while the lush surroundings look like Alderaan. Oga's Cantina feels a lot like the one found on Tatooine. As you browse the Merchant Row, you'll see creatures and items from the entire Star Wars Universe. This includes species found around Jabba the Hutt's palace, like the amphibious Worrt (located in Oga's Cantina) and a Kowakian monkey-lizard (purchasable in the Creature Stall shop). There's even a "live" baby Sarlacc (the sand monster that ate Boba Fett in *Return of the Jedi*) in Dok-Ondar's Den of Antiquities.

Disney made it so that every crevice of Batuu is sprinkled with Star Wars charm. For anyone doubting that a land like this belongs in a Disney theme park, guess again. There's nothing but magic, fantasy, and dazzling storytelling throughout Galaxy's Edge. Even if you've never seen a *Star Wars* film, the spectacular production of the land is still mind-blowing. The world appears real, and the fun is abundant. No matter what your expectations are, you're certainly in for a wild ride.

MAP OF GALAXY'S EDGE

Toy Story Land
Entrance

Grand Avenue
Entrance

a. Star Wars: Rise of the Resistance (ride)
b. Market (shopping)
c. Docking Bay 7 Food & Cargo (dining)
d. Droid Depot (droid build)
e. Savi's Workshop (lightsaber build)
f. Millennium Falcon: Smugglers Run (ride)
g. Oga's Cantina (bar)
h. Milk Stand (drinks)

RIDES

There are two featured rides in Star Wars: Galaxy's Edge. The first is Millennium Falcon: Smugglers Run, a flight simulation ride where guests collaborate to fly Han Solo's famous ship. It's incredible to see that Disney built the Falcon from the ground up. We don't mean a *part* of it or a *model* of it. Disney built the entire ship *to scale* — and you get to fly it!

Seeing the Falcon for the first time brings many visitors to tears. It's like meeting a long lost friend in an unexpected place. Disney effectively unveils the ship by making visitors peek around a corner or step down stairs as it comes into view. After the initial shock, you might want to touch the thing, but there's a rusty-looking barrier surrounding the Falcon that keeps us humans at bay. Luckily, Disney photographers happily snap photos in front of her. Best of all, these shots don't get other guests in the background!

> ★ **Magic Tips** ★
> The MaxPass service works widely around Galaxy's Edge, including a spot in front of the Millennium Falcon. Photos taken by Disney photographers will show up on your Disney World mobile app usually within a couple of hours after being taken.

Finally, you get to fly the Millennium Falcon! But not so fast — there will likely be a wait. Luckily, the queue is riddled with Star Wars surprises. There are engine parts, defunct droids, and an unfinished game of Sabacc. Best of all, there are dozens and dozens of Easter eggs to look for when you're in the queue — what can you spot? (Hint: look for Porgs!)

Just before entering the Falcon, you'll meet Hondo Ohnaka, Disney's second-most advanced animatronic (the first being the singing Na'vi shaman in Pandora — The World of Avatar). The way that Hondo moves around the space makes him appear more like an actor than a robot. Hondo's believable performance is essential to the ride as he gives details about the mission. Finally, you'll walk into the famous halls of the Millennium Falcon and will receive a placeholder with one of three jobs: pilot, gunner, or flight engineer.

Each requires pushing buttons, flipping switches, and/or cranking the ship into hyperspace! Pilots have the most interactive job and they work together to fly the ship (one guest moves the ship left and right while the other moves up and down). Gunners and engineers sit in back of the pilots and press buttons to help destroy targets and repair ship damages.

Depending on how poorly you fly the Falcon, you may see damage in the hallway as you exit. However, if you perform well, you'll score points that are recorded on the Disney Play app (make sure you have Bluetooth enabled in the app).

* **Magic Tips** *
Flying the pilot position has the best views of the screens, but it also requires the most work. Sadly, you can't choose which job you play. If you want a specific position, you can always ask a Cast Member or switch with someone in your group. Engineers have the easiest job on deck, while pilots have the most work. If someone decides not to press buttons, the ship will automatically take over for them.

The Millennium Falcon ride experience also changes day and night. For example, fly during the day, and you'll see the sun out. At night, it's much darker around Black Spire Outpost!

The main attraction in Galaxy's Edge is Star Wars: Rise of the Resistance. This is a roughly 18-minute role-playing adventure with several ride experiences and plenty of jaw-dropping special effects. During the attraction, guests escape Batuu and find themselves in a dangerous encounter with the evil First Order.

Rise of the Resistance is part walk-through, part motion simulator, and part trackless ride adventure. You'll see real actors, animatronics, mind-blowing special effects, and more in this immersive attraction. We don't want to give away too much but Rise of the Resistance is a must-do experience. Overall, the ride is family-friendly, so most guests will enjoy the ride (it's about as thrilling as Indiana Jones Adventure but has less "dark" parts).

```
* Magic Tips *
Keep in mind, if you get motion sickness on
rides like Star Tours, you may want to avoid
the Millennium Falcon and Rise of the
Resistance.
```

MILLENNIUM FALCON: SMUGGLERS RUN
Best for: Kids, Tweens, Teens, Adults
Restrictions: 38" / 97cm
Lightning Lane: Yes, Disney Genie+

STAR WARS: RISE OF THE RESISTANCE
Best for: Kids, Tweens, Teens, Adults, Thrill Riders
Restrictions: 40" / 102cm
Notes: Due to the overwhelming popularity of Star Wars: Rise of the Resistance, guests may need a boarding pass to ride the attraction. We go over tips for obtaining a boarding group in a later chapter.
Lightning Lane: Yes, Individual

SHOWS
The shows of Galaxy's Edge don't have the same style as the traditional theatrical productions at Disney theme parks. Instead of running on a schedule, they appear to occur at random before unsuspecting guests. The main stage is Kylo Ren's ship where the First Order dramatically welcomes their leader to Batuu. After the show, guests can take photos with Kylo and his stormtroopers.

```
* Magic Tips *
Shows in Galaxy's Edge mostly occur during
the day, as do most character meetings
(though Rey and Chewbacca have been spotted
in the evenings). Just keep this in mind if
you are planning on visiting at night.
```

If you don't know who Vi Moradi is, you're not alone. She's a fairly new character, only having debuted in a *Star Wars* novel back in 2017. Vi Moradi, a rebel spy, is easy to pick out of a crowd. She has black and blue hair and usually wears a bright orange rebel vest. Vi was sent to Batuu by General Leia Organa to spy on Kylo and his troops.

We love the shows in Galaxy's Edge because guests become part of the storyline. Talk to Vi Moradi, and she might tell you about her mission. Kylo Ren also walks through the crowd as he looks for rebels. Additionally, you'll see characters like Rey and Chewbacca roaming Batuu during the day. These moments are ideal times to snap a photo with your favorite Star Wars characters.

DINING

Disney has created out-of-this-world dining experiences for Star Wars: Galaxy's Edge! There's a lively cantina serving alcoholic (and non-alcoholic) beverages, a rustic dining hall, and a stand with the famous blue milk!

The food in Galaxy's Edge is somewhat eclectic. Disney purposely made the flavors hard to place so that each bite seems foreign. For foodies, this is great. There are a wide variety of new treats in store for them across the entire land. For many children and picky eaters, getting something to tickle their tastebuds might be a bit challenging. If this pertains to your traveling party, we highly recommend reviewing the menu options on WaltDisneyWorld.com or the Walt Disney World app before visiting.

OGA'S CANTINA

This high-energy cantina feels incredibly authentic to the Star Wars Universe. The ancient-looking building houses a hodgepodge of equipment, creatures, and a droid DJ! The owner, Oga Garra, is a Blutopian who also runs the cantina. She doesn't take any sass and expects all guests to follow her rules. We never really see Oga, but her staff talks wildly about her as if she's a well-known threat.

For those who recall the captain of the first Star Tours attraction, you're in for a treat. DJ R-3X (voiced by Paul Reubens, a.k.a. "Pee-wee Herman") spins day and night as bartenders deliver fizzing, bubbling, and steaming drinks to their patrons. Each of the cocktails is named after a Star Wars theme or creature—and comes with a high price tag starting around $15 for an alcoholic beverage.

There are drinks for kids, too, like the Blue Bantha with a cookie on top!

OGA'S CANTINA RECOMMENDATIONS

+ **Fuzzy TaunTaun** (alcoholic beverage) – A sweet drink made with peach vodka, peach schnapps, orange juice, and cane sugar. There's a fun "Buzz Button Tingling" foam on top that numbs your lips!

+ **Dagobah Slug Slinger** (alcoholic beverage) – A semi-sweet beverage made with tequila, blue curacao, ginger, herbs, citrus juice, and bitters

+ **T-16 Skyhopper** (alcoholic beverage) – A bold drink made with vodka, melon liqueur, half and half, and served with a kiwi candy garnish

+ **Oga's Obsession** (non-alcoholic provision) – A gelatinous mix of lemonade and cotton candy flavors served with dried fruit eaten with a spoon

+ **Carbon Freeze** (non-alcoholic beverage) – Lemon-lime and wild strawberry juices with blueberry and green apple "popping pearls"

+ **Not Recommended:** The Jedi Mind Trick is just a bit basic and the Yub Nub is tasty but watch out—it's $45 (comes with a souvenir mug)!

> * **Magic Tips** *
> The Cantina may also limit your experience to two drinks per person and a 45-minute max time slot.

DOCKING BAY 7 FOOD & CARGO

This rustic quick-service diner serves a variety of alien eats for guests to enjoy. We think that the food here closely resembles Asian-fusion cuisine with some surprising twists. For example, the sweet and spicy Smoked Kaadu Ribs comes with a blueberry corn muffin. Additionally, there aren't forks and knives in Galaxy's Edge (for now). Instead, guests must use a spork-like utensil to cut, scoop, and eat. Yes, this can be a little tricky at first, but it doesn't take long to get the hang of the spork. It's these unexpected touches that give Black Spire Outpost its alien feel.

DOCKING BAY 7 DINING RECOMMENDATIONS

+ **Smoked Kaadu Ribs** (lunch/dinner entree) – Pork ribs slathered in a sweet and lightly spicy sauce and served with a melt-in-your-mouth blueberry corn muffin and cabbage slaw
+ **Batuuan Pot Roast Roast** (lunch/dinner entree) – Savory beef pot roast served over pasta with cooked kale and mushroom
+ **Endorian Roasted Chicken Salad** (lunch/dinner entree) – A hearty salad of mixed greens, roasted veggies, quinoa, and pumpkin seeds, topped with delicious marinated chicken, and tossed in green curry ranch
+ **Moof Juice** (non-alcoholic beverage) – A very sweet mix of fruit juices and chipotle-pineapple
+ **Oi-oi Puff** (dessert) – A delectable creamy raspberry puff with passion fruit mousse
+ **Not Recommended:** The Endorian Fried Chicken Tip-Yip is fairly bland

OTHER EATS

RONTO ROASTERS – This snacking spot is popular for its tangy sausage wraps served in a pita. However, we highly recommend the plant-based Ronto-less Garden Wrap with kimchi slaw—it's one of the best snacks in Disney's Hollywood Studios!

MILK STAND – Try blue and/or green milk from the *Star Wars* films. These are plant-based (dairy-free) drinks served like a cold slushy. Blue Milk has a berry flavor and Green Milk is more citrus. We recommend Blue Milk over Green.

Kat Saka's Kettle – Munch on a variety of flavored popcorn. We recommend the sweet and spicy Outpost Mix.

Jat Kaa's Coolers – Droid-driven carts serving drinks, including very popular round Coke bottles!

SHOPPING

There are seemingly infinite items to purchase in Galaxy's Edge including cute Porg plushies and Jedi robes! You can also purchase a Kowakian monkey-lizard puppet (the small creature found with Jabba the Hutt) that sits on your shoulder and moves with your commands. For more immersion, Disney sells an exclusive metal gift card in Galaxy's Edge called the Batuuan Spira. These gift cards are available at Droid Depot for about $5 and a minimum load of $100.

Sadly, some of the better experiences in Galaxy's Edge come at an extra cost. Savi's Workshop and the Droid Depot are amazingly fun, but you might spend hundreds of dollars entertaining your family. Here we review these experiences to help decide what's best for your visit.

SAVI'S WORKSHOP CUSTOM LIGHTSABERS

Savi's Workshop is a secret backdoor area—sort of like a speakeasy —where those seeking the Force can become a Jedi! In other words, you find a secret entrance in a scrap metal yard to build a custom lightsaber for around $220. Because of the hefty price tag, we only recommend this experience for those who are serious Star Wars fans.

These lightsabers are as good as real. They have metal hilts, and the blades make sounds as they draw in and out. You can choose one of four handles: Peace and Justice (Republic-era Jedi), Power and Control (dark side/Sith), Elemental Nature (wild Jedi), or Protection and Defense (ancient Jedi). There are also four different kyber crystals that change the color of the blade: blue, red, green, or violet.

The lightsaber building experience includes a moving preshow where guests are taught the ways of the Jedi until they are finally sworn in by a mystical guest (give you a hint of who it is, we will...). For true Star Wars fans, Savi's Workshop will be one of the best moments of their trip. Having a "working" lightsaber that both looks and feels real is one thing, but becoming part of the Jedi order is absolutely mind-blowing. John Williams, the original composer of the *Star Wars* films, scored new music to fit this stunning experience. While we wished for some extra animatronics, Savi's Workshop delivers with great storytelling through script, lighting, and sound. We believe that adults and kids 5 and older will greatly appreciate this experience. Savi's Workshop only allows one guest to accompany each builder, so plan accordingly.

> **⋆ Magic Tips ⋆**
> Savi's Workshop takes a limited number of guests per day. Thus, time slots can become full very quickly with demand. If you're planning on building a lightsaber, reserve your experience at **WaltDisneyWorld.com** up to 60 days in advance.
>
> If you want a different saber hilt, visit Dok-Ondar's Den of Antiquities and see if you can barter or trade for one. Individual lightsaber parts and pieces are sold outside of Savi's and are limited to two parts per receipt of a purchased lightsaber.

If you're not a big Star Wars fan, you might want to skip this one if $220 sounds out of your price range. Sure, it's a fantastic show, but some of the magic might be missed if you don't appreciate the folklore from this franchise. The lightsabers are also huge—about 45 inches (114 cm)—so small children will have a difficult time wielding these. Also keep in mind that your lightsaber doesn't easily break down, so something this size won't fit in a rental locker. For this reason, you may want to schedule Savi's Workshop around the end of the day or when you can take time to place it somewhere. Otherwise, you'll be riding rollercoasters like Space Mountain with it between your legs!

DOK-ONDAR'S DEN OF ANTIQUITIES

Our favorite shopping spot in Galaxy's Edge is Dok-Ondar's Den of Antiquities. Inside, you'll see an array of Star Wars-themed rarities and exclusive merchandise. Hardcore Star Wars fans will also enjoy the extensive collection of lightsaber hilts, kyber crystals, and holocrons for sale.

Most impressive is the animatronic Dok-Ondar, a finicky Ithorian who might trade with you for one of his prized lightsaber hilts —or you can uncover your own treasure within his collection. Dok-Ondar sells rare white and yellow kyber crystals that change the color of lightsaber blades. Additional blue, red, green, and violet crystals found in Savi's Workshop are sold, too!

```
* Magic Tips *
If you're looking for a less expensive
lightsaber, head over to Dok-Ondar's. He
sells kid-sized ones for a fraction of the
cost.

Those who buy a red kyber crystal may
discover a rare black one instead with a
special note! Additionally, some of the red
and green kyber crystals react differently
inside of a Sith or Jedi holocron.

There are seemingly countless collected
goods in Dok-Ondar's Den of Antiquities.
Look at the second level of the shop to spot
some classic Star Wars and other Lucasfilm
items.
```

DROID DEPOT

See a working factory where guests can make their very own remote-controlled droid! You pick the parts to customize a BB-8 or R2-D2 unit. The droids start around $100 each and are fun to build for kids and adults (we recommend ages 6 and older, though Disney lists 3 and older). The Droid Depot doesn't have the show elements found in Savi's Workshop, but it likely makes a better take-home toy. Kids might play with lightsabers a bit, but a remote-control toy is fun for just about everyone.

Droid Depot is also home to some luxury finds. Guests can buy and design a fully animatronic R2-D2 for $25,000! If you're dropping the dough on this one, R2 can be customized with personality and a battle-worn appearance. If $25,000 is just a *little* bit out of your price range, R2 also hangs out at the depot for pics and chats with guests!

THE MARKET

Black Spire's prime marketplace is home to a gallery of small shops. Set up like a co-op, guests can browse the shelves and hidden elements within these stores. Most of the items appear handmade so as to add to the authenticity of visiting an alien planet with realistic merchandise.

Black Spire Outfitters – Pick up a Jedi robe and other costumes inspired by characters like Rey and the dark-sided Sith. Clothing pieces come in multiple sizes for kids and adults. Unfortunately, Disney prevents those aged 14 and older from wearing these costumes throughout the park. This ban may be removed in the near future as demand increases for guests to live out their Star Wars story in full garb.

Creature Stall – Set up like a small pet store, this shop is filled with *Stars Wars*-inspired toys from porg puppets to plush tauntauns. There are also several small animatronics here including a sleeping loth-cat found in a crate near the entrance. Loth-cats are furry alien critters made famous from the animated series *Star Wars Rebels*. Outside of the Creature Stall is a small register with Kowakian monkey-lizards, sinister-looking critters that work as puppets that sit on guests' shoulders. These monkey-lizards—like the one found in Jabba the Hutt's palace in *Return of the Jedi*—run about $70 each.

Jewels of Bith – The Bith were an alien race from the planet of Clak'dor VII. They were known for their highly evolved mental and motor skills for playing music and creating fine wares. If you're looking for more day-to-day clothes, this store sells everything from T-shirts and jackets to hats and trinkets. Pick up misting fans, keychains, pins, and several other gifts in this shop. To keep with authenticity, nothing in this store will say "Star Wars: Galaxy's Edge" but instead read "Black Spire Outpost" or "Batuu." If you're looking for merchandise with "Star Wars: Galaxy's Edge" on it, check out the shops on Hollywood Boulevard near the park's entrance.

Toydarian Toymaker – Discover wooden and hand-sewn toys perfect for collectors of all ages. There are also instruments and games for sale here. The store gets its name from the flying alien species Toydarians, like Watto, who appeared as a junk dealer in *The Phantom Menace*. You can see the Toydarian shop owner, Zabaka, flying around her shop through a foggy window.

OTHER STORES

The Resistance Supply – Kiosks found near the Rise of the Resistance attraction selling various gifts, clothes, and toys.

First Order Cargo — A store near Kylo Ren's ship that sells goods fitted for the light or the dark side. Buy everything from clothing to trinkets made famous by Star Wars characters. Look above First Order Cargo and spot Stormtroopers on the roofs!

MORE TO EXPLORE

Data Pad Interactions
The Play Disney mobile application has a special data pad designed just for Galaxy's Edge. Open the app, click on the icon in Galaxy's Edge, and follow the instructions to hack, decode, and interact with the world around you. You'll earn points as you crack simple codes, and even make things like droids move around the land!

The Language
Learn the language of Batuu from the locals! They say many words and phrases that aren't used on Earth. Some are a bit self-explanatory while others can be somewhat confusing to hear for the first time. For example, there are several ways to say "hello" or "goodbye" when visiting Batuu. To keep you up to speed, here are several of the phrases we've gathered:

BATUUAN SPEAK	ENGLISH MEANING
Datapad	mobile device / phone / credit card machine
Credits	dollars (money)
Credentials	Disney discount card (VISA, DVC Card, etc.)

Credit Reducer	Disney discount card (VISA, DVC Card, etc.)
Hydrator	water fountain
Scans	photos
Image Data Card	Disney PhotoPass Card
Image Scanner	camera / phone camera
Cargo	personal items such as backpacks and cameras
Cargo Manifest	receipt
Holograms	Magic Shots (added effects to Disney PhotoPass images)
"Good Run!"	"Good Luck!"
"Bright Suns!"	"Good Day!" or "Hello!" said in the daytime
"Rising Moons!"	"Good Evening!" or "Hello!" said at night
"Under the Shadow of the Spire!"	"Cheers!"
"May the Spires Keep You!"	"Goodbye!"
"Till the Spire!"	"Goodbye!" or "Until We Meet Again!"
"Good Journey!"	"Goodbye!"
"For the Order!"	a First Order salute
"May the Force Be With You"	a Resistance salute
Travelers/Off-Worlders	park guests
Youngling/Padawan	child

ADVENTURE AWAITS...

Virtually every corner of Galaxy's Edge has some hidden surprises awaiting you. For example, drink from the water fountain near the Market and spot a dianoga—the trash monster found in the original *Star Wars* film! With so much to see and do, you'll want to set aside plenty of time (and maybe a chunk of cash) before visiting Galaxy's Edge. You might not be able to do it all in a single day, which will only increase your desire to return to this beautiful and unique land.

CHAPTER ELEVEN

DISNEY'S ANIMAL KINGDOM

INTRODUCTION

Completed in 1998, Disney's Animal Kingdom is a unique theme park dedicated to both the classic Walt Disney World attractions as well as animal conservation. With lions, tigers, and elephants living in the park, it would seem that Animal Kingdom is Disney's version of a zoo. That couldn't be further from the truth. Animal Kingdom is breathtaking in its seamless foliage between specialized lands and perfect environments for its animals. As you travel through the jungle, you'll meet Disney favorites like meerkats and warthogs as well as critically endangered species. Disney takes this park seriously and works its hardest to be the best for its animal inhabitants.

Set on more than 500 acres of land, Animal Kingdom is the largest theme park in the world! The centerpiece is the famous Tree of Life, a 14-story replica of the same tree from Disney's *The Lion King*. Animal Kingdom perfectly ties together fun and information in six distinct lands, including Pandora—The World of Avatar, an alien planet inspired by the James Cameron film, *Avatar.*

For first-time guests, Disney's Animal Kingdom always feels new and exciting. Perhaps it's that you are seeing the actual animals roam as you ride on an African-style safari while you learn about the many habits of the spectacular creatures before you. The fun blend of family-friendly attractions, beautiful animals, and expansive thrill rides has something for everyone visiting this unique theme park.

THE OASIS

The lush entrance to Disney's Animal Kingdom. Here you will find several walkways through bush and along rivers filled with exotic plants and animals that find their home here. The Rainforest Cafe is also located here. There are no rides in the Oasis, so this land feels a lot like a well-designed animal sanctuary.

Theme: Tropical oasis

ANIMALS
Mammals: Barbirusa, Giant Anteater, Swamp Wallaby
Reptiles: Florida Cooter, Rhinoceros Iguanas
Birds: African Spoonbill, Bufflehead, Chiloe Wigeon, Exotic Duck, Hooded Merganser, Indian Spotbill, Macaw, Medium Sulpher-crested Cockatoo, Reeves' Muntjac, Teal

DISCOVERY ISLAND

The centerpiece or "hub" of Animal Kingdom. It's home to several animals, shops, and the park's signature Tree of Life. Discovery Island is surrounded by the Discovery River and connects to nearly every land in the park.

Theme: An animal-inhabited island

SHOWS AND ATTRACTIONS

TREE OF LIFE AWAKENING
Best for: Everyone
Description: See the Tree of Life come to life with four different animations that magically project on the tree at night.
Level: Family

Recommendation: This nighttime show can best be seen as you walk toward it from the Oasis. Views and details are better seen closer to the tree. Since this show occurs throughout the night, crowds usually stop forming after the first hour or so.
Line Length: None / **Lightning Lane:** No

IT'S TOUGH TO BE A BUG!
Best for: Everyone
Description: A 9-minute family-friendly 4D show starring characters from Pixar's *A Bug's Life*. With special lighting effects and a large 3D screen, you'll feel as small as a bug as you laugh along to this hilarious attraction.
Level: Everyone
Recommendation: Though Disney originally planned this attraction to please families with kids, everyone appears to get a kick out of this attraction. The theatre is large, so if there ever is a wait, it's usually just until the next show loads. For the best viewing, we recommend sitting in the center of the 4th-7th rows.
Line Length: Short / **Lightning Lane:** Yes, Disney Genie+

WILDERNESS EXPLORERS
Best for: Young Kids, Kids
Description: Inspired by Pixar's Up, kids can earn up to 30 Wilderness Explorer badges by completing challenges.
Level: Kids
Recommendation: A playground for kids of all ages.
Line Length: Very Short / **Lightning Lane:** No

DISCOVERY ISLAND TRAILS
Best for: Everyone
Description: Follow pathways around the Tree of Life to see waterfalls, unique animals, and meet Timon.
Level: Everyone
Recommendation: Great for animal lovers. Check out the many carvings in the Tree of Life and watch them magically come to life at night!
Line Length: None / **Lightning Lane:** No

ANIMALS

Mammals: African Crested Porcupine, Otters, Axis Deer, Cotton-top Tamarin, Lemur, Kangaroo
Birds: Black Neck Swan, Cockatoo, Exotic Duck, Teals, West African Crowned Crane, White Stork
Reptiles: Galapagos Tortoise, Lappet Face Vulture, Flamingo, Macaw, Saddle-Billed Stork

AFRICA

A popular land for safari excursions, African animals, and eateries, Africa is centered around Harambe, a fictional Kenyan village. This area has the most animals spread throughout its unique attractions. The best way to see the most animals is on the family-friendly Kilimanjaro Safari ride. Many of these animals can also be seen from the Pangani Forest Exploration Trail.

Theme: African village and safari

RIDES

KILIMANJARO SAFARIS
Best for: Everyone
Description: Hop aboard a guided caravan tour of Africa. From the jungles to the savanna, you'll see everything from wildebeest and giraffes to rhinos and lions. The animals are in "cage-less" enclosures (except for the carnivores, of course), so watch them roaming free before your eyes.
Level: Everyone
Recommendation: The Kilimanjaro Safaris is one of the best attractions in Animal Kingdom. This ride does get a bit bumpy, so
beware in case you have issues with that.
Disney also just opened the ride for nighttime safaris. Sadly, most of the animals are almost impossible to see at night, and portions of the ride are closed as well.

Line Length: Medium / **Lightning Lane:** Yes, Disney Genie+

ANIMALS

Mammals: Addax, African Elephant, African Wild Dog, Antelope, Ankole-Watusi, Bong, Bontebok, Cheetah, Duiker, Eland, Giraffe, Greater Kudu, Hippopotamus, Hyena, Impala, Lion, Okapi, Oryx, Ostrich, Mandrill, Nyala, Rhinoceros, Waterbuck, Warthog, Wildebeest, Zebra

Birds: African Ducks, African Geese, African Pelican, African Pintail, African Stork, Blue Crane, Flamingo, Helmeted Guineafowl, Teal, White-breasted Cormorant

Reptiles: Nile Crocodile

SHOWS AND ATTRACTIONS

FESTIVAL OF THE LION KING

Best for: Young Kids, Kids, Tweens, Adults 30+

Description: An interactive 30-minute stage show set to the characters and music of Disney's *The Lion King*.

Level: Family

Recommendation: Easily one of Walt Disney World's best live shows, the Festival of the Lion King entertains guests with dancing, puppetry, and fantastic costumes. We highly recommend seeing this one! The theatre is divided into four sections, so depending on where you sit, you'll have a slightly different experience. Each section is represented by an animal and the show's four hosts interact with their respective section.

Line Length: Short / **Lightning Lane:** Yes, Disney Genie+

PANGANI FOREST EXPLORATION TRAIL

Best for: Everyone

Description: Walk along the Kilimanjaro Safaris to see animals you can't explore from the caravan. There are more primates, reptiles, and even insects on this trail. There's also a large aviary filled with African birds.

Level: Everyone

Recommendation: We recommend this to anyone craving to see more African animals. The walk is short at little over 1/3 of a mile, so kids will love this one.

Line Length: None / **Lightning Lane:** No

ANIMALS

Mammals: Colobus Monkey, Duiker, Gerenuk, Gorilla, Hippopotamus, Lion, Meerkat, Naked Mole Rat, Okapi, Oryx, Zebra
Birds: African Duck, African Geese, African Parrot, African Pigeon, African Pelican, African Pintail, African Starling, African Stork, Blake Crake, Brimstone Canary, Blue Cran, Collared Kingfisher, Hamerkop, Hoopoe, Kori Bustard, Shrikes, Taveta Weaver, Teal, White-bellied Go-Away-Bird
Reptiles: Boa Constrictor, Shield-tailed Agama, Spiny-tailed Lizard
Arachnids and Fish: Lake Victoria Cichlid, Tarantula

WILD AFRICA TREK – VIP EXPERIENCE

If you're looking for an expanded safari experience, we highly recommend this attraction. Get closer to the animals, move across rope bridges through the jungle, and ride on a specialized caravan safari during the second half. This is a 3-hour tour with a separate cost.

Recommendation: Because this VIP excursion is so long, we don't recommend it for kids or those who have trouble walking. Guests must be at least 18 or older, or 8 years old with an adult. You must be able to wear harness gear and weigh under 300 lbs.
Pricing: $189-$249
Booking: (407) 939-8687

RAFIKI'S PLANET WATCH

A section connected to Africa that highlights how to practice conservation to save the Earth's animals from harm and extinction. Guests must take a train to get to this land.

Theme: Africa / Global Conservation

RIDES

WILDLIFE EXPRESS TRAIN
Best for: Young Kids, Adults 50+

Description: A slow-paced steam railroad to Rafiki's Planet Watch. The 7-minute ride (5-minute return) takes guests behind the scenes of the habitats before emptying onto the Planet Watch.
Level: Family
Recommendation: If you have curiosity about Rafiki's Planet Watch and want to see some behind-the-scenes areas where the animals live, we recommend this ride.
Line Length: Short / **Lightning Lane:** No

CONSERVATION STATION

Conservation Station is a special care facility designed to help animals in the park. You can interact with some of them as well as watch a 3D movie about the rainforest, see backstage cameras, see cases with crawling insects, and watch the veterinarians care for animals.

ANIMATION EXPERIENCE AT CONSERVATION STATION
Best for: Young Kids, Kids, Tweens
Description: Here guests learn to draw Disney characters based on animals here at the Animation Experience.
Level: Family
Recommendation: Great for those who love animals and who want to learn how to draw Disney characters.
Line Length: Short / **Lightning Lane:** Yes, Disney Genie+

HABITAT HABIT! — Walk along trails to discover cotton-top tamarin monkeys playing.

AFFECTION SECTION — Pet and feed cows, donkeys, goats, pigs, and sheep in this petting corral.

> **· Magic Tips ·**
> We recommend most of the attractions in Conservation Station for kids ages 3-8. However, older kids and teens may enjoy the Wildlife Express Train and the Animation Experience.

ASIA

Discover the fictional Asian land of Anandapur (Sanskrit for "Place of Many Delights") as you journey along a river village and deep into the Himalayan mountains. Asia is home to unique animals from beautiful tigers to stunning birds, as well as rides that can thrill the entire family.

Theme: Asian villages and the Himalayas

RIDES

EXPEDITION EVEREST
Best for: Tweens, Teens, Adults
Description: Costing Disney $100 million to make, Expedition Everest is one of the world's most expensive roller coasters! Lift high into the peaks of a mythical mountain deep in the Himalayas. You'll cruise at high speeds and end up rolling backward when attacked by the mountain's terrifying resident—a yeti!
Level: Thrill Riders
Recommendation: Perfect for those who enjoy high-speed rollercoasters. Expedition Everest also offers a Single Rider Line. Put this to use on busy days! To access the Single Rider line, look for the sign next to the regular queue entrance.
Line Length: Long / **Lightning Lane:** Yes, Individual

> **· Magic Tips ·**
> Expedition Everest is scheduled to close from January 4th through mid-April 2022.
>
> This ride allows guests to choose a front or back row seat! Just ask the Cast Member right before you board the coaster to get placed in a separate queue for these seats.

KALI RIVER RAPIDS
Best for: Kids, Tweens, Teens, Adults

Description: A family-friendly raft ride through the Asian jungle. You will likely get soaked on this 12-person water ride!

Level: Families, Thrill Riders

Recommendation: This wet ride is great for hot days! There are dips and spills, so if you're not looking to get wet, you might want to avoid this one.

Line Length: Medium / **Lightning Lane:** Yes, Disney Genie+

· **Magic Tips** ·

Kali River Rapids has shorter lines in the morning when it's cooler and very long lines in the hot afternoons. The shortest wait times are at night, just before Animal Kingdom closes.

SHOWS AND ATTRACTIONS

DISNEY KITETAILS

Best for: Families with Young Kids

Description: See wind kites shaped like popular Disney characters sail over the water.

Level: Everyone

Recommendation: The show might entertain small children but it's not very exciting. Overall, this just feels like a filler attraction until a new show is added to Disney's Animal Kingdom.

Line Length: Very Low / **Lightning Lane:** No

MAHARAJAH JUNGLE TREK

Best for: Everyone

Description: A walking trail slightly over 1/3 of a mile, showcasing some of the most exotic animals in all of Asia. From tigers to komodo dragons, the Maharajah Jungle Trek is both informative and delightful for all.

Level: Everyone

Recommendation: Not to be missed for those looking to see spectacular and rare animals.

Line Length: None / **Lightning Lane:** No

UP! A GREAT BIRD ADVENTURE

Best for: Young Kids

Description: A stage show with live birds and characters from Pixar's *Up*!
Level: Family
Recommendation: Best for kids 8 and under!
Line Length: Short / **Lightning Lane:** No (may be added later)
Holiday Script: This show spreads holiday cheer beginning in November.

ANIMALS
Mammals: Banteng, Bengal Tiger, Gibbon, Malayan Flying Fox, Sumatran Tiger, Water Buffalo
Reptiles: Komodo Dragon
Birds: More than 50 Species of Asian birds like Starling, Duck, Parrot, Peafowl, Pheasant, Barbet, and Kingfisher.

DINOLAND U.S.A.

This land takes guests on a journey to the past when the magnificent —and sometimes terrifying—dinosaurs roamed the Earth! There are dino-themed rides, fossil replicas, and a carnival-themed area.

Theme: Dinosaur museum and roadside attraction

RIDES

DINOSAUR
Best for: Kids, Tweens, Teens, Adults, Thrill Riders
Description: Get sent back to the age of the dinosaurs in a special SUV time machine. Themed after Disney's *Dinosaur* film, there's rocky terrain in this unique dark ride similar to Disneyland's Indiana Jones Adventure.
Level: Thrill Riders (must be 40" / 102cm or taller)
Recommendation: Perfect for Thrill Riders though some Kids may become frightened of the scarier dinosaurs.

Line Length: Medium / **Lightning Lane:** Yes, Disney Genie+

TRICERATOP SPIN
Best for: Young Kids, Kids
Description: Similar to Dumbo's Flight at the Magic Kingdom, riders control brightly colored triceratops as they soar in the air.
Level: Kids
Recommendation: A perfect ride for Young Kids.
Line Length: Short / **Lightning Lane:** No

SHOWS AND ATTRACTIONS

FINDING NEMO – THE MUSICAL
Best for: Young Kids, Kids, Tweens, Adults 50+
Description: A family-friendly musical stage show.
Level: Family
Recommendation: Finding Nemo – The Musical is scheduled to reopen sometime in 2022. Though many of the popular songs will return, it's expected to be a completely different and much shorter version of the previous show.

MORE ATTRACTIONS

THE BONEYARD
Parents, take a break while kids run around these dino dig-site playground!

DINO-SUE
A replica of one of the largest Tyrannosaurus Rex fossils ever found. It's impressive to stand next to Sue, the massive T-Rex!

DONALD'S DINO BASH!
Meet Donald Duck and his family (including rare characters like Scrooge McDuck) as they celebrate their ancestral connection to dinosaurs! Other characters greet guests here, too, like Chip and Dale in their dino suits!

FOSSIL FUN GAMES
Family-friendly carnival games with stuffed animal prizes. Each game costs money to play.

PANDORA – THE WORLD OF AVATAR

Enter a breathtaking alien world with mysterious flora and fauna that welcome you to their planet! See the famous floating mountains and experience some of the newest, state-of-the-art adventure rides anywhere in the world! Based around James Cameron's *Avatar* film series, Pandora is a not-to-be-missed land at Animal Kingdom.

Theme: Alien planet based on the *Avatar* film series

RIDES

AVATAR FLIGHT OF PASSAGE
Best for: Thrill Riders, Tweens, Teens, Adults
Description: Fly high on a winged alien banshee as you soar over Pandora's nature in this unique flight simulator.
Level: Thrill Riders (must be 44" or taller)
Recommendation: If you like rides like Star Tours and Soarin', Flight of Passage takes this simulation experience to the next level!
Line Length: Very Long / **Lightning Lane:** Yes, Individual

NA'VI RIVER JOURNEY
Best for: Young Kids, Kids, Adults 50+
Description: Explore the bioluminescent world of Pandora in this serene boat "dark ride."
Level: Everyone
Recommendation: This is a fun and gentle boat ride with some very cool Disney magic! The animatronics are awesome and the lighting is breathtaking!
Line Length: Very Long / **Lightning Lane:** Yes, Disney Genie+

PANDORA'S SECRETS

Pandora is an incredibly immersive land! We recommend taking your time to explore the walkways and other parts of the area. High above, you'll see amazing waterfalls coming from the floating mountains. However, some of the higher ones are actually just spinning wheels that simulate rushing water!

On the ground, look for the tracks of several wild animals. You can spot many of them in the water and hear them singing from the mountains. You also may be able to touch some of the plant life and interact with them. The massive plant near the attraction's entrance is called Flaska Reclinata. It may steam and squirt water when someone touches its pink and purple flesh!

When the sun goes down, the world of Avatar changes. Watch the bioluminescent world come to life under the stars as the magnificent creatures and plants light up in stunning ways. We don't want to give away too much more, but we highly recommend that you make your way to this unique land at night for some unforgettable magic!

· **Magic Tips** ·
Need water? Check out the water bottle refill stations at the drinking fountains in Pandora. It's a free and easy way to keep hydrated.

DISNEY WATER PARKS

INTRODUCTION

Walt Disney World opened its original water park, Disney's River Country, in 1976. This park has since been closed (as of 2001), as the massive popularity of its newer parks, Typhoon Lagoon (1989) and Blizzard Beach (1995), conquered the scene. Combined, the Disney water parks bring in nearly 5 million visitors annually—with Typhoon Lagoon being slightly more popular. Each water park is set in a different location within the Walt Disney World Resort. Typhoon Lagoon is near Disney Springs, and Blizzard Beach is on the other end near Animal Kingdom and between the All-Star Sports Resort and Disney's Coronado Springs Resort hotels.

Typhoon Lagoon is themed after a paradise bay—shortly after a storm has hit! There are pirate ships, streams, waterfalls, palm trees, and dozens of attractions. Blizzard Beach pulls its theme from ski lodges where the snow melts in the summer heat. It's an interesting hodgepodge of ideas with log cabins and snowy slopes— only without the cold! Each park has a similar layout with a mountain peak in the center, a wave pool below, and a lazy river around the perimeter.

Many adults who visit without children may want to skip the water park and just lounge at the pools in their resort hotel. Remember, most of the hotels have their own waterslides. In fact, if you are staying less than five nights, it may be difficult to fit a full day in at the water parks and still see all of the theme parks. It's tricky to choose, so we give you concise information on which slides and attractions will benefit your vacation.

KEEP IN MIND

1. During the winter, water parks may close for refurbishment.
2. The line lengths for water parks can change frequently (but expect up to 30-minute wait times during the summer peak season for the most popular slides). Since everyone can go at their own pace, the water parks are a perfect time to find relaxation during your stay.
3. If you are feeling adventurous, you can do both water parks in one day. We recommend spacing these out by going at opening to one and heading over to the next in the afternoon when the crowds have lessened. Just remember that you might not get your choice of lounging area at the second park you choose.
4. There are no Disney Genie+ selections for Typhoon Lagoon, as the average wait time is usually only 10-15 minutes (with some of the popular attractions having 30-minute waits).
5. Get to the water parks at opening to reserve the best lounge chairs for your family. Prime spots are near the wave pool or just outside of it near the lazy rivers.
6. Keep your belongings safe. There's a general safe feeling all around the park, so you can leave some items like sunscreen and visors unattended (or under your towel). We recommend storing away your cellphone and car keys in a rental locker.

· **Magic Tips** ·

The Disney water parks may shut down due to cold or severe weather. Have a backup plan just in case this occurs.

WHAT TO BRING

The water parks have nearly everything you'll need for poolside fun—but with a cost. That's why we recommend bringing these items with you into the parks:

1. Sunscreen – You'll be out in the sun all day, after all.
2. Beach towels – Rentals are available. You can bring the towels from your hotel if you want, though Walt Disney World doesn't recommend this (and we're not saying that you should). However, people do it from time to time.
3. Change of clothing – It's not vital, but we recommend it if you plan to go somewhere afterward. If you forget anything, the shops at the water parks sell quality sunscreen, sunglasses, and visors—for a premium price.

RENTALS

LOCKERS

We highly recommend keeping your things here. There are two locker rental stations in each park near the entrance. Pricing is $10/day for a regular locker (12.5 inches by 17 inches) and $15/day for a large (15.5 inches by 17 inches). Lockers take credit cards and cash and your items are kept safe with a 4-digit code that you set. Lockers can sell out, so make sure you get to the park early to reserve one.

CABANAS

The Beachcomber Shacks at Typhoon Lagoon and the Polar Patios at Blizzard Beach are reserved areas that come with lounge chairs, a personal locker, and a cooler for up to 6 guests (though you can pay more for 7-10 guests). Prices vary (usually $200-$350), and spaces are limited, so reserve yours as early as possible before your visit by calling: (407) 939-7529.

UMBRELLA AND LOUNGE CHAIRS

If you don't want to fork out the money for a cabana, you can always reserve an umbrella. These come with two loungers, two chairs, and towels for up to 4 guests. If you have two adults, we recommend splitting up at the start of the day to reserve a locker and lounge chairs. Sometimes the "rope drop" at the start of the day can get crowded. Have one person reserve the chairs in your desired section and the other rent a locker. You don't want to miss out on either! If we had to pick one over the other, we'd pick a lounging space and take our chances that the lockers will still be available. Pricing varies from $40-$50 per reservation. Like the cabanas, these are limited, so call ahead to reserve: (407) 939-7529.

TYPHOON LAGOON

Escape to the wild tropics in this water park built around a Caribbean beach, complete with a sunken ship perched high on a mountain!

Theme: Post-typhoon Caribbean beach

Note: Typhoon Lagoon did not reopen in 2021 and may remain closed for part of 2022.

RIDES AND ATTRACTIONS

TYPHOON LAGOON SURF POOL
Best for: Tweens, Teens, and Adults
Description: A wave pool with waves that reach up to 6 feet.
Level: Everyone
Recommendation: This massive pool is wildly popular. Kids, Tweens, Teens, and Adults will love to splash in the blue waves. The waves aren't constant, as they come every couple of minutes. Young Kids should be kept near the beach part where the waves are just a couple of inches in height.

CASTAWAY CREEK
Best for: Family, Adults
Description: An expansive, 2000-foot-long lazy river that slowly travels around the perimeter of Typhoon Saloon. The entire journey takes about 20 minutes. Hop aboard one of the many floating rafts as you cruise down this gentle river.
Level: Everyone
Recommendation: Best for adults looking to relax, though Young Kids and Kids enjoy splashing around this area as well. You can stay in Castaway Creek for as long as you'd like. There are several entry points for all to enjoy.

KETCHAKIDDEE CREEK
Best for: Young Kids, Kids
Description: A water play area perfect for Young Kids under 48 inches.
Level: Young Kids and Kids
Recommendation: A great space to take your kids who want to ride water slides and splash in an area designed for them.

KEELHAUL
Best for: Kids, Tweens, Teens, Adults, Thrill Riders
Description: A beautiful waterslide with an inner tube.
Level: Family
Recommendation: Perfect for Kids to Adults, but Young Kids may want to sit this one out.

MAYDAY FALLS
Best for: Kids, Tweens, Teens, Adults, Thrill Riders
Description: A rapids-themed waterslide on a tube. Go over bumps and small drops as you adventure quickly down a river.
Level: Family
Recommendation: Great for Kids to Adults, but Young Kids may want to sit this one out. This one can be a bit rough!

GANGPLANK FALLS
Best for: Kids, Tweens, Teens, Adults, Thrill Riders
Description: A giant inner tube that seats four takes you down a wide waterslide.
Level: Family
Recommendation: Perfect for Kids to Adults, but Young Kids may want to sit this one out.

HUMUNGA KOWABUNGA
Best for: Tweens, Teens, Adults
Description: One of the park's steepest slides—and it's in the dark. Travel alone through a treacherous path that leads to a plunge.
Level: Thrill Riders (must be 48" or taller)
Recommendation: Best for those looking for a thrill.

STORM SLIDES
Best for: Tweens, Teens, Adults, Thrill Riders
Description: A set of three waterslides that plummet from the ship-wrecked mountain top. Each of them dunk into a pool.
Level: Family
Recommendation: Best for those looking for a family-fun thrill.

CRUSH 'N' GUSHER
Best for: Tweens, Tween, Adults, Thrill Riders
Description: A high-speed "water coaster" on a raft that holds 2-3 people.
Level: Thrill Riders
Recommendation: A fun bobsled waterslide experience!

BAY SLIDES
Best for: Young Kids, Kids
Description: A water play area perfect for Young Kids under 60 inches.
Level: Young Kids and Kids
Recommendation: A great space to take your kids who want to ride water slides and splash in an area designed for them.

MOUNTAIN TRAIL
Best for: Young Kids and Adults 30+
Description: Green, tree-filled walkways beneath Typhoon Lagoon's famous mountain. There are palm trees, beautiful Caribbean structures, and rope bridges.
Level: Everyone
Recommendation: Perfect for those looking for a stroll, though we recommend this part mostly for Adults, as Kids and Teens may find it boring.

MISS ADVENTURE FALLS
Best for: Kids, Tweens, Tween, Adults, Thrill Riders
Description: The newest slide at Disney's Typhoon Lagoon! Discover the legend of Captain Mary Oceaneer as you discover her fabled lost fortune in this unique attraction. Disney designed Miss Adventure Falls with the entire family in mind. Hop aboard a family-sized raft and climb to the top before descending into a raging river.
Level: Family / Thrill Riders
Recommendation: Great for those wanting to board with their entire family.

MORE ATTRACTIONS

SURF LESSONS
Learn to surf in Typhoon Lagoon's signature wave pool! Hop aboard a surfboard in a 3-hour event for swimmers of all surf levels. Disney stops the guest list at 25 people so that everyone has ample time to catch waves. The instructors are fantastic and make the experience enjoyable for all! Lessons are $190 per person for guests ages 8 and older. Booking: (407) 939-7529

H2GLOW NIGHTS
During the summer months, Disney's Typhoon Lagoon throws a rave-style nighttime party. The entire resort glows with neon lights and most of the attractions are open. See special characters, usually from Pixar, in festive rave-style gear while music bumps in the background. With advanced tickets ranging from about $60-$70 a night, this event is a lot of fun for the entire family. The warm Orlando weather during these nights also makes jumping in a wave pool and heading down a waterslide even more enjoyable—and you don't have to worry about a sunburn! Hours run from 8pm-11pm on select nights usually from May through August. Early entry begins at 6pm.

BLIZZARD BEACH

Enter a ski resort on the brink of summer as the snow melts into a stunning water park! Disney's Blizzard Beach is as fun as it sounds–but without the cold! And what's ice and Disney without a little *Frozen*? Yes, there are also areas designed after one of the world's most beloved animated films. The park is built around a snowy summit with three color-coded sections: the Green Slopes, the Purple Slopes, and the Red Slopes.

Theme: Snowy ski resort water park

RIDES AND ATTRACTIONS

MELT-AWAY BAY
Best for: Kids, Tweens, Teens, and Adults
Description: A wave pool filled with rafts and small waves along rocks.
Level: Family
Recommendation: This large pool is wildly popular for families. The waves are constant, but are small and easy to ride.

CROSS COUNTRY CREEK
Best for: Family, Adults
Description: A calm, winding river journey that expands for 3,000 feet around the perimeter of Blizzard Beach. Hop aboard one of the many floating rafts as you cruise down this gentle river near waterfalls, lush foliage, and some of the thrill rides.
Level: Everyone
Recommendation: Best for adults looking to relax, though Young Kids and Kids enjoy splashing around this area as well. You can stay in Cross Country Creek for as long as you'd like. There are 7 points around the creek to enter.

SKI PATROL TRAINING CAMP
Best for: Kids, Tweens
Description: A water play area, short slides, and an obstacle course that's perfect for Kids and Tweens under 60 inches.
Level: Kids
Recommendation: A great space to take your kids who want to ride water slides and splash in an area designed for them.

TIKE'S PEAK
Best for: Young Kids, Kids
Description: A water play area perfect for Young Kids under 48 inches. There are mini water slides with and without rafters, shallow pools, and soft ground in case small kids slip!
Level: Young Kids and Kids
Recommendation: A great space to take your kids who want to ride water slides and splash in an area designed for them.

GREEN SLOPE

SUMMIT PLUMMET
Best for: Thrill Riders
Description: A single body slide that takes thrill riders through a high-speed plunge from the park's centerpiece, Mt. Gushmore.
Level: Thrill Riders (must be 48 inches or taller)
Recommendation: Thrill Riders only.

SLUSH GUSHER
Best for: Thrill Riders
Description: A body slide that takes thrill riders through a high-speed plunge from this 90-foot tall slide.
Level: Thrill Riders (must be 48 inches or taller)
Recommendation: Thrill Riders only.

TEAMBOAT SPRINGS
Best for: Kids, Tweens, Teens, Adults, Thrill Riders
Description: A massive inner tube that seats 6 as it takes you down a long, wide waterslide.
Level: Family
Recommendation: Perfect for the family, but you might want to leave the Young Kids out of it as it does get a bit scary.

CHAIRLIFT
Best for: Kids, Tweens, Teens, Adults, Thrill Riders
Description: What's a ski resort without a ski lift? Take the Chairlift to the top of Mt. Gushmore to ride the Green Slope Rides.
Level: Family (must be 32" or taller)
Recommendation: A fun way to the top, but we don't recommend heading up there if you have a fear of heights.

PURPLE SLOPE

TOBOGGAN RACERS
Best for: Kids, Tweens, Teens, Adults, Thrill Riders
Description: Fly down wavy slopes on slick mats—a family favorite!
Level: Family and Thrill Riders
Recommendation: Perfect for Kids and older. The hills are steep, so if someone has an issue with heights, this might not be the ride for them.

SNOW STORMERS
Best for: Kids, Tweens, Teens, Adults
Description: Built to look like sledding slopes in the snow, Snow Stormers is another fun mat slide.
Level: Everyone
Recommendation: Great for those who want to try a mat slide without the scary heights. We don't recommend this ride for Young Kids.

DOWNHILL DOUBLE DIPPER
Best for: Tweens, Teens, Adults, Thrill Riders
Description: Race against friends and family in these side-by-side, snow-covered tubes in the wilderness.
Level: Thrill Riders (must be 48 inches or taller)
Recommendation: These are short slides with drops, and are very fun to race. The height requirement won't allow many Kids to ride, though they may want to.

RED SLOPE

RUNOFF RAPIDS
Best for: Kids, Tweens, Tween, Adults, Thrill Riders
Description: Three different slides change up the thrills as you travel on inner tubes over and through the lush wilderness of Disney's Blizzard Beach. Each slide carries you in fun swirls down Mt. Gushmore.
Level: Family
Recommendation: Each slide is different, but all empty into a large pool. This ride allows you to travel alone or with a companion in a double tube. The center slide is completely enclosed (and dark) and made to look like there are stars coming through from the outside light. The outer slides open with different paths down the mountain.

CHAPTER THIRTEEN

HOTEL GUIDE

INTRODUCTION

Booking the right accommodations for your trip is important for your comfort outside of the parks. While we've heard many future guests downplay the importance of a hotel, we believe that after a tiresome day at the parks, you'll desire a nice space to sleep. For this reason, we recommend carefully building a list of your top-choice hotels.

The Walt Disney World Resort is home to dozens of hotel and resort options. Each offer great service, unique rooms, and plenty of charming amenities. Best of all, you'll be in the heart of the Walt Disney World Resort with complimentary transportation to all of its tourism destinations. However, staying on property can be pricey. For this reason, we also list great surrounding hotels from big-name brands to boutique hot spots.

THE DISNEY RESORTS

Disney puts its hotels into four different categories: Value, Moderate, Deluxe, and Villa. Prices, amenities, and proximity to the parks are all factored into these categories. Depending on your desires and budget, you might choose one category over another. While most guests would prefer to stay in a Deluxe hotel or Villa because of the amenities, all Disney-owned hotels share some amazing perks.

DISNEY-OWNED HOTEL BENEFITS

When staying at a Disney-owned hotel, you can expect friendly service, themed dining, comfy rooms, and several in-room amenities. However, there are also some great perks that you may not be able to find outside of Disney's Resort bubble.

✦ **Early Theme Park Entry** – Perhaps one of the biggest perks for staying on property. All Disney Resort guests have access to the four main theme parks an hour before the general public! Heading to the parks early can save you hours of waiting in lines, especially during popular days.

✦ **Complimentary Theme Park Parking** – While guests must pay nightly parking rates at the hotels, the theme parks are free!

✦ **Proximity** – Some hotels are within walking distance to the theme parks while others are just a short gondola, boat, monorail, or bus trip away. Because the parks are so spread apart, you won't find a hotel within walking distance to every theme park. In fact, the only way to visit Disney's Animal Kingdom is by bus or car—even from Disney's Animal Kingdom Lodge. Conversely, some Value resorts are very far away from the parks, even though they are still on Walt Disney World Resort property.

✦ **Disney Theming** – Each hotel has its own distinct theme and most have rooms that match the aesthetic. However, some use more Disney characters than others.

✦ **Stunning Pools** – Every Disney-owned hotel has at least one pool and most have waterslides!

✦ **Disney Dining Plan** – To take advantage of Disney's prepaid dining plan, you'll need to stay at a Disney resort. The Disney Dining Plan is a fan favorite as it allows guests to use points to dine around Disney World. More about this in the Dining chapter.

✦ **Merchandise Delivery** – When shopping in the parks, many stores will deliver your purchases straight to your hotel! The following day you can pick packages up from your hotel's bell services. Just ask the store cashier at checkout for this option.

✦ **Discounted MagicBands** – Disney hotel guests may have the option to purchase MagicBands at a discounted rate! We recommend ordering these weeks ahead of your trip to ensure timely delivery.

✦ **More Amenities** – All Disney resorts have access to complimentary Wi-Fi and resort-wide transportation—including the Disney Skyliner, monorail, and Epcot ferries. Resort guests may also have early access to event tickets.

RESORT TYPES

Of the four different Disney resort types, each have their own pros and cons. For example, Moderate resorts are often closer than Value ones, but guests often receive more Disney theming at a Value hotel.

DISNEY DELUXE RESORTS

Starting at about $440/night (before discounts)

The Walt Disney World Resort's premier properties are the most expensive. From our experience, the service at Deluxe resort hotels is the best in Disney World. Deluxe resorts are located in prime locations with several transportation choices to the parks, including the monorail system, boats, gondolas, or via walking dedicated paths. Guests staying at a Deluxe resort may have access to amenities like gyms, spas, excellent dining, room balconies, several pools (including a water slide), and even golf courses. In addition, Deluxe-level resorts have exclusive access to extended evening park hours on select nights that the other tier resorts do not.

DISNEY DELUXE VILLAS

Starting at about $435/night (before discounts)

Designed as Disney Vacation Club timeshares, Villas offer both the amenities of a hotel and home—like washers and dryers. Most Villas are available for booking to standard hotel guests. All Villas have a kitchen or kitchenette and are considered a Deluxe-level hotel. Thus, guests staying in a Villa have access to extended evening park hours when available. Many Villas are located at an existing Deluxe hotel like the Grand Floridian, Beach Club, or Polynesian. However, others like Old Key West and Saratoga Springs are on the outskirts and don't have quick access to the theme parks. Nevertheless, these resort hotels can be the most relaxing due to their laid-back vibe.

> **· Magic Tips ·**
>
> Many guests love staying in a Villa because they can cook for their family in the kitchen. Get your groceries delivered to the lobby via Garden Grocer: www.gardengrocer.com.

MODERATE

Starting at about $270/night (before discounts)

Guests staying at the Moderate resort level have several dining options located on property. Rooms here typically don't have much

Disney theming. However, with plenty of amenities, Moderates can feel very close in comfort level and service to the Deluxe level. All Moderate properties have access to multiple pools, including at least one with a waterslide.

DISNEY VALUE RESORTS
Starting at about $135/night (before discounts)
Value resorts are designed to give guests a distinct Disney feel but without the giant price tag. These resorts are further away from the parks and have fewer amenities. One of the biggest downsides of the Value resort is the limited dining options. However, all of these resorts have large, welcoming pools and beautiful scenery.

> **· Magic Tips ·**
> If you're staying at a Value or Moderate resort, Disney may give you the option to suspend Mousekeeping (room cleaning services) for credit. When checking in, look for a card near your television with an invitation to skip Mousekeeping in exchange for a Disney gift card! These cards are usually worth $10 a day (not including your checkout day). If you don't see the card, call the front desk or concierge and ask if this option is available for your stay.

ROOM TYPES

When booking your accommodations, you may notice a vague room description along with varying price differences. Rooms with the best views and locations are usually more expensive.

✦ **Standard** – These rooms often have views of the parking lots or parts of the hotel buildings. However, you sometimes spend half the cost of a room with a better view.

> **· Magic Tips ·**
> Some standard rooms have views of theme parks or other in-demand sights. If you're staying at a Deluxe resort, you can always request a higher floor and hope for a better view.

✦ **Garden, Pool, Lake, & Theme Park Views** – For those looking for scenery outside of your room window, getting a view of the garden, pool, or body of water may be your top choice. Often, the garden view rooms aren't much more than the cost of a standard view. Keep in mind that garden views aren't always spectacular. You may only see hedges and some grass—but to many, that's better than a view of a parking lot! Still, we've discovered that the pool and lake views are usually very stunning (though they do come with a much higher price tag). If you can grab a room with a theme park view, you'll pay a premium, but will likely have views of the fireworks at night. Near the Magic Kingdom, there's something special about seeing the Cinderella Castle in the distance.

✦ **Studios** – Deluxe Villa resorts offer small studio rooms that often have Moderate-level price tags. Most studios have small kitchenettes with mini fridges, microwaves, and sinks. Disney's Riviera has the smallest studios on property that can only house two people. However, the larger studios at Disney's Old Key West have two large queen-sized beds and feel very spacious!

✦ **Suites** – Guests needing more space may find that a suite will suit their needs. In many instances, these house nine guests or more with several beds and pull-outs in the rooms. Most suites are located at Deluxe Resorts and can cost well over $1,000 per night. Nonetheless, larger families can book a Value-level suite at Disney's Art of Animation Resort.

✦ **Preferred Rooms** – Since many of the Disney-owned resorts are fairly spread out, rooms closer to amenities like bus stops, restaurants, and gondola transports may cost more. We recommend preferred rooms for anyone who plans to stay at the parks for most of their trip.

✦ **Club Level** – Guests staying in these rooms have access to a concierge service and a lounge with light bites and cocktail hours. Club levels can cost twice that of a standard room, and are not always worth the extra expense. Often, you can pay for the Disney Dining Plan for your entire family for the same price. All Disney Deluxe resorts offer club level rooms except for the Disney Deluxe Villas.

✦ **Treehouse, Bungalow, Cabin** – These special themed rooms are larger and contain more beds than a standard room. Often, they come with a high, premium price for their adventurous feel and spaciousness. The Polynesian Village Bungalows are popular for their on-the-water island vibes and unmatched views of the Magic Kingdom!

MORE TO CONSIDER

PARKING FEES

RESORT TYPE	Nightly Rate	Vallet
Value	$15	-
Moderate	$20	-
Deluxe	$25	$33
Deluxe Villa	$25	$33

HOTEL AAA DIAMOND RATINGS
The AAA Automobile Club ranks hotels based on their amenities, features, and value. Disney Resort hotels have a status of 3-Diamonds or higher. These luxury levels suggest that the hotels will have a prominent elegance and several amenities for guests to enjoy. The 4-Diamond award is given to more stylish hotels with a bump in service and refineries not found in 3-Diamonds. AAA is a bit vague on how they determine these rankings, but the differences often mean more amenities with each higher level.

REFURBISHMENT
Like the attractions in the parks, the hotels also undergo refurbishment. This process may seem unsavory, but these can often work in your favor! Some of the nicer hotels may have discounted rooms during refurbishing periods. Best of all, you may not even notice the construction. Disney often lists hotel refurbishments on their booking pages.

ROOM REQUESTS
Disney will rarely upgrade your room for free, but guests can specify location during check-in. Look for the drop-down menu to make room level and accessibility requests. If you don't see the room request, contact Disney by phone at least 5 days ahead: (407) 939-1936.

· **Magic Tips** ·

Rooms near the pool and those with theme park views may be much noisier than rooms with garden views.

SPLIT STAYS

If you're staying a week or longer, you may want to consider booking a split stay at multiple hotels. We highly recommend split stays because they are a fun and adventurous way to enjoy more of Walt Disney World. Disney will also transport your belongings from one resort hotel to the next—we just recommend tipping bell services $1-$2 a bag.

HOTEL BOOKING DISCOUNTS

1. Always check third party travel websites for better deals (Orbitz.com, Priceline.com, Expedia.com) and compare to WaltDisneyWorld.com.
2. Sometimes you can save quite a bit per night with third-party websites. Click on their "deals" or "promotions" tab to find discount coupons on the sites.
3. Though many websites offer package deals, sometimes these are not the lowest cost. We recommend checking the pricing of hotels and flights separately before you commit to a vacation package.
4. Seasonally, WaltDisneyWorld.com will offer discounted hotel pricing (usually 20-30% off). We recommended booking early when you see these deals! When you book online on the website or over the phone, you can often just put $200 down on a reservation (this includes any bundled park tickets and added items such as Memory Maker) and pay the remaining balance closer to your arrival date.

· **Magic Tips** ·

Some social distancing guidelines may impact bell services in delivering your luggage. In addition, bell services will not deliver perishable goods between hotels.

DISNEY DELUXE RESORTS

DISNEY'S ANIMAL KINGDOM LODGE

Best for: Everyone (especially animal lovers)
Theme: African Savanna Lodge
AAA Rating: 4-Diamond
Location: Furthest west, close to Disney's Animal Kingdom Park
Pool: Yes, with Waterslide
Transport to Parks: Bus only
Amenities: Wi-Fi, Paid Laundry and Dry Cleaning, Multiple Pools, Waterslides, Jogging Trails, Movie Nights at the Pool, Playground, Club Level Rooms, Fitness Center, and Arcade

OUR REVIEW

The Animal Kingdom Lodge is gorgeous! You'll feel transported to Africa with over thirty species of wildlife roaming outside of your hotel room window. The savanna view rooms are breathtaking and an unforgettable experience. The animals range from zebras and giraffes to warthogs and exotic birds. The animals are in a "fenceless" savanna that comes right up to your room (a hidden fencing system keeps the animals from getting too close). While it's the closest hotel to the Animal Kingdom Park, it's still about a mile (1.5 km) away by bus. The AK Lodge feels like a wilderness hotel with a breathtaking entrance, well-decorated rooms, authentic African art, views of the savanna, and a massive pool with a waterslide and real flamingoes. However, the rooms aren't as big as some of the other Deluxe resorts and the bathrooms could use brighter lighting.

Animal Kingdom Lodge is split into two properties: Jambo House and Kidani Village. Most of the activity and restaurants are in Jambo House, the main area of the resort. Kidani Village has the perks of Disney Vacation Club rentals with condo-like villas equipped with kitchens. If your family needs a little more room, you may want to book at Kidani Village, though the rooms are further away from many of the resort's amenities (but Kidani does have its own pool). Jambo House also has villas with a bit more space.

The hotel has a smaller pool (with its own waterslide), because a bigger space is set aside for the savanna. The hotel is beautiful, but if you don't have a savanna-facing room, we don't think it's worth the cost. We wish that the Lodge and Villas were within walking distance to Animal Kingdom, but we've found that this resort has the most efficient bussing system in all of Walt Disney World. Some of the non-savanna facing rooms still have partial views of the animals. Request one of these rooms if you can, through it's not guaranteed. Otherwise, each floor has a balcony that faces the savanna.

> · **Magic Tips** ·
> Some of the other standard rooms also have partial views of the savanna! If you're willing to risk it, save money and book a standard room. Then, 5-7 days before your trip, call Disney and request a room with a partial view of the savanna. Of course, this is not guaranteed.

BOTTOM LINE

A gorgeous, African-inspired resort with a collection of on-property animals. However, Animal Kingdom Lodge is far from the theme parks, so only the savanna-facing rooms are worth the price tag.

> · **Magic Tips** ·
> The animals aren't as active in the mornings as they are in the afternoons and evenings. To see them better, take a midday break and head back to your room for viewing. At night, ask a Cast Member for night vision goggles!

PROS

- Stunning African savanna views with over 200 animals
- Multiple pools, one with waterslide
- Several great dining options
- Gorgeous lobby and rooms
- Early Theme Park Entry

CONS

- Far away from theme parks
- Bus is the only transport
- Poor room lighting (though this was done on purpose for the animals)
- Only savanna-view rooms are worth the price

DISNEY'S BEACH CLUB RESORT

Best for: Teens, Adults, Epcot Fans
Theme: Beach Resort
AAA Rating: 4-Diamond
Location: Central to Epcot and Hollywood Studios
Pool: Yes, with Waterslide, Sand-bottom, and Lazy River
Transport to Parks: Boat, Walk, Busses, near Epcot Gondola
Amenities: Wi-Fi, Paid Laundry and Dry Cleaning, Multiple Pools, Waterslides, Jogging Paths, Movie Nights, Playground, Volleyball and Tennis Courts, Bike Rentals, Boat Rentals, Fishing, Club Access for Certain Rooms, Fitness Center, Mini Golf, and Arcade

OUR REVIEW

Beach Club is a charming, New England-style resort within walking distance to Epcot and Disney's Hollywood Studios. The resort has a quaint feel along a massive lake with water taxis taking guests to the nearby theme parks. There is a timeless beach appeal to the building that will be appreciated by adults and teens alike. Most of the standard rooms have Juliet balconies while larger rooms have full-sized balconies with seats.

Kids love the Stormalong Bay sand-bottom pool with a shipwreck-style waterslide! Adults will enjoy the spacious beach chairs, comfortable rooms, and fine dining in this large pool area. For nightlife, Disney's BoardWalk is just a ferry trip across the lake. Guests can also walk to Epcot in 5-10 minutes and Disney's Hollywood Studios within 15-20 minutes, depending where your room is located. If you're watching Harmonious at Epcot, walking to the Beach Club is great because you don't have to wait with other guests for the busses to return.

BOTTOM LINE

A Beautiful "seaside" resort with Disney's best pool and plenty of amenities. Guests can easily travel to Epcot, Disney's Hollywood Studios, and Disney's BoardWalk for dining.

PROS

• Multiple pools, including Stormalong Bay, a 3-acre water area with a sand-bottom pool, waterslide, beach loungers, bars, and lazy river with inner tubes

- Excellent dining options
- Gorgeous lobby and rooms
- Shared amenities with Disney's Yacht Club

- Short walk to Epcot and a quick boat ride to Disney's Hollywood Studios
- See the Epcot fireworks from the beach

CONS

- Longer bus wait times for the Magic Kingdom, Disney's Animal Kingdom, and Disney Springs

- Often difficult to book in advance
- Stormalong Bay can become very busy and loud

· **Magic Tips** ·

Guests at the Beach Club and Yacht Club share many amenities. For a less-crowded pool, head to Disney's Yacht Club next door!

DISNEY'S BOARDWALK INN

Best for: Kids, Teens, Adults
Theme: Coney Island Hotel
AAA Rating: 4-Diamond
Location: Central to Epcot and Hollywood Studios
Pool: Yes, with Waterslide
Transport to Parks: Boat, Walk, Busses
Amenities: Wi-Fi, Paid Laundry and Dry Cleaning, Multiple Pools, Waterslides, Jogging Paths, Movie Nights, Playground, Tennis Courts, Bike Rentals, Boat Rentals, Fishing, Club Access for Certain Rooms, Fitness Center, Valet, Mini Golf, and Arcade

OUR REVIEW

Disney's BoardWalk Inn is styled after an old Coney Island hotel. However, Disney updated its pool area with newer images of Mickey Mouse to freshen up the aesthetic. The BoardWalk Inn is directly across from Disney's Beach Club and easily walkable to Disney's Hollywood Studios and Epcot. Kids will enjoy this pool—especially the Keister Coaster water slide. Being able to walk or boat to Epcot or Hollywood Studios is a huge benefit, and the boardwalk-facing rooms are stunning if you don't mind a little noise. However, the rooms here are a bit plain and lack the character of properties like the nearby Beach Club or Yacht Club.

BOTTOM LINE
Fun, central property that appeals to families with kids more than the Yacht Club or Beach Resort.

PROS
- Rooms have balconies
- Carnival-themed pool area with waterslide
- Fun boardwalk arcades, dining, and dancing
- Gorgeous lobby
- 10-minute walk or boat ride to Epcot
- 15-minute walk or boat ride to Hollywood Studios
- See the Epcot fireworks from the beach

CONS
- Longer bus wait times to Magic Kingdom and Animal Kingdom
- Very spread out
- Plain room decor

DISNEY'S CONTEMPORARY

Best for: Teens, Adults
Theme: Contemporary Hotel
AAA Rating: 4-Diamond
Location: Next to Magic Kingdom
Pool: Yes, with Waterslide
Transport to Parks: Monorail to Magic Kingdom and Epcot, Boat, Busses, and Pedestrian Walkway to the Magic Kingdom
Amenities: Wi-Fi, Paid Laundry and Dry Cleaning, Multiple Pools, Waterslides, Jogging Trails, Movie Nights, Playground, Volleyball and Tennis Courts, Cabana Rentals, Fishing, Club Access for Certain Rooms, Fitness Center, Salon, Child Care, and Arcade

OUR REVIEW
The Contemporary Resort opened the same year as the Magic Kingdom Park in 1971 and is based on the design concepts in Tomorrowland. The hotel has kept its charm over the years, even when something contemporary could feel dated, it doesn't. The resort décor is clean and bright and everything feels streamlined and somewhat futuristic—the monorail even goes through it!

The Contemporary feels like a high-end condo building or Las Vegas hotel (without the casino and cigarette smoke). Best of all, it's walking distance to Magic Kingdom. Though guests like to take the monorail over to the park, we recommend skipping the morning monorail rush and walking to the theme park by foot. However, we highly recommend taking the monorail to Epcot if you're headed in that direction. The character dining experience, Chef Mickey's, is a fun stop before heading to the parks in the morning. At night, the California Grill is a hotspot for elegant dates.

The Contemporary recently received an *Incredibles*-themed renovation to add some character to the design. Some of the rooms also offer stunning views of the Magic Kingdom with fireworks at night. If this doesn't interest you, book a standard or lake view instead to save some money.

BOTTOM LINE
A beautifully designed modern resort with a monorail system to Magic Kingdom and Epcot.

· Magic Tips ·
Disney's Electrical Water Pageant is a charming nighttime light parade on the Seven Seas Lagoon. Guests staying here can often see the show float by from their rooms!

PROS
- Monorail to Magic Kingdom and Epcot
- 10-15 minute walk to Magic Kingdom
- Gorgeous lobby and rooms
- Fine dining and character dining
- Boat to Polynesian, Fort Wilderness, or Grand Floridian
- See the Magic Kingdom fireworks from this resort
- See the Electrical Water Pageant from the bay

CONS
- Not as close to the other parks (other than Magic Kingdom)
- Very expensive
- May not be ideal for larger groups and families

DISNEY'S GRAND FLORIDIAN RESORT

Best for: Tweens, Teens, Adults
Theme: Sophisticated Southern Resort
AAA Rating: 4-Diamond
Location: Next to the Magic Kingdom Park
Pool: Yes, with Waterslide
Transport to Parks: Monorail to Magic Kingdom and Epcot, Boat, Busses, and Pedestrian Walkway to the Magic Kingdom
Amenities: Wi-Fi, Turn Down Service, Paid Laundry and Dry Cleaning, Multiple Pools, Waterslides, Jogging Trails, Movie Nights, Playground, Volleyball and Tennis Courts, Private Cabana Rentals, Boat Rentals, Club Access for Certain Rooms, Spa and Fitness Center, and Arcade

OUR REVIEW

Disney's Grand Floridian is the most elegant hotel on property! With a magnificent Southern theme, you'll feel swept away by the magic and pristine styles of this resort hotel. The Grand Floridian is the most expensive property per night, so we only recommend it if you are looking for a more romantic feel to your stay.

The Grand comes with a certain prestige from Disney fans, and that status often adds to its appeal. Some of the best dining in Disney is located here—including the 5-Star restaurant, Victoria & Albert's. Though this hotel is a bit far from parks other than Magic Kingdom, its impeccable service and beautiful grounds make it a wonderful stay.

BOTTOM LINE

The Grand Floridian is the most prestigious resort on property with excellent amenities, elegant rooms, and unmatched dining.

PROS

- Gorgeous lobby, rooms, and exquisite décor
- Walkway to the Magic Kingdom
- Views of the Electrical Water Pageant

- Fine dining and character dining
- Monorail to Magic Kingdom and Epcot
- Boat to Magic Kingdom
- See the Magic Kingdom fireworks from this resort

CONS

- Not as kid-friendly as other hotels
- Far from the theme parks (other than Magic Kingdom)

DISNEY'S POLYNESIAN VILLAGE

Best For: Everyone
Theme: Island-themed Resort
AAA Rating: 4-Diamond
Location: Near Magic Kingdom
Pool: Yes, with Waterslide
Transport to Parks: Monorail to Magic Kingdom and Epcot, Boat, and Busses
Amenities: Wi-Fi, Multiple Pools, Waterslide, Jogging Trail, Movie Nights, Playground, Volleyball Court, Boat Rentals, Fishing, Club Access for Certain Rooms, and Fitness Center access at Disney's Grand Floridian

OUR REVIEW

Disney's Polynesian Village is beautiful, fun, and wonderfully relaxing. The tropical plants and island smells in the lobby instantly transport you to the Pacific islands. In fact, with Florida's humidity, you might actually feel like you're *in* Hawaii!

We love the Poly because it's close to the Magic Kingdom and has monorail service around the area. There's also great themed dining here including the family-style 'Ohana and Jungle Cruise-themed bar, Trader Sam's Grog Grotto.

The price tag is high at the Poly because of its many amenities. There are *Moana*-themed rooms, a large pool area, and even a beach with the Magic Kingdom fireworks displaying most nights. If your group needs more space, the Bora Bora Bungalows on the water sleep up to eights guests in beautiful rooms. While the Poly has beautiful landscaping, it can feel a bit spread out. Yet, the rooms are spacious, especially the bungalows.

BOTTOM LINE

Disney's Polynesian perfectly replicates an island feel with its stunning scenery, relaxing vibe, and fantastic dining options.

PROS

- Beautiful scenery and gorgeous lobby
- Fantastic dining
- *Moana*-themed rooms
- Monorail to Magic Kingdom
- Boat to Magic Kingdom
- See the Magic Kingdom fireworks from this resort
- On-the-water bungalows
- See the Electrical Water Pageant from the bay

CONS

- No on-site fitness center (must use Grand Floridian's)
- Not as close to the other parks (other than Magic Kingdom)
- No easy walking to Magic Kingdom
- May have to walk far from the amenities to your room

DISNEY'S WILDERNESS LODGE

Best for: Everyone (especially wilderness lovers)
Theme: Forest Lodge
AAA Rating: 4-Diamond
Cost: Deluxe (more affordable than others in this category)
Location: Close to the Magic Kingdom Park
Pool: Yes, with Waterslides
Transport to Parks: Boat and Busses
Amenities: Wi-Fi, 2 Large Pools, Paid Laundry and Dry Cleaning, Valet, Waterslides, Jogging Trail, Movie Nights, Water Playground, Volleyball Court, Bike and Boat Rentals, Fishing, Club Access for Certain Rooms, and Fitness Center

OUR REVIEW

A beautiful lodge-themed resort set on the lake near the Magic Kingdom. The Wilderness Lodge is located on a massive piece of land known as Fort Wilderness, with campgrounds set in an evergreen forest. Sadly, the monorail doesn't travel to the Wilderness Lodge like it does to other resorts in the area. However, the great dining, gorgeous scenery, and excellent service bring it up to the Deluxe Resort status.

A popular time for the Wilderness Lodge is during the holiday season where the many fir trees come to life with Christmas lights and spirit. It's also a lot of fun to take a boat ride to Magic Kingdom. The busses can move a little sluggish when visiting other parks. Families with kids may like the Wilderness Lodge better because of the affordable cost and kid-friendly pool area.

Fire Rock Geyser
Between the main pool and the lake is the Fire Rock Geyser. This erupting beauty evokes the splendor of natural attractions such as Old Faithful in Yellowstone National Park. Fire Rock Geyser erupts every hour like clockwork.

· **Magic Tips** ·
Larger parties should consider a cabin at Copper Creek. These beautiful and stunning cabins sleep up to 8 adults and boast views of Bay Lake. They are also very close to the main pool area and the boats to the Magic Kingdom.

BOTTOM LINE
A forest-surrounded resort set on the lake that's a short ferry ride to the Magic Kingdom. The Wilderness Lodge is also one of the least expensive Deluxe Resort properties.

PROS
- Fine dining and character dining
- Gorgeous lobby and rooms
- Boat to Magic Kingdom
- Stunning at Christmas time
- Most rooms aren't far from lobby or amenities
- Ferry to Magic Kingdom
- See the Electrical Water Pageant from the bay

CONS
- Not walking distance to any theme parks
- Sometimes long bus wait times to all parks

DISNEY'S YACHT CLUB

Best for: Adults
Theme: New England Beach Resort
AAA Rating: 4-Diamond
Cost: Deluxe
Location: Epcot area
Pool: Yes, including access to Beach Club pools
Transport to Parks: Boat, Walk, Busses
Amenities: Wi-Fi, Paid Laundry and Dry Cleaning, Multiple Pools, Valet, Waterslides, Jogging Paths, Movie Nights, Playground, Volleyball and Tennis Courts, Bike Rentals, Boat Rentals, Fishing, Club Access for Certain Rooms, Spa and Fitness Center, Child Care, Mini Golf, and Arcade

OUR REVIEW

The Yacht Club is similar to the Beach Club but with an even more tranquil atmosphere that often appeals to adults. Both resort hotels were built in the same year and have many of the same features, layout, and amenities. In fact, these properties share the stunning Stormalong Bay pool, but the Yacht Club also has its own quiet pool near the back. This property is a bit spread out and walking to the rooms from the lobby, pool, or busses can be a bit of a journey. Still, the rooms are beautifully decorated with several Hidden Mickeys in the décor. You'll find spacious rooms and quiet at the Yacht Club all while being centrally located to Epcot and Disney's Hollywood Studios.

BOTTOM LINE

Disney's Yacht Club is a quieter sister hotel to the Beach Club that also shares many of its amenities.

· **Magic Tips** ·
Yacht Club charges significantly more for rooms with a view of the water. However, many times these rooms only have a view of a very basic pool. We recommend saving money and booking a Garden/Woods or Standard room instead.

PROS

- Access to Disney's Beach Club's huge Stormalong Bay (5-10 minute walk)
- Fine dining and character dining
- Beautiful lobby and rooms

- 5-minute walk or boat ride to Epcot
- 15-minute walk or boat ride to Hollywood Studios
- See the Epcot fireworks from the beach
- Tranquil feel

CONS

- Longer bus wait times
- No quick-service restaurants (only at Beach Club, Disney's Boardwalk)

- Often very difficult to book in advance

DISNEY DELUXE VILLAS

All rooms in this category come with home amenities like a full kitchen, washer, and dryer. However, the studios may have kitchenettes with smaller fridges and may lack the washer and dryer units.

DISNEY'S OLD KEY WEST RESORT

Best for: Adults, Older Adults
Theme: Florida's Key West
AAA Rating: 3-Diamond
Location: Isolated, closer to Disney Springs
Pool: Yes, with Waterslide
Transport to Parks: Busses to Parks, Boat to Disney Springs
Amenities: Wi-Fi, Paid Laundry and Dry Cleaning, Multiple Pools, Jogging Trail along a Golf Course and Canals, Tennis, Volleyball, Basketball, Fishing, Bike Rentals, Playgrounds, Outdoor Movies by the Pool, Old Key West Campfires, Fitness Center, and Arcade

OUR REVIEW

Disney's Old Key West Resort was the original Disney Vacation Club property and feels like a country club with a tranquil atmosphere. Guests who stay here are looking to get away from the bustle and noise of the parks for a relaxing stay. While there are some amenities for kids, Old Key West has several tennis courts and serene pools that appeal mostly to an older crowd. Additionally, boats run from Old Key West to Disney Springs for shopping and entertainment.

The rooms are large and typically inexpensive for their size. There are also larger villas with a full-sized kitchen that sleeps up to nine. There are also several restaurants here and a riverboat to Disney Springs.

BOTTOM LINE

Old Key West is a laid-back resort that can feel somewhat isolated from the parks. However, adults typically love the charm and tranquility of this Disney Vacation Club property.

PROS

- Laid-back atmosphere with beautiful scenery
- Boat to Disney Springs
- Huge rooms
- Several basketball, tennis, and volleyball courts
- Gym
- Home-like rooms with full kitchens or kitchenettes

CONS

- Longer bus wait times for both leaving and returning
- Larger, spread out area that may require a lot of walking
- Far from the theme parks with bus-only transport
- Not as many dining options compared to other Deluxe resorts

DISNEY'S SARATOGA SPRINGS

Best for: Adults, Older Adults
Theme: 19th Century Upstate New York
AAA Rating: 3-Diamond
Location: Near Disney Springs
Pool: Multiple Pools, with Waterslide
Transport to Parks: Busses to Parks, Boat or Walking to Disney Springs

Amenities: Wi-Fi, Paid Laundry and Dry Cleaning, Multiple Pools, Jogging Trail along a Golf Course and Canals, Tennis, Basketball, Fishing, Bike Rentals, Playgrounds, Outdoor Movies by the Pool, Campfires, Full-service Spa, Fitness Center, and Arcade

OUR REVIEW

The equestrian-themed Saratoga Springs Resort is by far the quietest Walt Disney World Resort hotel. Similar to the Old Key West Resort, Saratoga feels like a country club with a serene environment. Older crowds will enjoy the lax pools, scenery, golf courses, spa, and quiet away from the parks.

Saratoga Springs is large and very spread out, which can be both good and bad qualities. However, shopping is just a short walk or boat ride away at Disney Springs. The rooms are large and typically inexpensive for their size. The Treehouse Villas sleep up to nine guests.

· **Magic Tips** ·

The Congress Park area of Saratoga Springs is the closest to Disney Springs and has a short walking distance.

BOTTOM LINE

A peaceful resort with an old country club feel. Though it's very close to Disney Springs, Saratoga is very spread out and can feel isolated.

PROS

- Walking distance or boat ride to Disney Springs
- Golf course
- Full-service Spa
- Quiet atmosphere
- Beautiful scenery and serene walkways
- Gym
- Home-like rooms with full kitchens or kitchenettes

CONS

- Longer bus wait times for both leaving and returning
- Larger, spread out area that may require a lot of walking
- Not very close to any of the parks, so you have to take the bussing system

DISNEY'S RIVIERA RESORT

Best for: Teens, Adults
AAA Rating: N/A
Cost: Deluxe / Disney Vacation Club
Location: Epcot area
Pool: Two, one with Waterslide
Transport to Parks: Skyliner Gondola to Epcot and Hollywood Studios, Busses to other parks
Amenities: Rooftop Bar, Wi-Fi, Paid Laundry and Dry Cleaning, Multiple Pools, Jogging Trail, Volleyball Courts, Playgrounds, Outdoor Movies, Campfires, Spa and Fitness Center, and Arcade

OUR REVIEW

While many other Disney hotels don't exceed two stories in height, the gorgeous Riviera Resort offers spectacular views of Epcot and Hollywood Studios. The resort is inspired by a trip Walt Disney took to the French Riviera in 1935. It also hosts beautiful pools, easy access to the Disney Skyliner gondolas, and a rooftop restaurant, Topolino's Terrace (named after the Italian word for Mickey Mouse).

From its stunning lobbies to European-style rooms, Disney's Riviera Resort is beautiful. The Tower Studio rooms here are smaller, less-expensive spaces with Murphy beds. At around 250 square feet, these rooms are tiny. Disney designed them for traveling guests wishing to stay at a Deluxe resort without the huge price tag. Though the Tower Studio bathrooms are fairly large and each room has a small balcony, these are only worthwhile if you don't spend much time in your room. If you're booking a Tower Studio, ask for a view of the gondolas.

BOTTOM LINE

A beautiful tower hotel with sweeping views of Walt Disney World. Guests can take dedicated gondolas to Epcot and Disney's Hollywood Studios.

PROS

- Some rooms have views of Epcot fireworks
- Fantastic pools
- Gondolas connect to Epcot and Hollywood Studios
- Great dining

CONS

- Less of a "resort feel" than other Disney hotels
- Standard rooms don't have much of a view
- Standard rooms can also feel lacking in unique decor

OTHER VILLAS

Though a few Disney Villas have their own dedicated hotels, most do not. The other Villas are located in previously mentioned Deluxe resort hotels. Some of these properties may be difficult to book since Disney Vacation Club occupies many of the rooms.

- **Bay Lake Tower at Disney's Contemporary Resort** – A separate tower from the Contemporary that is much closer to the Magic Kingdom. However, you'll have to walk to the Contemporary for dining and monorail access.
- **Boulder Ridge Villas at Disney's Wilderness Lodge** – A set of Villas just outside of the main Wilderness Lodge building. You may have to walk further to the amenities than other rooms.
- **Copper Creek Villas & Cabins at Disney's Wilderness Lodge** – A separate set of rooms within the main Wilderness Lodge building. Some have excellent views of the lake and fireworks!
- **Disney's Animal Kingdom Villas (Jambo House)** – Guests can book rooms within the main Animal Kingdom Lodge building that have access to kitchens and more.
- **Disney's Animal Kingdom Villas (Kidani Village)** – Like a sister hotel to Jambo House, Kidani Village spreads out with its own set of savannas. All rooms here are Villas and often have more availability than Jambo House.
- **Disney's Beach Club Villas** – Located on an adjoining wing to the Beach Club resort, these villas are a closer walk to Epcot.
- **Disney's BoardWalk Villas** – A set of villas closer to Disney's Hollywood Studios. However, there are room types with views of the pool and Disney's BoardWalk.
- **Disney's Polynesian Villas & Bungalows** – Close to the tickets and transportation center but far from other Poly resort amenities. The Poly's Bungalows are considered large Villas.
- **The Villas at Disney's Grand Floridian Resort & Spa** – Villas here are closer to the Beach Pool and Senses Spa. However, the walking path is on the opposite end of the resort.

DISNEY MODERATE RESORTS

DISNEY'S CARIBBEAN BEACH

Best for: Kids, Adults (especially pirate lovers)
Theme: Caribbean Resort
AAA Rating: 3-Diamond
Cost: Moderate
Location: Isolated, to the south of Epcot
Pool: Several, one with Waterslides
Transport to Parks: Skyliner Gondola to Epcot and Hollywood Studios, Busses to other parks
Amenities: Wi-Fi, Paid Laundry and Dry Cleaning, Multiple Pools, Jogging Trail, Bike Rentals, Volleyball Courts, Playgrounds, Fishing, Outdoor Movies, Campfires, and Arcade

OUR REVIEW

Disney's Caribbean Beach is a colorful, moderately priced resort to the southeast of Epcot. Set on a stunning lake, there are several vibrant Caribbean-style buildings. The rooms here are fairly standard with a few island-themed details. Those looking for more theming may want to book a pirate room with a boat-like bed. Though kids may love these rooms, they are some of the furthest away from the amenities. But no matter when you stay, there are bus stops all around the resort.

Caribbean Beach is one of the more popular Moderate resorts because of its easy gondola access to the parks. Its gondola transport is the intersection between the Epcot line and the Disney's Hollywood Studios line, so you'll have quick access to both. Caribbean Beach is also very popular with families, so that could either be a good or bad fit depending on your desires.

BOTTOM LINE

A Caribbean-style hotel with moderately priced simple rooms. Guests might feel that their room isn't close enough to the amenities, but the Disney Skyliner station here has quick access to Epcot and Disney's Hollywood Studios.

PROS

- Gondola system to Epcot and Hollywood Studios
- 45-acres of beautiful Caribbean scenery
- Island with playgrounds
- Multiple pools and beach areas
- Pirate-themed rooms

CONS

- Boring standard rooms
- Long bus wait times
- Larger, spread out area that may require a lot of walking
- Often busy and sometimes noisy

> **· Magic Tips ·**
>
> If you're staying at the Riviera side of Caribbean Beach, you can easily walk to its Skyliner gondola station. The Riviera tends to have much shorter wait times and less congestion to Epcot.

DISNEY'S CORONADO SPRINGS

Best for: Adults
Theme: Latin American Resort
AAA Rating: 3-Diamond
Location: Isolated, to the east of Animal Kingdom
Pool: Yes, with Waterslide
Transport to Parks: Busses
Amenities: Wi-Fi, Paid Laundry and Dry Cleaning, Multiple Pools, Jogging Trail, Volleyball Courts, Playgrounds, Outdoor Movies, Campfires, Spa and Fitness Center, and Arcade

OUR REVIEW

Our favorite feature of Disney's Coronado Springs Resort is the Lost City of Cibola pool. There is a Mayan-style pyramid with a waterfall next to a long waterslide and a large, beach-like swimming area. The rest of the resort is very spread out. In fact, it can feel impossible to walk the entire thing in an afternoon. With several buildings located around a large lake, Coronado Springs brings a Latin flare to Disney World.

The Gran Destino Tower has a stunning two-story lobby, new restaurants, and sweeping views from its rooms. There is club access to the tower and most of the artwork was inspired by Walt Disney's love of Salvador Dali paintings (the hotel was named after one). The better dining options are available in the Gran Destino Tower. If you're looking for a sophisticated style with a moderate price tag, book a room in the fabulous Gran Destino Tower at Coronado Springs.

· Magic Tips ·

Compared to club level rooms in Disney Deluxe Resorts, the Gran Destino Tower's club rooms are about half the cost. Guests booking these rooms can enjoy refreshments, snacks, and complimentary booze (like mimosas for guests 21 and older). However, the Cronos Club has limited hours.

BOTTOM LINE
A moderate resort with a great pool and stylish Gran Destino tower.

PROS
- Fantastic pools
- Beautiful Gran Destino Tower with sweeping resort views
- Top-notch dining
- Club Level access for select rooms in a moderate resort
- Low price tags for standard rooms

CONS
- Standard rooms are lackluster
- Long bus wait times
- Very spread out
- Requires bussing to all parks and Disney Springs
- Water view rooms in the Gran Destino Tower can cost as much as a Deluxe Resort

DISNEY'S FORT WILDERNESS
CABINS AND CAMPGROUNDS

Best for: Large Groups and Families
Theme: Camping in the Woods
AAA Rating: 3-Diamond
Location: Close to the Magic Kingdom Park

Pool: Yes, with Waterslide
Transport to Parks: Boats to Magic Kingdom and Busses to others
Amenities: Wi-Fi, Pool with Waterslide, Paid Laundry and Dry Cleaning, Animals at Tri-Circle-D Ranch, Jogging Trail, Holiday Sleigh Rides (seasonal), Archery, Wagon Rides, Movies in an Outdoor Theater, Campfire, Sing-a-longs, Fishing, Volleyball and Basketball Courts, Playgrounds, and Arcade

OUR REVIEW

Cabins – If you've ever heard of "glamping" (glamorous camping), this is the Disney version. Stay in a 750-acre forest with your family in a specially designed cabin. These aren't as glamorous as the Copper Creek Cabins, but they have a charming feel to them with a much lower price tag.

Campgrounds (considered a Value-level accommodation) – If you would rather pitch your own tent or bring an RV, check out the Fort Wilderness campgrounds. With all of the same perks of the cabins, just without the housing, you'll be able to sleep in tent, plug in your RV, or stay inside a pop-up tent deep in the woods of Walt Disney World. Campsites include a picnic bench, grill, and television, as well as electrical, water, and sewage hookups for RVs. The surrounding foliage is placed to give you extra privacy while you stay.

BOTTOM LINE
Affordable, spacious cabins and campgrounds in the woods for those who like "roughing" it.

PROS
- Quick-Service dining and BBQ available
- Spacious cabins sleep up to six
- Several Christmas events during the Holiday season including sleigh rides
- Boat to Magic Kingdom or bus to the other parks
- Cook your own meals to save cash on your trip
- Each cabin has its own driveway for cars
- Unique activities from pony rides to archery
- See the Electrical Water Pageant from the water
- Dogs are allowed in some of the campgrounds
- Complimentary parking for campsites (1 vehicle per reservation)

CONS

- Longer bus wait times and you have to walk far to the stops
- Smaller bed sizes in the cabins

- Lacks some of the dining options that other Moderate resorts have

DISNEY'S PORT ORLEANS
FRENCH QUARTER & RIVERSIDE

Best for: Everyone
Theme: New Orleans Hotel and Resort
AAA Rating: 3-Diamond
Location: Isolated, to the north of Disney Springs
Pool: Multiple Pools, with Waterslides
Transport to Parks: Busses, Boat to Disney Springs
Amenities: Wi-Fi, Paid Laundry and Dry Cleaning, Multiple Pools, Jogging Paths, Playgrounds, Fishing, Bike Rentals, Horse-Drawn Carriage Rides, and Arcade

OUR REVIEW

French Quarter – This part of the Port Orleans Resort is central to the lobby and feels like a Louisiana neighborhood. Out of all of the Disney Moderate hotels, we recommend French Quarter the most. It's less spread out than the Riverside and has one large pool. Guests can also hop on a ferry to Disney Springs. Also, make sure to get a hot beignet at the Scat Cats Club near the French Quarter lobby!

Riverside – Spread out along the waterways of Port Orleans, Riverside is a charming bayou retreat. Several bus stops and boat docks take guests from Riverside to the parks or Disney Springs. Kids will love the Royal Guest rooms with added Disney artwork. The standard rooms are slightly less thrilling, but better for vacationing adults who may find the Royal Guest rooms a bit overly themed. The touches on the standard room moldings and bathroom sink area are very sweet. Riverside's pool is located on an island in the middle of the river.

BOTTOM LINE
Port Orleans is our favorite Moderate resort with its stunning landscapes and well-designed rooms. The French Quarter is our top

choice with great food and easy access to the bus stops to the parks. Both hotels can ferry on the water to Disney Springs.

PROS

- Stunning landscapes and rivers
- Riverboat cruise to Disney Springs with a port in both Riverside and the French Quarter (about 20 minutes)

- French Quarter requires less walking than Riverside
- King beds available in the French Quarter
- Bussing system feels faster than other Moderate resorts
- Several great restaurants

CONS

- Riverside can feel very spread out
- French Quarter can book quickly

- Bus-only transport to the parks

DISNEY VALUE RESORTS

DISNEY'S ALL-STAR RESORTS
ALL-STAR MUSIC, SPORTS, & MOVIES

Best for: Families with Kids ages 3-10
Themes: Colorful hotels with Disney characters
AAA Rating: 3-Diamond
Location: Furthest south. Animal Kingdom is the nearest park, but it's nowhere near walkable. These Resort hotels are also close to the ESPN Wide World of Sports Complex and Disney's Blizzard Beach.
Pool: Yes (no Waterslides)
Transport to Parks: Bus only
Amenities: Wi-Fi, Paid Laundry, Two Pools, Jogging Trail, Movie Nights, Playground, and Arcade

BUILDING THEMES
The three hotels have several buildings, each with a different theme:

✦ **All-Star Music** – Calypso, Jazz, Country Fair, Broadway, and Rock
✦ **All-Star Sports** – Surfing, Baseball, Football, Tennis, and Basketball
✦ **All-Star Movies** – Toy Story, Fantasia, Love Bug, Mighty Ducks, and 101 Dalmatians

· **Magic Tips** ·
Disney's All-Star Sports Resort may open later in 2022.

OUR REVIEW
Disney created the All-Star hotels to accommodate guests who wanted to stay at a Disney-owned property at a lower price point. Families enjoy the three All-Star resorts because they have heavy Disney theming and a variety of rooms to choose from. You can snag a room here for a fraction of the Deluxe or Moderate Resort prices, while still receiving several amenities like Early Theme Park Entry.

The All-Star hotels are clustered together at the very southern part of the Walt Disney World Resort. While its guests stay the furthest from the Magic Kingdom and the other parks, they still receive plenty of Disney magic. The All-Star Resorts have the appeal of eye-popping Disney-themed buildings with bright character paintings on the walls. We recommend families on a tight budget with young kids to stay here. There are two pools in each hotel and plenty of busses traveling to the theme parks. The hotels are broken up into themed hotel towers that spread around the pools.

Other than the distance from the parks, the All-Star hotels have very few dining options. The food courts here mostly serve American favorites like burgers and sandwiches.

BOTTOM LINE
Get several Disney amenities and lots of theming at a lower price. These resorts are also very far from the theme parks and have few dining options.

PROS
- The least expensive Disney-owned rooms on property
- Two pools at each hotel
- Food court and pizza room delivery options
- Disney themes with large statues and decorative spaces that are perfect for kids
- All-Star Music has family suites that sleep up to six

CONS

- Very far from the theme parks
- Only transport option is the busses, and every All-Star Resort hotel shares the same bus line, so they can feel crowded
- Adults may find these rooms cheesy
- Some rooms require a lot of walking to the amenities
- Limited dining options
- Often noisy with kids

DISNEY'S ART OF ANIMATION

Best for: Families with Kids ages 3-12
Themes: Disney animated films
AAA Rating: 3-Diamond
Location: South of Hollywood Studios and north of ESPN Wide World of Sports Complex
Pool: Yes (no Waterslides)
Transport to Parks: Skyliner Gondola, Bus
Amenities: Wi-Fi, Paid Laundry and Dry Cleaning, Several Pools, Jogging Trail, Movie Nights by the Pool, Bike Rentals, Playground, and Arcade

BUILDING THEMES

- **Cars**
- **Finding Nemo**
- **The Lion King**
- **The Little Mermaid**

OUR REVIEW

Disney's Art of Animation is perfect for families who want heavy Disney theming in the rooms and more space to spread out. The suites here are designed after Disney and Pixar animated films including *The Lion Kong*, *Cars*, and *Finding Nemo*. Guests can also stay in *Little Mermaid* standard rooms.

Kids will likely love these vibrant, themed rooms. For example, the Cars suite features toolshed-like dressers, and the Lion King suites have jungle print curtains. The design here feels almost like a kids playground, which is great for families, and not-so-great for traveling adults. But if you're looking for a room with two bathrooms and plenty of beds at a low price, Art of Animation is a great deal.

Like other Value resorts, Art of Animation has limited dining options. However, it has easy access to the Disney Skyliner gondolas that transport guests to Disney's Hollywood Studios and Epcot. The only downside here is that you have to switch to another line at Disney's Caribbean Beach before hopping to one of the parks.

BOTTOM LINE
A hotel with plenty of suites designed for families traveling on a budget. Rooms feature heavy Disney theming based on animated films. Though the Art of Animation lacks dining options, it has quick and easy access to the Disney Skyliner.

PROS
- Inexpensive rooms
- Disney Skyliner gondola access to Epcot and Disney's Hollywood Studios
- Multiple pools
- Food court and pizza room delivery options
- Heavy Disney theming
- Family Suites sleep up to 6 at the Art of Animation
- Closer to the parks than the All-Star Resorts

CONS
- Far away from the parks
- Busses can become crowded
- Adults may find the themed rooms in the Art of Animation cheesy
- Can feel spread out with some rooms far from the amenities
- Often noisy with kids
- More expensive than other Value resort hotels

DISNEY'S POP CENTURY

Best for: Families with Young Kids, Kids, and Tweens
Themes: 20th Century Pop Culture
AAA Rating: 3-Diamond
Location: South of Hollywood Studios and north of ESPN Wide World of Sports Complex
Pool: Yes (no Waterslides)
Transport to Parks: Skyliner Gondola, Bus
Amenities: Wi-Fi, Paid Laundry and Dry Cleaning, Several Pools, Jogging Trail, Movie Night, Bike Rentals, Playground, and Arcade

BUILDING THEMES
+ **'50s**
+ **'60s**
+ **'70s**
+ **'80s**
+ **'90s**

OUR REVIEW
Disney's Art of Animation and Pop Century resorts face one another over the Hourglass Lake (named for its shape). Each building is themed after decades and pop culture from the 20th century. There are '50s, '60s, '70s, '80s, and '90s-themed buildings.

No matter which building you stay in, your room will look roughly the same. The Pop Century rooms are stylish, comfortable, and usually feature two beds. There's plenty of storage space, a nice bathroom vanity, and rolling "barn" doors for privacy. The toilet and shower also have a separate door from the vanity area.

The biggest perk to staying at Pop Century is the quick access to the Skyler gondolas. Unfortunately, there aren't many dining options here. Nonetheless, you can score an inexpensive room with relatively fast travel by bus or gondola to all of the parks.

BOTTOM LINE
Pop Century is a great deal for couples and other small travel parties on a budget. The Disney Skyliner really adds value to this hotel with fewer dining options than Moderates or Deluxes.

PROS
- Inexpensive rooms
- Disney Skyliner gondola access to Epcot and Disney's Hollywood Studios
- Multiple pools
- Food court and pizza room delivery options
- Fun Disney theming that isn't overbearing
- Closer to the parks than the All-Star Resorts

CONS
- Far away from the parks
- Busses can become crowded quickly
- Can feel spread out with some rooms far from the amenities
- More expensive than other Value resort hotels

MORE RESORTS

SWAN, DOLPHIN, & SWAN RESERVE

Best for: Tweens, Teens, Adults
Theme: Premium Hotel
AAA Rating: 4-Diamond
Location: Central, walking distance to Epcot and Disney's Hollywood Studios
Pool: Yes, with Waterslide
Transport to Parks: Boat, Walk, Busses
Amenities: Wi-Fi, Paid Laundry and Dry Cleaning, Pools with Waterslides and Waterfall, Jogging Paths, Movie Nights, Playground, Volleyball, Basketball, Tennis, Bike Rentals, Boat Rentals, Fishing, Club Access for Certain Rooms, Spa and Fitness Center, Child Care at Camp Dolphin, Mini Golf, and Arcade

OUR REVIEW

The Swan, Dolphin, and Swan Reserve are three sister hotel towers near Epcot and Disney's Hollywood Studios. These hotels are not run by Disney. Instead, they are leased to another corporation and run by Marriott. Because of this, these hotels do not receive all of Disney's amenities like discounted Magic Bands and the Disney Dining Plan. Still, guests may prefer to stay here because of the lower price point and close proximity to Epcot and Hollywood Studios.

These three hotels also provide guests with designated travel to the parks and Early Theme Park Entry (when applicable). The boats also stop in front of the Swan and Dolphin for easy planning.

BOTTOM LINE

Stylish hotels within walking distance to Epcot and Disney's Hollywood Studios. These two hotels are leased out by Disney to other companies, so guests will have different transports to the park.

PROS

- Early Theme Park Entry and Extended Evening Hours
- Walking distance to Hollywood Studios and Epcot

- Less expensive than Disney Deluxe Resorts
- Full-service spa (in Dolphin)
- Gym
- Great hotel dining
- Close to Disney's BoardWalk
- Designated busses that run to the Magic Kingdom and Disney's Animal Kingdom every 20-25 minutes

CONS
- Very little Disney theming
- Rooms feel a little dated
- Parking costs more than other hotels at $29/day or $39/day for valet

BOOKING
You'll have to book your Swan or Dolphin hotel room through a separate website: www.swandolphin.com.

SHADES OF GREEN

Best for: Military Families
Theme: Golf Resort
Location: West of Magic Kingdom Park, near the golf courses
Pool: Yes, with Waterslide

OUR REVIEW
Shades of Green is a family resort with tennis courts, a pool, and golf courses. It's set up to give discounted vacations to those who serve in the military for the United States. Meals tend to be very inexpensive and the rooms are nice and big for the price. You might also want to use your military discount to stay closer to the parks.

PROS
- Beautiful landscaping with golfing
- Large rooms for the price
- Inexpensive dining in the hotel
- Exclusive busses to the parks and Disney Springs
- Early Theme Park Entry
- Extended Evening Hours

CONS
- Far away from the theme parks
- Very little Disney theming

BOOKING
Active and retired military can book at: www.shadesofgreen.org

STAR WARS: GALACTIC CRUISER

Boarding begins March 1, 2022

This Star Wars-themed hotel is perfect for guests wanting a more immersive theme park experience. However, is not your typical Disney hotel. Think of the Galactic Cruiser like a 2-night role playing adventure on a cruise ship!

After booking, guests will arrive at a terminal outside of Disney's Hollywood Studios and be transported onto the Galactic Starcruiser. Guests can choose to play an exotic alien or simply be themselves. The Starcruiser boasts top-level service, excellent themed dining, and plenty of unique experiences. Guests choose their own itineraries from training with a realistic lightsaber to becoming a socialite in the lounge. During the day, guests can complete missions on board or travel to Star Wars: Galaxy's Edge via transport. In the evening, danger could be afoot as Kylo Ren and the First Order threaten all who are on board!

While all of that sounds amazing, the Star Wars: Galactic Starcruiser comes with a steep price tag. Guests can expect to pay a starting price of about $6,000 for a family of four. These rooms aren't very large and will certainly feel like a cruise ship. Still, for hardcore Star Wars fans, this experience might be worth every penny! We mostly recommend the Galactic Starcruiser for adults and teens. However, Star Wars fans ages 7 and older may also have a great appreciation for this immersive experience.

For more details, cabin choices, costume guidelines, and booking, visit: www.starwarsgalacticstarcruiser.com.

· **Magic Tips** ·

Disney encourages guests to dress up for the Galactic Starcruiser! We recommend creating your own character rather than dressing up as Han Solo or Princess Leia so that you can add to the on-going story.

There's also a special "Captain's Table" for guests to have extra entrees and experiences during their cruise. There are only a small number of seats per dining experience, and the additional cost is $30 per person. Reserve this experience when booking your stay.

MORE HOTEL TIPS

Check-in – You can easily check-in to your Walt Disney World Resort hotel room via the Walt Disney World application. You can also do this days before your arrival. Your room number will be displayed in the app when it's time to check in (3pm, and 4pm for Deluxe Villas).

Checkout – The checkout process is automatic at the Walt Disney World Resort. You will be delivered an itemized final bill on the morning of your departure. You will not need to manually checkout, call, or visit the front desk. Checkout time is 11am. For Late Checkout, call the front desk on the morning of your departure. If they have availability, you might be able to checkout as late as 1pm. Bell services will also hold your belongings if you have a later departure time (we recommend tipping $1-$2 per bag).

Room Upgrades – Based on availability, you may be able to upgrade your room. Most of the time, Disney will charge for this. If you checkin at the front desk, you can always ask for availability and an upgrade.

EVEN MORE HOTELS

Staying on property at the Walt Disney World Resort may be too expensive for your budget and needs. While we usually recommend staying on-property for all of Disney's benefits, there are several properties in and around Walt Disney World that make fantastic options. Here we list our most-recommended of these hotels.

$\sum$ = Hotels that receive Early Theme Park Entry

DISNEY SPRINGS AREA HOTELS

If you're looking to stay close to the theme parks but in a deluxe or moderate-style hotel without the premium cost, Disney Springs houses several nearby hotels in its "Hotel Plaza" area. Each of these properties is endorsed by Walt Disney World and can often come with Disney theming. At times, Disney Springs resorts will have Early Theme Park Entry for their guests.

B Resort & Spa Σ
1905 Hotel Plaza Blvd., Lake Buena Vista, FL 32830
(888) 246-8357 / www.bhotelsandresorts.com/b-resort-and-spa

Star Rating	Our Rating	Price	Shuttle to Disney Parks	Pool
4	B+	Moderate	Yes	Yes

Pros: Affordable and stylish rooms. On-site spa with shuttle to and from Disney theme parks. You can also ask for a gaming console to play in your room.
Cons: Resort fee, inconsistent customer service

Best Western Lake Buena Vista
2000 Hotel Plaza Blvd., Lake Buena Vista, FL 32830
(407) 828-2424 / www.lakebuenavistaresorthotel.com

Star Rating	Our Rating	Price	Shuttle to Disney Parks	Pool
3	B	Economic	Yes	Yes

Pros: Affordable rooms with shuttle to and from Disney theme parks. There is also a fitness center. AAA discount available.
Cons: Further away from Disney Springs, Resort fee, hotel appears dated

---

DoubleTree Suites by Hilton Orlando Σ
2305 Hotel Plaza Blvd., Lake Buena Vista, FL 32830
(407) 934-1000 / www.doubletree.com

Star Rating	Our Rating	Price	Shuttle to Disney Parks	Pool
3	B+	Economic	Yes	Yes

Pros: Affordable rooms with shuttle to and from Disney theme parks. There is also a fitness center and Hilton Honors members can get discounts on rooms and earn points.

Cons: Further away from Disney Springs, inconsistent customer service

---

Hilton Orlando Buena Vista Palace ∑
1900 E. Buena Vista Dr, Lake Buena Vista, FL 32830
(407) 827-2727 / www.buenavistapalace.com

Star Rating	Our Rating	Price	Shuttle to Disney Parks	Pool
4	A	Moderate	Yes	Yes

Pros: Affordable and stylish 4-star rooms with a view. Offers shuttle to and from Disney theme parks, a fitness center, and Hilton Honors members can get discounts on rooms and earn points. Very close to Disney Springs.
Cons: May not live up to other Hilton hotels in terms of service and room style.

Hilton Orlando Lake Buena Vista ∑
1751 Hotel Plaza Blvd, Lake Buena Vista, FL 32830
(407) 827-4000 / www.hilton.com

Star Rating	Our Rating	Price	Shuttle to Disney Parks	Pool
4	A-	Moderate	Yes	Yes

Pros: Affordable 4-star rooms with a view. Offers shuttle to and from Disney theme parks, a fitness center, and Hilton Honors members can get discounts on rooms and earn points. Very close to Disney Springs. Adults-only pool available.
Cons: May not live up to other Hilton hotels in terms of service and room style. High parking fees.

Holiday Inn Orlando ∑
1805 Hotel Plaza Blvd, Lake Buena Vista, FL 32830
(407) 828-8888 / www.hiorlando.com

Star Rating	Our Rating	Price	Shuttle to Disney Parks	Pool
3	A	Economic	Yes	Yes

Pros: Very affordable and simple rooms. Offers shuttle to and from Disney theme parks and fitness center.
Cons: Parking costs extra and high resort fees. Rooms could use updating.

Wyndham Garden Lake Buena Vista ∑
1850 Hotel Plaza Blvd, Lake Buena Vista, FL 32830
(407) 842-6644 /www.wyndhamlakebuenavista.com

Star Rating	Our Rating	Price	Shuttle to Disney Parks	Pool
3	B-	Economic	Yes	Yes

Pros: Very close to Disney Springs. Offers shuttle to and from Disney theme parks and fitness center. Rooms are clean and affordable.
Cons: Rooms are nothing special. Resort needs updating.

MORE NON-DISNEY HOTELS

These hotel properties are a bump up in price, but offer more amenities. Overall, they can still save you money in comparison to staying at a Disney Resort.

Margaritaville Resort Orlando
8000 Fins Up Circle, Kissimmee, FL 34747
(407) 479-0950 / www.margaritavilleresortorlando.com

Star Rating	Our Rating	Price	Shuttle to Disney Parks	Pool
4	A	Moderate	Yes	Yes

Pros: An island-themed resort hotel with "lagoon-style" sand pools, a luxury spa, signature dining, and the 14-acre Island H2O Live! water park. Margaritaville is designed both for family fun and relaxation. Disney's Animal Kingdom theme park is only about 5 miles away. Larger groups may want to consider renting a cottage located on property.
Cons: Rates can skyrocket during the summer and holiday seasons. At times, the party scene near the pools can become noisy.

Hyatt Regency Grand Cypress
1 Grand Cypress Blvd, Orlando, FL 32836
(407) 239-1234 / www.hyatt.com

Star Rating	Our Rating	Price	Shuttle to Disney Parks	Pool
4	A	Deluxe	Yes	Yes

Pros: Beautiful property and rooms. Shuttle service to and from Disney theme parks, on-site spa, nearby golfing, rock climbing, and 24-hour fitness center. Pet accommodations available.
Cons: Can be expensive and have a very high resort fee. About a 5 to 10-minute drive to Disney Springs and 20-minute drive to the Magic Kingdom.

Waldorf Astoria Orlando ∑
14200 Bonnet Creek Resort Ln, Orlando, FL 32821
(407) 597-5500 / www.waldorfastoriaorlando.com

Star Rating	Our Rating	Price	Shuttle to Disney Parks	Pool
5	A+	Luxury	Yes	Yes

Pros: Beautiful and affordable 5-star hotel property and rooms. Shuttle service to and from Disney theme parks, on-site spa, nearby golfing, and 24-hour fitness center. Hilton Honors members can get discounts on rooms and earn points. Excellent staff.
Cons: About a 10- to 15-minute drive to the Magic Kingdom.
Walt Disney World Perks: This hotel receives Early Theme Park Entry benefits.

Gaylord Palms Resort
6000 W. Osceola Parkway, Orlando, FL 32821
(407) 586-0000 / www.gaylordpalms.com

Star Rating	Our Rating	Price	Shuttle to Disney Parks	Pool
4	A-	Luxury	Yes	Yes

Pros: Beautiful and affordable 4-star hotel property and rooms. Unique theming including an indoor restaurant on a boat. Shuttle service to Disney theme parks, on-site spa, pools with waterslides, wave pool, on-site alligators, nearby golfing, and 24-hour fitness center. Marriott Rewards members can get discounts on rooms and earn points. 10-minute drive to Epcot.

Cons: Hotel can sell out during popular months. Parking is expensive and can become backed up on busy weekends and holidays.

Hilton Orlando Bonnet Creek ∑

14100 Bonnet Creek Resort Ln, Orlando, FL 32821-4023
(407) 597-3600 / www.hiltonbonnetcreek.com

Star Rating	Our Rating	Price	Shuttle to Disney Parks	Pool
4	A-	Deluxe	Yes	Yes

Pros: Clean and affordable 4-star hotel property and rooms. Oasis-like pool with lazy river, golf course, fitness center, jogging track, arcade, and bike rental. Shuttle service to Disney theme parks. Hilton Honors members can get discounts on rooms and earn points. 10-minute drive to Epcot.

Cons: May not live up to typical Hilton hotel styles. Rooms by pools can become very noisy.

Walt Disney World Perks: This hotel receives Early Theme Park Entry benefits.

Rosen Shingle Creek ∑

9939 Universal Blvd, Orlando, FL 32819
(866) 996-9939 / www.rosenshinglecreek.com

Star Rating	Our Rating	Price	Shuttle to Disney Parks	Pool
4	A+	Luxury	Paid	Yes

Pros: We believe that the Rose Shingle Creek is one of the better deals for a luxury vacation stay outside of the Walt Disney World Resort. Beautiful and affordable 4-star hotel property and rooms. On-site spa, on-site golfing, and fitness center. Close to Universal Orlando (5-10 minute drive). Excellent staff.

Cons: Paid shuttle service through Mears to theme parks. A bit far from Walt Disney World (20-25 minute drive to the Magic Kingdom).

Walt Disney World Perks: This hotel receives Early Theme Park Entry benefits.

Ritz-Carlton Grande Lakes
4012 Central Florida Pkwy, Orlando, FL 32837
(407) 206-2400 / www.ritzcarlton.com

Star Rating	Our Rating	Price	Shuttle to Disney Parks	Pool
5	A	Luxury	Yes	Yes

Pros: Elegant 5-star hotel property and stunning rooms. Shuttle service to and from Walt Disney World theme parks, Universal Orlando, and SeaWorld. On-site spa, butterfly garden, kids play area, bocce ball courts, 18-hole golfing, and fitness center. Superior service.

Cons: Expensive, so if you're looking for a bargain on a 5-star resort, you may want to try the Waldorf Astoria (though we prefer the Ritz Carlton or the Four Seasons). About 20- to 25-minute drive to the Magic Kingdom, Epcot, or Universal Orlando.

Four Seasons Resort Orlando ∑
14200 Bonnet Creek Resort Ln, Orlando, FL 32821
(407) 597-5500 / www.fourseasons.com/orlando

Star Rating	Our Rating	Price	Shuttle to Disney Parks	Pool
5	A+	Luxury	Yes	Yes

Pros: Elegant 5-star hotel property and stunning rooms. Several pools with lazy river, adults-only pool, splash zone, bocce ball, movies by the pool, and game room. Complimentary "luxury motor coach" to and from the Disney parks. Private car service available. Closer to the parks than the Ritz-Carlton (about 10 minutes to the Magic Kingdom or Epcot). Superior service.

Cons: Very expensive, so if you're looking for a bargain on a 5-star resort, you may want to try the Waldorf Astoria or the less-expensive Ritz-Carlton (though we prefer the Four Seasons). About 20 to 25-minute drive to the Magic Kingdom, Epcot, or Universal Orlando.

Walt Disney World Perks: This hotel receives Early Theme Park Entry benefits.

INTRODUCTION

Like many shopping locations in America, Disney Springs has gone through radical transformations. Originally known as Lake Buena Vista Shopping Village when it opened in 1975, this section of the Walt Disney World Resort has always focused heavily on dining and shopping experiences. Soon after its inception, the shopping area transformed into Walt Disney World Village, Disney Village Marketplace, and Downtown Disney before coming to its latest name in 2015.

Disney Springs is designed for wandering. Visitors will discover fun new shops, premium restaurants, and dazzling entertainment. Whether you're looking for a Disney-themed gift, a romantic dinner, or an unforgettable show, Disney Springs has it all.

For the most part, Disney Springs is a beautiful outdoor mall with chain stores as well as unique boutiques. Restaurants fill much of the area that's covered in waterways, bridges, and stunning Floridian scenes. The scene comes to life with beautifully paved walkways filled with music, glowing ponds, and spectacular banners. Here, we explore some of Disney Springs' unique shopping and dining experiences based on our top recommendations.

NOTE: There are 100 stores and small shops located in Disney Springs. Because there are so many, we cover the highlights.

GETTING TO DISNEY SPRINGS

Disney Springs is located on property, but a bit far away from the Magic Kingdom and Animal Kingdom. If you're driving, parking at Disney Springs is free in any of their lots or garages. There are a few ways to travel there without a car:

+ **Boat** – There is free water transport from the Disney's Port Orleans Resort (French Quarter and Riverside), Disney's Old Key West Resort, and Disney's Saratoga Springs Resort.
+ **Bus** – Perhaps the least glamorous way, but it's efficient. Travel to Disney Springs from any of the resort parks or hotels for free with the Disney Bus system.
+ **Walk** – From Disney's Saratoga Springs Resort, you can walk directly to Disney Springs in about 15 minutes.

UNIQUE SHOPS

There are dozens of shops at Disney Springs—and it's still growing! Since many of them are found in retail locations around the world, we've just listed the unique shops dedicated to pleasing visitors of Walt Disney World.

THE ART OF DISNEY
Get Disney-themed gifts from art to fineries. You won't find anything like these pieces of art anywhere else!

BIBBIDI BOBBIDI BOUTIQUE
Perfect for Kids looking to get a makeover to look like their favorite Disney Princess. It's a replica of the one also offered in the Magic Kingdom Park. We recommend booking an appointment if you'd like a makeover. Otherwise, this Boutique gives free spritzes of pixie dust to any visitor!

BUILD A DINO
The makers of Build-A-Bear Workshop bring you a prehistoric version of the same concept. Make your own dinosaur toy or plush, or build one as a gift. Kids will go crazy for this experience.

COCA-COLA STORE
Everything Coca-Cola from clothing to unique flavors can be found in this well-themed store.

DISNEY'S CANDY CAULDRON
Discover an array of delicious Disney desserts including their famous hand-designed caramel apples. Mobile ordering may be available here using the Walt Disney World app!

DISNEY'S DAYS OF CHRISTMAS
A magic emporium where the holidays never end. Relive your Christmas spirit any day of the year in this stunning shop.

DISNEY'S PHOTOPASS STUDIOS
Looking for the perfect Disney photo experience? Search no further because you can have everything from classic Disney backdrops to *Frozen* wonderlands created in this professional photo studio.

DISNEY PIN TRADERS
Search through a seemingly endless supply of pins to buy and trade with people all over the Walt Disney World Resort. The largest Disney pin board is at the Disney Pin Trading Company Store in Disney Springs. While this board is only on display during part of each day, pin traders will drop their jaw after spotting it!

DISNEYSTYLE
Find clothing and accessories to fit your ideal Disney outfit! There's also fantastic nostalgic items from the parks inside this store.

DISNEY'S WONDERFUL WORLD OF MEMORIES
If scrapbooking is your thing, then there is no better place in all of Walt Disney World. Commemorate your vacation with unique Disney-style stickers, pages, and more to complete your beautiful scrapbook.

GHIRARDELLI ICE CREAM & CHOCOLATE SHOP
Try world-famous chocolate, ice cream, and sodas in this classic chocolate shop. The smell of this shop is also heavenly! If you're just stopping by, you'll receive a free square of chocolate to sample.

GOOFY'S CANDY COMPANY
A great spot for delicious candy! We highly recommend Goofy's Sour Gummy Worms as a perfect gift—or just a treat for yourself. Guests

can also stop by and try a free piece of candy here! Mobile ordering available with the Disney World app.

THE LEGO STORE
We can't think of a better way to bribe kids to go shopping than with the magic of LEGO! This store has it all from individual pieces to unique sets. You can also design your own figurines to buy. Even adults will be stunned by the amazing LEGO collections.

M&MS STORE
Enter the colorful world of M&Ms to pick out your favorite flavors and snag specialty apparel.

STAR WARS GALACTIC OUTPOST
The destination for Star Wars apparel! Buy everything from artwork to T-shirts and toys that range in theme from every *Star Wars* movie ever made.

SUPER HERO HEADQUARTERS
Power up with loads of Marvel merchandise in this specially themed store.

TREN-D
Disney-inspired fashion with designs mostly aiming at tweens, teens, and young adults.

UNIQLO
This multi-level apparel destination will remind first-time visitors of retail giants like H&M. However, UNIQLO is also a fantastic place to purchase inexpensive Disney-branded clothing and accessories. They have everything from Mickey Mouse to Star Wars for kids and adults!

· **Magic Tips** ·
Many of the shops in Disney Springs have hotel delivery free of charge for those staying on property! We love this feature and highly recommend using it.

WORLD OF DISNEY
This may be the most popular store in all of the Walt Disney World Resort—and for a good reason. Pick from an overabundance of Disney merchandise from pins and toys to clothing and kitchenware.

There's something for every Disney fan in here and we highly recommend that you pay World of Disney a visit.

> **· Magic Tips ·**
> The Guest Services booth at Disney Springs can be a lifesaver. If you have any issues with your mobile app or vacation planning, head over there and a Disney Cast Member will take care of you.

MORE NOTABLE SHOPS

Alex and Ani – Charm bracelets and more

Anthropologie – Women's apparel

The Art of Shaving – Bath products aimed at men

Basin – Soaps and body care items

Coach – Designer purses, bags, and other accessories

Crystal Arts by Arribas Brothers – Beautiful crystal collectables, including ones with Disney characters

Fit2Run – Shop for athletic apparel and related goods

Happy Hound – A kiosk with adorable pet accessories

Kate Space New York – Designer purses and other accessories

Lovepop – Fun cards for any occasion

Marketplace Co-Op – Find several small stores, including ones with Disney products, in this indoor shopping space.

Sephora – A wide variety of makeup and beauty products

Sunglass Icon – Designer sunglasses

Superdry – Trendy clothing and accessories

Tommy Bahama – Island-inspired apparel

UGG – Comfortable boots and more

Volcom – Clothing inspired by music and skate scenes

Zara – High-fashion apparel at an affordable cost

ATTRACTIONS

AEROPHILE

Fly up to 400 feet into the air on a giant helium balloon, and get stunning views of the Walt Disney World Resort. Prices are $20 for adults and $15 for kids ages 3-9. Cloudy and foggy days may have limited viewing. Also, weather can prevent the balloon from taking off. We also recommend booking a dinner somewhere at the Gran Destino Tower in Coronado Springs or the Riviera Resort's rooftop for amazing views and a delicious meal.

GO BOWLING

Splitsville has luxury bowling lanes that are fun for the entire family! Dine and bowl—or just come for the bowling. Splitsville has extended hours usually from 10:30am - 1am.

DRAWN TO LIFE BY CIRQUE DU SOLEIL

Walt Disney Animation Studios and Cirque du Soleil have teamed up to bring a one-of-a-kind theatrical production to life! In *Drawn to Life*, Disney animated characters will interact with the performers to make this a touching and magical experience for all!

Tickets: Start around $80

Booking: https://disneyworld.disney.go.com/entertainment/disney-springs/cirque-du-soleil

INTRODUCTION

You may have come to the Walt Disney World Resort for the world-class attractions and themes. However, there's a hidden gem just awaiting you. The Walt Disney World Resort is home to some of the best food in the world with cuisine you'll be raving about well after your trip has come to an end. That is, *if* you know where to go. It's true that there are many quick-service stands with bland hamburgers and forgettable fries. However, there are places in the resort with some of the *best* burgers, fries, and churros. You just need to know where these places are. In this chapter, we adventure through Walt Disney World eating spots. Whether it's hotel dining or Epcot cuisine, we review all that can tickle your tastebuds.

DINING TYPES

A listing of the different categories of restaurants. Walt Disney World keeps it simple by bringing you only a few types of eateries: Quick-Service, Table Service, and Fine Dining. It may be difficult to know the pricing based on their recommendations, so we've broken it down further here.

+ **Quick-Service** – Meals that you can order and then typically seat yourself soon after ordering.

✦ **Table Service** – Restaurants with a waiter. It is suggested that you tip based on the service you receive.

✦ **Fine Dining or Signature Dining** – The best that the Walt Disney World Resort has to offer with elegant décor and excellent, world-class courses. Fine Dining restaurants come with a premium price and often a dress code.

✦ **Snack** – Carts, shacks, and huts serving snacks and drinks.

✦ **Bars and Lounges** – Calm areas with open seating and typically a full bar. Lounges typically have more seating than bars.

BOOKING A RESERVATION

We highly recommend that you book reservations in advance before you go. Reservations typically drop between 5:30am and 7:00am EST. Getting a dining reservation to a popular spot can be very frustrating because they often book up very quickly. We recommend setting your alarm and making sure you're up in time to reserve your spot with the app.

> **· Magic Tips ·**
>
> Disney Dining Reservations can be made in advance using the Disney World app or via WaltDisneyWorld.com. Before the park closures, Disney offered 180-day advanced dining reservations. However, after reopening, Disney dropped its dining reservations to 60 days in advance. It's unclear at the time of this publication if Disney will extend reservations back to 180 days in 2022.

MOBILE ORDERING

The Walt Disney World App is your ticket to fast and easy ordering to some of the best dining locations in the parks! Not every restaurant has this option, but some with infamously long lines now have a way for you to cut ahead! We highly recommend mobile ordering instead of waiting. Disney has streamlined this system to make it quick and easy for your food availability.

Using Mobile Ordering:

1. Log into the Walt Disney World App
2. Tap the + menu sign, followed by "Order Food"
3. Choose your dining spot and arrival time
4. Select your items

5. Review the order and purchase with credit card
6. When your order is ready, head to the restaurant and alert a Cast Member that you have arrived for pickup!

> We've marked all restaurants with mobile ordering using this icon: ‡ — Disney will likely add more restaurants and possibly change options, so use the app for a more up-to-date list.

Note: Walt Disney World's soda fountains and bottled waters are Coca-Cola products. The resort's domestic beer is typically Budweiser.

· **Magic Tips** ·
If you don't find your requested restaurant reservation time, there's a small trick that might work in the app. Instead of selecting "lunch" or "dinner" time slots, choose individual times. Something may pop up that wasn't there before! If not, keep checking because you can pick up a reservation that another party cancels.

OUR RESTAURANT PRICING

Walt Disney World only has 3 tiers of pricing on their website. We don't think it's enough. To the savvy traveler, there is a big difference between something under $10 and something over $10. There's also a big difference between a table-service meal that will cost you $15-$25 versus well over $25 per person.

$ – Under $10 (typically snack carts)
$$ – $10-$15 (typically Quick-Service Restaurants)
$$$ – $15-$30 (Table Service Restaurants)
$$$$ – $30-$60 (Dinner Buffets, Fine and Signature Dining)
$$$$$ – $60 or more (Dining experiences)

OUR FAVORITES
We list our favorites food items and locations from snacks to dining. Just look for the ❤ next to the item!

ALLERGY AND DINING REQUESTS

Disney is happy to accommodate special dining requests and wants to ensure that your food is safe for you to eat. If you have a dietary need or request, inform your waiter or the quick-service dining spot. Many times, the wait staff will ask before you're seated if you have any food allergies. To pre-plan, we recommend reviewing the menus of each dining spot before attending (these can be found on the Walt Disney World mobile app and WaltDisneyWorld.com). If Disney cannot meet your dietary needs, you may bring food with you to the parks. Your travel safety is important, so please reach out to Disney with any questions: special.diets@DisneyWorld.com

> **· Magic Tips ·**
> Disney's commitment to the environment has taken its theme parks away from using many plastics. This means Quick-Service dining spots distribute soft drinks without a plastic lid or straw. If you'd like a paper straw, ask a Cast Member at your dining location.

BOOKING DINING

The popular restaurants fill up quickly, so don't forget to book in advance. The easiest way to book dining is through the Walt Disney World mobile app or online on Disney World's website. If you need assistance, call **(714) 781-DINE** to book.

DISNEY DINING PLAN

INTRODUCTION

The Walt Disney World Resort offers special dining packages for guests staying on property. The Disney Dining Plans (DDP) are designed for guests to pre-pay for the food that they plan to enjoy during their vacation. While Disney touts DDP as a way to save money, for many guests, this simply isn't the case. So, think of DDP as more of an "all-inclusive" cost rather than a way to save money. We've discovered that DDP *can* save you a load of cash or end up costing you more, depending on your plan. Overall, we like DDP a lot, and with our tips, you can take maximum advantage of this program.

USING DISNEY DINING PLAN

You may redeem your DDP points at one of 200 dining spots around Walt Disney World that take part of the program. These spots include the four theme parks, water parks, Resort hotels, and Disney Springs. Each meal or snack becomes 1 credit on your reservation. A Table Service credit and a Quick-Service credit are separate points. Snack credits are also separate points. Signature Dining restaurants require 2 Table Service credits to dine. Your MagicBand can be scanned to use your credits.

Quick-Service meals come with an entree and a drink. Table Service Meals come with 1 entree, 1 dessert, and 1 beverage—or you can use 1 Table Service credit toward a buffet. Snack credits can be used toward items like popcorn, ice cream, chips, coffee, and drinks. Different snack locations will offer various items. For Table Service and Quick-Service, adults ages 21 and older can use their drink credit for an alcoholic beverage.

All credits of one party are linked to a single account, therefore someone in your group can borrow from the entire pool. This can be a bit tricky for those with large groups, so it's important to keep this in mind before purchasing DDP. Guests will not be able to break up these dining credits across multiple locations. Meaning, you cannot redeem 1 Quick-Service credit for an entree at one restaurant and a drink at another.

Additionally, the Walt Disney World mobile app keeps track of your used and remaining dining credits. After using a credit, your receipt will also show your party's remaining credits. If you have trouble accessing this information, you can also receive a breakdown from your hotel concierge.

QUALIFICATIONS

To buy one of the Disney Dining Plans, you'll need to book a package through Disney with a room and theme park tickets. Those staying with Disney Vacation Club may not have to purchase the theme park tickets to buy a DDP.

DINING PLAN TYPES

There are three types of Disney Dining Plans and each offer different meals depending on your needs. If you tend to eat at Quick-Service burger and sandwich places, you might want to skip the more expensive meal plans. If you enjoy eating at several of Disney's themed Table Service dining experiences, you may want an upgraded plan.

ALL PLANS

All dining and snack credits and other perks are valid through midnight of the day you check out. Each Dining Plan comes with a refillable mug per person that can be used for fountain drinks at Resort hotels.

DISNEY QUICK SERVICE PLAN

2 Quick-Service Meals and 2 Snacks per person, per night. Quick-Service meals are spots without a waiter and are scattered around the Walt Disney World Resort. These are also the least expensive meals. You will not be able to use this plan at Table Service, Character Dining experiences, or Signature restaurants.
Cost per day: $55.50/adult (ages 10+) and $26.00/child (ages 3-9)

DISNEY DINING PLAN

1 Quick-Service Meal, 1 Table Service Meal, and 2 Snacks per person, per day. Table Service meals are restaurants with a waiter or a buffet. You can also use 2 of your Table Service credits for a Signature Dining experience like the California Grill or the Yachtsman Steakhouse.
Cost per day: $78.01/adult (ages 10+) and $30.51/child (ages 3-9)

DISNEY DINING PLAN PLUS

2 Meals (either Table Service or Quick-Service), and 2 Snacks per person, per day. This package is the best deal for those needing flexibility and not nearly as much food as the Deluxe Dining Plan provides.
Cost per day: $94.61/adult (ages 10+) and $35.00/child (ages 3-9)

DISNEY DELUXE DINING PLAN

3 Meals (either Table Service or Quick-Service), and 2 Snacks per person, per day. If you are planning on dining at table service restaurants more than once a day, we recommend this package. Or, if you plan on dining at several Signature Dining locations, we also recommend this package.
Cost per day: $119.00/adult (ages 10+) and $47.50/child (ages 3-9)

MORE TIPS

DDP is relatively flexible. Each night you stay gives you dining credits. So, you can use as many or as little of your credits each day. For example, you can choose to use one Quick-Service credit and one Table Service credit per day, or use two Quick-Service one day and two Table Service another. You can also use two Table Service and one Quick-Service in a day. Really, the choice is yours. If you run out of credits, you will be billed. Tip is also not included with DDP, so we recommend bringing cash or charging your room or credit card upon receipt.

> **· Magic Tips ·**
> If you're traveling with a group, the Disney Dining Plans make paying easy! You won't have to worry about splitting bills since you're using one credit per person.

DINING PLAN CONS

As we've said before, depending on your needs, the Dining Disney Plan may not save you money. It may also cost you more than just paying out of pocket for your meals. If you're not interested in planning all of your dining before you head to the parks, we don't recommend DDP. It might feel overwhelming to pre-plan your vacation, meal by meal for each day. The Quick-Service DDP may work for your needs in this occasion. That way, you can grab food when you're hungry.

Children ten and older with smaller appetites may end up costing you more than they'll eat. While some ten-year-olds eat as much as an adult, many do not. Nonetheless, you'll pay the same for a ten-year-old boy as you would an adult man. Children who are picky and inconsistent eaters may not benefit from DDP. Make sure you review kids' menus before booking.

Furthermore, the reliable drink mug that comes with each dining plan is very, very small. They hold about one can of Coke, which is fine for children and those who don't drink very many liquids. Most guests wishing to fill their mugs, even with filtered drinking water, will find themselves bouncing back and forth between their hotel room and the refill station near the lobbies.

We also wish that the Table Service credits could have a choice of appetizer instead of dessert. Most guests don't feel like eating 2-3 desserts a day. Some restaurants will allow those with the Deluxe Dining Plan to get both an appetizer and a dessert with each meal at no additional cost.

Overall, the Disney Dining Plan comes with *a lot* of food. Will you want to eat an entree, dessert, and specialty beverage more than once a day? If the answer is yes, then we highly recommend DDP for you.

DINING PLAN TIPS

1. Book your restaurant reservations well in advance to secure your top dining choices.
2. Snack credits can be used in a variety of ways, including for a Starbucks coffee or pastry.
3. Snack credits can be redeemed at many locations at Epcot's famous Food & Wine Festival. You can also use 1 Quick-Service credit as 3 snack credits at participating locations!
4. At Table Service locations, you can always ask your waiter to substitute your food. It's not a guarantee, but if you don't feel up for dessert, you may ask to change it for an appetizer.
5. Dinner buffets are always a great idea to get your money's worth. These usually cost about $60 per adult for a dinner buffet. 1 Table Service credit is all that you need to redeem at most of these locations!
6. When dining for dinner, order a steak; it's the best value for an entree that you can find.
7. Snacks credits are the biggest items that go to waste while using DDP. If you don't use all of them, you can redeem Snack credits at most hotel shops. These can be used for candy bars and other to-go items.
8. Snacks can be used for specialty drinks and desserts. This includes popular items like Dole Whips and LeFou's Brew at Gaston's Tavern in Fantasyland (Magic Kingdom)!
9. Watch your credits! Since you pay with DDP at the end of your meal, you may find yourself with a surprise bill if you've run out of dining credits (keep track on the Walt Disney World app).

FREE DINING PLAN DEAL

Almost every year, Walt Disney World releases a very limited discount where guests staying at select Disney Resort properties get a Disney Dining Plan for free! Of course, there are limitations. Often these include a minimum of a four-night stay and park hopper tickets for each person in your group. These deals are often released in April for travel in August through December (with October, Thanksgiving, and Christmas weeks usually excluded). We've done the math and it usually saves hundreds of dollars for a family of four, even in contrast with booking a discounted room.

Most of the time, Pop Century or Old Key West are the best options for this dining deal. Pop Century is centrally located to many of the attractions and comes with the Quick-Service Dining Plan. Old Key West is also centrally located and comes with the Disney Dining Plan (with Table Service) at a much lower rate. Disney's BoardWalk Inn comes at a close second to Old Key West.

· **Magic Tips** ·
We update our free e-mail newsletter when the free dining deal becomes available: **www.magicguidebooks.com/list**

TABLES IN WONDERLAND

Florida residents, Walt Disney World Passholders, and Disney Vacation Club Members can join a unique discounted dining program called Tables in Wonderland. Save 20% on food *and* alcohol for your party at over 100 Walt Disney World restaurants. This is a great option for guests with larger groups who might consume alcohol, as Passholder and DVC discounts don't cover adult beverages. One Tables in Wonderland pass works for up to 10 guests or you can combine two passes for up to 20 guests on one bill.

Tables in Wonderland is $175 for Florida Residents and $150 for Passholders and DVC members. Booking: **http://tablesinwonderland.com**

MAGIC KINGDOM DINING

‡ **ALOHA ISLE** ❤
Adventureland
Description: Grab a famous Dole Whip here. One of the best treats in all of Walt Disney World.
Type: Snack
Price: $ / **Dining Plan:** Yes
Menu Items: Dole Whip, Juice, Water, Pineapple
Recommendation: Pineapple Float ❤

AUNTIE POLLY'S DOCKSIDE INN
Frontierland
Description: Seasonal snack stand
Type: Snack
Price: $ / **Dining Plan:** No
Menu Items: sandwiches, brownie, root beer float, pretzel sticks
Recommendation: This seasonal snack stand rarely opens in Frontierland, but serves delicious biscuit sliders and root beer floats

AUNTIE GRAVITY'S GALACTIC GOODIES
Tomorrowland
Description: Ice cream stand
Type: Snack
Price: $ / **Dining Plan:** No
Menu Items: Ice cream, floats, muffins, fruit, smoothies, soda pop
Recommendation: Hot Fudge Sundae

BE OUR GUEST RESTAURANT ❤
Fantasyland
Description: Not to be missed! A dazzling restaurant with three main dining areas: the dark west wing, the ballroom, and the rose gallery. It has some of the best food in the Magic Kingdom.
Type: Quick-Service (breakfast and lunch) / Table Service (dinner)
Price: $$$-$$$$ / **Dining Plan:** Yes
Menu Items:
Breakfast: eggs, bacon, croissant doughnut, ham, breakfast sandwiches, vegetable quiche, fries, soda pop, coffee, milk
Kids: crepes, French toast, eggs, cereal
Lunch: soups, sandwiches, salad, desserts, soda pop, coffee, tea, beer, wine
Kids Lunch: sandwiches, shrimp, pasta, chicken, grilled cheese
Dinner (3-course, prix fixe meal): escargot, French onion soup, lobster bisque, salad, filet mignon, lamb chops, ricotta tortellini, chicken, roasted pork, seafood bouillabaisse, desserts, wines, beers
Kids Dinner: chicken, beef tenderloin, shrimp skewer, macaroni and cheese
Recommendations: Get a reservation! You won't be able to dine here without one. Eat in the west wing of the Be Our Guest Restaurant—it's dark and beautifully decorated. Thunder and lightning clash every few minutes near the red rose with the wilting petals. For dinner, we recommend the Center-Cut Filet Mignon.

‡ CASEY'S CORNER ❤
Main Street, U.S.A.
Description: Quick-grab hot dogs and drinks
Type: Quick-Service
Price: $$ / **Dining Plan:** Yes
Menu Items: hot dogs, pulled pork, brownie, soda pop, lemonade, juice, hot chocolate, coffee, iced tea
Recommendation: Corn Dog Nuggets ❤

> **· Magic Tips ·**
> Looking for a spot to eat? Eat on the grass near the hub in front of the castle. It's a comfortable place to rest.

CHESHIRE CAFE
Fantasyland
Description: *Alice in Wonderland*-themed snacks and treats
Type: Snacks
Price: $ / **Dining Plan:** No
Menu Items: cereal, muffin, fruit, soda pop, lemonade, juice, hot chocolate, coffee, iced tea
Recommendation: Cheshire Cat Tail

CINDERELLA'S ROYAL TABLE
Fantasyland
Description: A fanciful castle feast with Disney Princesses
Type: Character Dining
Price: $$$-$$$$ / **Dining Plan:** Yes
Menu Items:
Breakfast: eggs, bacon, ham, beef, French toast, shrimp and grits, quiche, soda pop, coffee, milk, juice
Kids Breakfast: eggs, bacon, waffle
Lunch & Dinner: pork, chicken, vegetable couscous, fish, beef and shrimp, salad, desserts, soda pop, coffee, milk, juice, various desserts
Kids Lunch & Dinner: salad, turkey pot pie, chicken nuggets, chicken leg, beef tenderloin
Recommendation: Chef's Tasting Platter

‡ COLUMBIA HARBOUR HOUSE ❤
Liberty Square
Description: The best place for American-style seafood in the Magic Kingdom

Type: Quick-Service
Price: $$ / **Dining Plan:** Yes
Menu Items: lobster roll, sandwiches, chicken nuggets, fried shrimp, chicken pot pie, salad, battered fish, grilled salmon, clam chowder, fries, chili, various desserts, soda pop, iced tea, juices, coffee
Kids Menu: sandwiches, salad, chicken nuggets, fish
Recommendations: Lobster Roll ❤ and Slushy Lemonade

COOL SHIP
Tomorrowland
Description: Snack
Type: Snacks
Price: $ / **Dining Plan:** No
Menu Items: Mickey pretzel, soda pop, lemonade, juice, hot chocolate, coffee, iced tea

‡ COSMIC RAY'S STARLIGHT CAFE
Tomorrowland
Description: Futuristic hamburger fast-food joint
Type: Quick-Service
Price: $$ / **Dining Plan:** Yes
Menu Items:
Lunch & Dinner: burgers, chicken, hot dog, sandwiches, fries, cheese dip, various desserts, soda pop, iced tea, juices, coffee
Kids Lunch & Dinner: sandwiches, salad, macaroni and cheese, chicken nuggets
Recommendation: Bland food, try another spot

THE CRYSTAL PALACE
Main Street, U.S.A.
Description: Beautiful, Victorian-style character buffet with Winnie the Pooh and friends
Type: Character Buffet
Price: $$$ / **Dining Plan:** Yes
Menu Items:
Breakfast: fruit, cereals, pastries, custom scrambled eggs and omelets, potatoes, other changing breakfast choices
Lunch & Dinner: salad, carved meats, shrimp, chicken, beef, fish, vegetables, pastas, various desserts, wine, beer, hard cider
Drinks: soda pop, lemonade, juice, hot chocolate, coffee, tea, wine, beer, hard cider

THE DIAMOND HORSESHOE
Liberty Square

Description: Old West dining and music hall with American eats
Type: Quick-Service
Price: $$ / **Dining Plan:** Yes
Menu Items:
Lunch & Dinner: salad, carved meats, corn, beans, sausage, pulled pork, macaroni and cheese, braised beef, brownie
Drinks: soda pop, lemonade, juice, hot chocolate, coffee, tea
Recommendation: Barbecue Pulled Pork

‡ THE FRIAR'S NOOK
Fantasyland
Description: Mac and cheese and more American bites to eat
Type: Quick-Service
Price: $ / **Dining Plan:** Yes
Menu Items: macaroni and cheese, hot dogs, various desserts, soda pop, lemonade, juice, hot chocolate, coffee, iced tea, milk
Recommendation: Creamy Bacon Macaroni & Cheese Tots

GASTON'S TAVERN
Fantasyland
Description: *Beauty and the Beast*-inspired tavern where you can meet Gaston and try snacks
Type: Quick-Service
Price: $ / **Dining Plan:** No
Menu Items: cinnamon rolls, pretzels, chocolate croissant, specialty drinks, soda pop, lemonade, juice, hot chocolate, coffee, iced tea, milk
Recommendations: Mac and Cheese-stuffed Pretzel and Warm Cinnamon Roll
Skip: LeFou's Brew, unless you really like very sweet apple juice. If you just want to try it, there's enough to share.

GOLDEN OAK OUTPOST
Frontierland
Description: Old West quick-service with American eats
Type: Quick-Service
Price: $ / **Dining Plan:** Yes
Menu Items: chicken nuggets, waffle fries, chocolate chip cookies, soda pop, lemonade, juice, hot chocolate, coffee, iced tea, milk

JUNGLE NAVIGATION CO. LTD. SKIPPER CANTEEN
Adventureland
Description: Food inspired by Asia, South America, and Africa in a jungle outpost setting

Type: Table Service
Price: $$$ / **Dining Plan:** Yes
Menu Items: pot stickers, salad, falafel, soup, beef, fried fish, steak, shrimp, noodle bowls, pasta, fried chicken, vegetable stew, various desserts, specialty drinks, soda pop, lemonade, juice, hot chocolate, coffee, iced tea, milk
Kids Menu: fish, chicken noodle soup, steak, salad, macaroni and cheese, crispy chicken
Recommendation: Gyoza Pot Stickers (appetizer), Char Siu Pork (entree), Kungaloosh! (dessert)

LIBERTY SQUARE MARKET
Liberty Square
Description: American Snacks
Type: Snacks
Price: $ / **Dining Plan:** No
Menu Items: hot dogs, turkey leg, fruit, soda pop, lemonade, juice, hot chocolate, coffee, iced tea, milk

LIBERTY TREE TAVERN ❤
Liberty Square
Description: Colonial style dining area with New England eats
Type: Table Service
Price: $$$ / **Dining Plan:** Yes
Menu Items: clam chowder, soups, corn fritters, salad, pot roast, cheeseburger, grilled chicken, turkey, pork sandwich, pastas, various desserts, specialty drinks, soda pop, lemonade, juice, hot chocolate, coffee, iced tea, milk, beer, cider, wines
Kids Menu: pot roast, turkey, pasta, macaroni and cheese
Recommendation: Patriot's Platter (a delicious all-you-can-eat Thanksgiving turkey dinner)

‡ THE LUNCHING PAD
Tomorrowland
Description: Futuristic fast-food snacks
Type: Quick-Service
Price: $$ / **Dining Plan:** Yes
Menu Items: hot dog, pretzels, chips, soda pop, lemonade, juice, hot chocolate, coffee, iced tea, milk
Recommendation: Ham and Cheese-stuffed Pretzel

MAIN STREET BAKERY (STARBUCKS)
Main Street, U.S.A.
Description: Starbucks coffee and pastries

Type: Quick-Service
Price: $ / **Dining Plan:** Yes
Menu Items: Starbucks-brand coffees and specialty drinks, smoothies, Teavana Iced teas, hot chocolate

‡ PECOS BILL TALL TALE INN AND CAFE
Frontierland
Description: Old West saloon with Southwest flavors
Type: Quick-Service
Price: $$ / **Dining Plan:** Yes
Menu Items: nachos, burgers, fajitas, burrito, salad, desserts, soda pop, lemonade, juice, hot chocolate, coffee, iced tea, milk
Kids Menu: macaroni and cheese, mini corn dogs, sandwich
Recommendation: Beef Nachos

‡ PINOCCHIO VILLAGE HAUS
Fantasyland
Description: Dining inspired by Disney's Pinocchio
Type: Quick-Service
Price: $ / **Dining Plan:** Yes
Menu Items: flatbreads, chicken parmesan, pasta, chicken nuggets, salad, fries, tomato soup, breadsticks, various desserts, soda pop, lemonade, juice, hot chocolate, coffee, iced tea, milk
Kids Menu: macaroni and cheese, pizza, chicken nuggets, sandwich
Recommendation: Village Haus is notoriously bland. The Sausage and Pepper Flatbread is okay.

PLAZA ICE CREAM PARLOR
Main Street, U.S.A.
Description: Classic American ice cream shop
Type: Quick-Service
Price: $ / **Dining Plan:** No
Menu Items: various ice cream flavors, sundaes, kids' ice cream cone, floats, toppings, bottled water

---

· Magic Tips ·
Walt Disney World has a strict no-sad-faces policy—we're not kidding! If your child spills an ice cream cone, tell a Cast Member at the point of purchase and they will happily replace it for free.

THE PLAZA RESTAURANT
Main Street, U.S.A.
Description: Classic American dining
Type: Table Service
Price: $$ / **Dining Plan:** Yes
Menu Items:
Breakfast: steak and eggs, Mickey waffles, omelets, bacon, eggs, sausage, fruit, oatmeal, cocktails, juice, coffee, tea, soda
Lunch & Dinner: steak, salad, fries, fried green tomatoes, sandwiches, pork chop, meatloaf, salad, vegetarian bangers and mash, desserts, sundaes, soda, beer, wine
Kids Lunch & Dinner Menu: sandwiches, burgers, chicken strips
Recommendations: All-American Breakfast Platter (breakfast), Baked Honey-Barbecued Brisket Macaroni & Cheese

PRINCE ERIC'S VILLAGE MARKET
Fantasyland
Description: Fruit cart
Type: Snack
Price: $ / **Dining Plan:** No
Menu Items: fruit, hummus, chips, lemonade, bottled water

‡ SLEEPY HOLLOW ❤
Liberty Square
Description: Waffle sandwich house
Type: Snacks
Price: $ / **Dining Plan:** No
Menu Items: waffle sandwiches, funnel cake, cookies, soda pop, lemonade, juice, hot chocolate, coffee, iced tea, milk
Recommendation: Fruit Waffle Sandwich ❤

SPRING ROLL CART ❤
Adventureland (near the entrance)
Description: Snack
Type: Snacks
Price: $ / **Dining Plan:** No
Menu Items: spring rolls, soda, water
Recommendation: The Spring Roll Cart in Adventureland offers delicious new twists on the classic egg roll. Rotating egg roll flavors include bacon mac 'n' cheese, cheeseburger, Philly cheesesteak, and buffalo chicken!

STORYBOOK TREATS
Fantasyland

Description: Ice cream and floats
Type: Snacks
Price: $ / **Dining Plan:** No
Menu Items: sundaes, floats, soft-serve ice cream, soda pop, hot chocolate, coffee, iced tea, milk
Recommendation: Peter Pan Float (key lime ice cream and Sprite)

‡ SUNSHINE TREE TERRACE
Adventureland
Description: Ice cream and slushies
Type: Snacks
Price: $ / **Dining Plan:** No
Menu Items: slushies, soft-serve ice cream in a cup, soda pop, hot chocolate, coffee, iced tea, milk

‡ TOMORROWLAND TERRACE RESTAURANT
Tomorrowland
Description: Futuristic fast food dining
Type: Quick-Service
Price: $$ / **Dining Plan:** Yes
Menu Items: burgers, chicken strips, sandwiches, lettuce wraps, salads, soda pop, coffee, iced tea, milk
Kids Menu: macaroni and cheese, chicken strips
Recommendation: Kids may like it, but the food is nothing special.

TONY'S TOWN SQUARE RESTAURANT
Main Street, U.S.A.
Description: *Lady and the Tramp*-inspired Italian Restaurant
Type: Table Service
Price: $$ / **Dining Plan:** Yes
Menu Items: steak, spaghetti, shrimp scampi, pizza, pasta, salads, soda pop, hot chocolate, coffee, iced tea, milk
Kids Menu: macaroni and cheese, chicken strips, sandwich
Recommendation: Chicken Fettuccini Alfredo or Roman-style Steak

TORTUGA TAVERN
Adventureland
Description: Pirate-themed American eats
Type: Quick-Service
Price: $$ / **Dining Plan:** Yes
Menu Items: sandwiches, salads, soda pop, hot chocolate, coffee, iced tea, milk
Kids Menu: macaroni and cheese
Recommendation: The Brisket

WESTWARD HO
Frontierland
Description: Snack
Type: Snacks
Price: $$ / **Dining Plan:** No
Menu Items: corn dog, chips, chocolate chip cookie, soda pop, hot chocolate, coffee, iced tea, milk
Kids Menu: macaroni and cheese
Recommendation: Guests love the delicious corn dogs or corn dog nuggets served here.

EPCOT DINING

AKERSHUS ROYAL BANQUET HALL
World Showcase – Norway
Description: Dine while you meet your favorite Disney princesses in this Norwegian castle. The food has a Norwegian flare.
Type: Character Dining
Price: $$$$ / **Dining Plan:** Yes
Menu Items:
Breakfast: eggs, sausage, bacon, potato casserole, salami, turkey, corn, fish, cheeses, punch
Lunch & Dinner: salmon, chicken, pork, pasta, meatballs, shrimp, assorted desserts, punch, specialty cocktails, wine
Kids Lunch & Dinner: macaroni and cheese, meatballs, pizza, chicken, salmon, beef
Recommendation: Traditional Kjottkake (meatballs, gravy, and mashed potatoes)

> **· Magic Tips ·**
> Akershus Royal Banquet Hall is a great way to meet several Disney Princesses like Belle, Ariel, and Rapunzel, all in one sitting! Characters subject to change.

BIERGARTEN RESTAURANT ❤
World Showcase – Germany
Description: German feasts in a nighttime village

Type: Character Dining
Price: $$$$ / **Dining Plan:** Yes
Menu Items: schnitzel, salad, sausage, greens, soup, chicken, potato, macaroni and cheese, cheese platter, meatballs, spätzle, ham, meat loaf, assorted desserts, beer, wine, schnapps
Recommendation: Pork Schnitzel ❤

BLOCK AND HANS

World Showcase – American Adventure
Description: American beer stand
Type: Quick-Service
Price: $$ / **Dining Plan:** Yes
Menu Items: beer, pretzels, bottled water
Recommendation: Order a beer with a Mickey-shaped Pretzel and cheese sauce.

CHEFS DE FRANCE ❤

World Showcase – France
Description: French cuisine restaurant
Type: Fine Dining
Dress Code: Park attire
Price: $$$ / **Dining Plan:** Yes
Menu Items: French onion soup, escargot, salad, flatbread, lasagna, baked macaroni
Recommendations: Everything here is great, and we recommend the Gratin de Macaroni (Baked Macaroni and Cheese), Boeuf Bourguignon (Beef Short Ribs), or Filet de Boeuf Grille (Grilled Tenderloin) ❤

CHOZA DE MARGARITA

World Showcase – Mexico
Description: Outdoor margarita hut
Type: Snack
Price: $-$$ / **Dining Plan:** No
Menu Items: margaritas, beer, Mexican fruit punch, empanadas, pork tacos
Recommendation: Any flavor of Signature Margarita

COOL WASH

World Discovery
Description: Slushy Station
Type: Snack
Price: $ / **Dining Plan:** No
Menu Items: slushies, chips, alcoholic floats, soda pop, water

CORAL REEF RESTAURANT
World Nature
Description: Restaurant with a massive aquarium wall filled with exotic fish and other sea life
Type: Table Service
Price: $$$ / **Dining Plan:** Yes
Menu Items: salad, octopus, calamari, fondue, soups, pork, chicken, fish, shellfish, steak, assorted desserts, beer, wine, specialty cocktails
Kids Menu: macaroni and cheese, steak, fish and chips, pork, chicken tenders
Recommendation: This spot is fantastic for unique dining. We recommend the Crispy Rhode Island Calamari.

FIFE AND DRUM TAVERN
World Showcase – American Adventure
Description: American favorite snacks
Type: Snack
Price: $ / **Dining Plan:** Yes
Menu Items: turkey leg, popcorn, soft-serve ice cream, soda pop, slushies, beer, wine, hard root beer
Recommendations: Disney has some delicious popcorn! The American Dream slushy is a good one, too.

> **· Magic Tips ·**
> Disney's snack stands sell souvenir popcorn buckets in the shape of popular characters. While these buckets can cost more than $20 each, they usually come with inexpensive refills and a lid to protect kids from spilling.

FUNNEL CAKE ❤
World Showcase – American Adventure
Description: American desserts
Type: Snack
Price: $ / **Dining Plan:** No
Menu Items: funnel cake, bottled water
Recommendation: Funnel cake with sugar ❤

GARDEN GRILL ❤
World Nature

Description: Rotating restaurant serving freshly picked food while overlooking Living with the Land
Type: Character Dining
Price: $$$ / **Dining Plan:** Yes
Menu Items:
Breakfast Buffet: sticky buns, fruit, potatoes, scrambled eggs, bacon, ham, Mickey waffles, juices, coffee, tea
Lunch & Dinner Buffet: salad, turkey, beef, macaroni and cheese, fries, vegetables, stuffing, sausage, shortcake, punch, beer, wine
Recommendation: All of the buffets are delicious ❤

GELATERIA TOSCANA
World Showcase – Italy
Description: Italian gelato
Type: Snack
Price: $ / **Dining Plan:** No
Menu Items: gelato, sorbet, bellini, beer, wine, espresso, cappuccino
Recommendation: Any of the Gelati Creations

JOY OF TEA
World Showcase – Japan
Description: Tea hut
Type: Snack
Price: $ / **Dining Plan:** No
Menu Items: Pork buns, egg rolls, curry chicken pockets, tea, slushies, ice cream, wine, beer, mixed drinks
Recommendations: Pork and Vegetable Egg Rolls

KABUKI CAFE
World Showcase – Japan
Description: Japanese sushi and soda bar
Type: Snack
Price: $ / **Dining Plan:** No
Menu Items: sushi, edamame, shaved ice, bottled soda, hot chocolate, bottled water
Recommendation: Try a shaved ice. Adults might like the Sake Mist, an alcoholic shaved ice.

KATSURA GRILL
World Showcase – Japan
Description: Japanese restaurant in a tranquil garden
Type: Quick-Service
Price: $ / **Dining Plan:** Yes

Menu Items: sushi, noodles, miso soup, edamame, rice, teriyaki, chicken, shrimp, bottled soda, hot chocolate, bottled water, beer, wine, juice, tea, various desserts
Kids Menu: chicken, beef, or shrimp teriyaki
Recommendations: Chicken and Beef Teriyaki

KRINGLA BAKERI OG KAFE

World Showcase – Norway
Description: Norwegian cafeteria-style cuisine
Type: Quick-Service
Price: $$ / **Dining Plan:** Yes
Menu Items: sandwiches, meatballs, biscuit, pastries, salad, fish, soda pop, hot chocolate, bottled water, beer, wine, juice, tea, various desserts
Recommendation: School Bread

L'ARTISAN DES GLACES

World Showcase – France
Description: Ice cream parlor
Type: Ice Cream Shop
Price: $ / **Dining Plan:** No
Menu Items: ice cream, macaron, bottled water

LA CANTINA DE SAN ANGEL

World Showcase – Mexico
Description: Mexican cafeteria-style cuisine
Type: Quick-Service
Price: $$ / **Dining Plan:** Yes
Menu Items: tacos, nachos, salad, churro, juices, coffee, various desserts, beer, margarita
Kids Menu: empanadas, chicken tenders
Recommendations: Tacos de Barbacoa, Churros with Caramel Sauce

LA CAVA DEL TEQUILA

World Showcase – Mexico
Description: Underground tequila bar
Type: Lounge
Price: $$ / **Dining Plan:** No
Menu Items: tequila
Recommendation: Hibiscus tequila

LA CREPERIE DE PARIS

World Showcase – France

Description: French crepes
Type: Snack
Price: $-$$ / **Dining Plan:** No
Menu Items: crepes, drinks
Recommendation: Savory Saumon (smoked salmon) and Sweet Pomme (caramelized apples)

LA HACIENDA DE SAN ANGEL
World Showcase – Mexico
Description: Mexican restaurant
Type: Table Service
Price: $$ / **Dining Plan:** Yes
Menu Items: gorditas, empanada, steak, short ribs, fried shrimp, chicken, pork confit, tacos, fish, margaritas, tequila, beer, wine, various desserts
Kids Menu: salad, fruit cup, grilled chicken, tacos, quesadilla, fish, churros, ice cream
Recommendation: Taquiza Taco Sampler

THE LAND CART
World Nature
Description: Fruit cart
Type: Snack
Price: $ / **Dining Plan:** No
Menu Items: fruit, cheese plate, vegetable plate, pretzels, hummus, soda pop, juice, beer

LE CELLIER STEAKHOUSE ❤
World Showcase – Canada
Description: French Canadian restaurant
Type: Fine Dining
Dress Code: Business Causal, though the dress code is not always enforced; don't wear tank tops, hats, cut-off clothes, or sports clothing

Price: $$$$ / **Dining Plan:** Yes
Menu Items: cheeses, steak, pork rib, chicken breast, tofu, halibut, fries, mashed potatoes, macaroni and cheese, scallops, poutine, various desserts, wine, teas
Kids Menu: cheddar soup, salad, grilled chicken, salmon, pasta, sirloin with french fries, chocolate "moose" ice cream
Recommendations: Le Cellier is known for its poutine and steaks. We highly recommend the Signature Poutine ♥ (French fries with cheese, truffles, and a red wine sauce) and Le Cellier Filet Mignon

LES HALLES BOULANGERIE-PATISSERIE ♥
World Showcase – France
Description: Fast French Favorites
Type: Quick-Service
Price: $$ / **Dining Plan:** Yes
Menu Items: French sandwiches, salad, croissant, quiche, lobster bisque, pastries, various desserts, soda pop, champagne, mimosa, beer, wine, coffees, milk, smoothies, teas
Recommendations: Croque Monsieur, Crème Brûlée

LES VINS DES CHEFS DE FRANCE
World Showcase – France
Description: Fast French Favorites
Type: Snack
Price: $-$$ / **Dining Plan:** No
Menu Items: French cocktails, wines, and alcoholic slushies
Recommendations: Le Geant Slush

LOTUS BLOSSOM CAFE
World Showcase – China
Description: American takes on Chinese Favorites
Type: Quick-Service
Price: $$ / **Dining Plan:** Yes
Menu Items: egg rolls, pot stickers, orange chicken, shrimp fried rice, salad, ice cream, soda pop, beer, coffees, milk, hot chocolate
Kids Menu: pot stickers, spring rolls, sweet-and-sour chicken
Recommendation: Pork and Vegetable Egg Rolls
Skip: The Orange Chicken, especially if you like the one at Panda Express. You'll be disappointed.

OASIS SWEETS & SIPS
World Showcase – Morocco
Description: Moroccan pastries and drinks
Type: Quick-Service

Price: $ / **Dining Plan:** No
Menu Items: pastries, beers, mixed drinks, tea, soda
Recommendations: One of the pastry assortments

NINE DRAGONS RESTAURANT ❤

World Showcase – China
Description: Chinese Dining
Type: Table Service
Price: $$$ / **Dining Plan:** Yes
Menu Items: spring rolls, pot stickers, dumplings, Asian chicken, fried rice, Asian beef, lo mein, tofu stir fry, salad, various desserts, soda pop, specialty cocktails, smoothie, beer, wine, teas
Recommendation: Pork Belly Bao Buns (appetizer), Honey Crispy Chicken (entree), Banana Cheesecake Eggrolls (dessert)

· **Magic Tips** ·
Nine Dragons offers partial views of the Epcot nighttime show. Request a table near the windows for 30-45 minutes before showtime. The lights will dim and a soundtrack for the show will play as you watch the fireworks during dinner.

POPCORN IN CANADA

World Showcase – Canada
Description: Popcorn cart
Type: Snack
Price: $ / **Dining Plan:** No
Menu Items: popcorn, beer, whisky, bottled water
Recommendation: Walt Disney World has great popcorn!

PROMENADE REFRESHMENTS

World Showcase – Canada
Description: Snack House / **Type:** Snack
Price: $ / **Dining Plan:** Yes
Menu Items: hot dogs, chips, ice cream, beer, soda pop,
Recommendation: Chili Hot Dog

‡ REGAL EAGLE

World Showcase – American Adventure
Description: Muppet-themed American Barbecue
Type: Quick Service
Price: $$ / **Dining Plan:** Yes

Menu Items: ribs, smoked chicken, burgers, brisket, greens, onion rings, juice, soda, wine, cocktails, beer
Recommendation: Though we adore the Muppet theming, the food here is a bit underwhelming. If you're craving barbecue, head to The Polite Pig in Disney Springs. For quick drinks, head to the walk-up bar next to the Regal Eagle.

REFRESHMENT OUTPOST
World Showcase – American Adventure
Description: Quick snacks
Type: Snack
Price: $ / **Dining Plan:** Yes
Menu Items: hot dogs, chips, ice cream, beer, soda pop, slushy, hot chocolate, bottled water

REFRESHMENT PORT
World Showcase – Canada
Description: Snack House
Type: Snack Shack
Price: $ / **Dining Plan:** Yes
Menu Items: croissant doughnut, chicken nuggets, ice cream, french fries, beer, soda pop, slushy, hot chocolate, bottled water
Recommendation: Croissant Doughnut ❤

RESTAURANT MARRAKESH
World Showcase – Morocco
Description: Moroccan dining experience with belly dancers
Type: Table Service
Price: $$$ / **Dining Plan:** Yes
Menu Items: chicken skewers, beef rolls, salad, roast lamb, lemon chicken, couscous, kebab, beer, mixed drinks, soda pop, various desserts
Kids Menu: chicken tenders, hamburger, pasta
Recommendation: Try a skewer and baklava for dessert.

ROSE AND CROWN DINING ROOM ❤
World Showcase – United Kingdom
Description: Authentic British restaurant with excellent food and beer
Type: Table Service
Price: $$$ / **Dining Plan:** Yes
Menu Items: soup, salad, fish and chips, shepherd's pie, burger, corn beef and cabbage, bangers and mash, beer, mixed drinks, soda pop, various desserts

Kids Menu: fish and chips, bangers and mash, steak and chips, turkey meatballs, grilled chicken, baked fish
Recommendations: Fish and Chips, Bangers and Mash

· **Magic Tips** ·
The Rose and Crown has an excellent view of the Epcot fireworks. Book a dining reservation just before showtime to have an awesome view while you dine!

ROSE AND CROWN PUB
World Showcase – United Kingdom
Description: Authentic British pub with a wide variety of beers
Type: Lounge
Price: $$ / **Dining Plan:** No
Menu Items: scotch egg, fish and chips, beer, mixed drinks, soda pop, wine, whiskey
Recommendation: Fish and Chips

SAN ANGEL INN RESTAURANTE
World Showcase – Mexico
Description: Indoor Mexican dining
Type: Table Service
Price: $$$ / **Dining Plan:** Yes
Menu Items: soup, queso, quesadilla, steak, tacos, chicken, various desserts, margarita, soda pop
Kids Menu: tacos, grilled tilapia, cheese quesadilla
Recommendation: Skip this one. The atmosphere is fun but the food is bland and inauthentic. You can walk inside here to check out the scenery and shops without dining.

‡ SOMMERFEST
World Showcase – Germany
Description: Fast German Favorites
Type: Quick-Service
Price: $$ / **Dining Plan:** Yes
Menu Items: bratwurst, frankfurter, potato salad, pretzel, baked macaroni, various German desserts, beer, wine, soda pop, bottled water

SPACE 220 ❤
World Discovery
Description: An impressive restaurant aboard a space station!

Type: Table Service
Price: $$$$ / **Dining Plan:** TBA
Menu Items: calamari, salad, steak, salmon, duck, fish, bolognese, desserts, soda, cocktails, wine, beer
Recommendation: An immersive dining experience where guests are transported to a space station restaurant with sweeping views of Earth on giant screens! We recommend sitting near the center of the restaurant for the best view of the "windows" into space. Space 220 serves a prix fixe menu, and we recommend the Starry Calamari, Slow Rotation Short Rib, and Carrot Cake.

· **Magic Tips** ·
We highly recommend booking your visit to Space 220 in advance. If you didn't grab a table, there's a lounge inside the space with bites and cocktails.

SPICE ROAD TABLE
World Showcase – Morocco
Description: Mediterranean Restaurant
Type: Table Service
Price: $$$ / **Dining Plan:** Yes
Menu Items: calamari, shrimp, skewers, fondue, lamb, chicken, vegetable platter, fish, various desserts, cappuccino, espresso, soda pop, sparkling water, beer, specialty drinks
Recommendation: Lamb Slider

SUNSHINE SEASONS
World Nature
Description: An indoor venue with serval snack options
Type: Quick-Service
Price: $$ / **Dining Plan:** Yes
Menu Items: chicken, fish, soups, salad, fish tacos, flatbread, stir-fry, various desserts, cappuccino, espresso, soda pop, bottled beer
Kids Menu: Mongolian beef, salmon, chicken, macaroni and cheese, cheese panini, sandwich
Recommendation: Fish tacos—fresh and delicious

TANGIERINE CAFÉ
World Showcase – Morocco
Description: Mediterranean Restaurant
Type: Quick-Service
Price: $$$ / **Dining Plan:** Yes

Menu Items: salad, falafel, shawarma, hummus, pastries, soda pop
Kids Menu: hamburger, chicken tenders
Recommendation: Mediterranean Falafel Wrap

TAKUMI-TEI
World Showcase – Japan
Description: If you're looking for an unforgettable Disney dining experience, we highly recommend Takumi-Tei. Styled after traditional Japanese tea-service meals, this restaurant delivers exquisite food. Each room of the restaurant is based around an element like water, wood, stone, or earth. The rooms also have accompanying features like an actual waterfall in the water room!
Type: Signature Dining / Table Service
Price: $$$$-$$$$$ / **Dining Plan:** No
Menu Items: wagyu beef, roasted duck, sushi, desserts, teas, cocktails, wines, Japanese beer, soda pop,
Kids Menu: shrimp, steak, chicken
Recommendations: Takumi-Tei is best for adults looking for an adventurous dining option. We recommend the Chef's Table in the Water Room. It's a 3-hour dining event with a wide range of Japanese bites from seafood to wagyu beef. The bites become more flavorful throughout the meal and are best enjoyed with a beverage pairing. Of course, an exquisite meal like this comes at a cost: $180 per person with beverage pairing at an additional $100 per person. For a less expensive Japanese dining option, try Teppan Edo or Tokyo Dining.

TOKYO DINING
World Showcase – Japan
Description: Traditional Japanese
Type: Table Service
Price: $$$ / **Dining Plan:** Yes
Menu Items: sushi, tempura, teriyaki chicken, noodles, desserts, tea, Japanese beer, wine, cocktails, soda pop
Kids Menu: shrimp, steak, chicken
Recommendations: The Chef's Creation Bento Box comes with an assortment of sushi, tempura, and steak

TEPPAN EDO ❤
World Showcase – Japan
Description: Authentic Japanese cuisine with amazing chefs that perform in front of you
Type: Table Service
Price: $$$ / **Dining Plan:** Yes

Menu Items: chicken, sushi, steak, seafood, sake, beer, various desserts, soda pop, tea, milk
Kids Menu: shrimp, steak, chicken
Recommendations: Teppan Edo is a must if you've never done Teppan-style Japanese dining before. These authentic Japanese chefs are incredible and put on a show like no other. Try the Filet Mignon and Lobster Tail. The green tea ice cream is also incredible.
Seating: Guests are typically seat in parties of eight. If your group is smaller than that, you may be seated near others.

TRAVELER'S CAFE (STARBUCKS)
Between World Showcase and World Celebration
Description: Starbucks coffee and pastries
Type: Quick-Service
Price: $ / **Dining Plan:** Yes
Menu Items: Starbucks-brand coffees and specialty drinks, smoothies, Teavana Iced teas, hot chocolate

TUTTO GUSTO WINE CELLAR
World Showcase – Italy
Description: Italian wine cellar that showcases over 200 bottles
Type: Lounge
Price: $$ / **Dining Plan:** No
Menu Items: wine, cheeses, bread, small plates, pasta, sliders, paninis, various desserts
Recommendation: Meatball sliders

TUTTO ITALIA RISTORANTE
World Showcase – Italy
Description: Authentic Italian Restaurant
Type: Table Service
Price: $$$ / **Dining Plan:** Yes
Menu Items: salad, calamari, chicken, pasta, seafood, various desserts, beer, cocktails, soda pop
Kids Menu: spaghetti, pizza, mozzarella sticks, chicken tenders
Recommendation: Meatball sliders

UK BEER CART
World Showcase – United Kingdom
Description: Beer Cart
Type: Snack
Price: $ / **Dining Plan:** Yes
Menu Items: beer, pear cider, bottled water

VIA NAPOLI RISTORANTE E PIZZERIA ❤

World Showcase – Italy
Description: Authentic Italian Pizzeria
Type: Table Service
Price: $$$ / **Dining Plan:** Yes
Menu Items: pizza, calamari, small plates, pasta, various desserts, beer, cocktails, soda pop
Kids Menu: spaghetti, pizza, salad
Recommendation: Their pizzas are amazing and authentic. We love creating our own Margherita pizza with meatballs ❤

> **· Magic Tips ·**
> Seasonally, Disney will open Pizza al Taglio, a quick-service pizza window next to Via Napoli. Get a delicious slice of pizza to go when this window is available!

‡ YORKSHIRE COUNTY FISH SHOP

World Showcase – United Kingdom
Description: British quick-service
Type: Quick-Service
Price: $ / **Dining Plan:** Yes
Menu Items: fish and chips, sponge cake, soda pop, beer
Recommendation: Fish and Chips

HOLLYWOOD STUDIOS DINING

50'S PRIME TIME CAFÉ ❤

Echo Lake
Description: Swanky mid-century American dining
Type: Table Service
Price: $$$ / **Dining Plan:** Yes
Menu Items: pot pie, pork chops, lasagna, pot roast, salad, fried chicken, fish, meatloaf, fries, onion rings, shakes, ice cream, various desserts, soda pop, hot chocolate, coffee, iced tea, milk, wine, beer, specialty cocktails
Kids Menu: salad, soup, salmon, spaghetti, meatloaf, chicken

Recommendations: Onion Rings, Aunt Liz's Golden Fried Chicken
❤, Peanut Butter and Jelly Milk Shake

‡ ABC COMMISSARY
Commissary Lane
Description: Fast dining with indoor seating
Type: Quick-Service
Price: $$ / **Dining Plan:** Yes
Menu Items:
Breakfast: avocado toast, fried chicken and doughnut, scrambled eggs, chilaquiles, eggs
Lunch & Dinner: BBQ ribs, burgers, sandwiches, salad, chicken strips, desserts, soda pop, sangria
Kids Menu: cheeseburger, sandwich

ANAHEIM PRODUCE
Sunset Boulevard
Description: Snacks
Type: Snack
Price: $ / **Dining Plan:** No
Menu Items: fruit, chips, snack bars, pretzels, granola, lemonade, soda pop, beer, margarita, hard cider, bottled water

‡ BACKLOT EXPRESS
Echo Lake
Description: Star Wars-themed fast food
Type: Quick-Service
Price: $$ / **Dining Plan:** Yes
Menu Items: burgers, sandwiches, chicken and biscuits, chicken tenders, salad, french fries, buttermilk biscuits, desserts soda, margaritas, mixed drinks
Kids Menu: chicken tenders, macaroni and cheese
Recommendation: The food here is impressively decorative, though much of the flavor is fairly bland.

BASELINE TAPHOUSE ❤
Grand Avenue
Description: American Gastropub / Lounge
Type: Quick-Service
Price: $-$$ / **Dining Plan:** No
Menu Items: pretzel, cheese plates, other small bites, beers and wines on tap, cocktails and ciders on tap, non-alcoholic specialty drinks

Recommendations: If you're looking for a stylish, new experience at the Walt Disney World Resort, look no further than the BaseLine Tap House. With excellent artisan cheeses and craft beers, it's the perfect hangout for adults. Try the California Cheese and Charcuterie Plate, and the Blue Sky Black Cherry Soda on Tap is delicious!

‡ CATALINA EDDIE'S
Sunset Boulevard
Description: Pizza shack
Type: Quick-Service
Price: $$ / **Dining Plan:** Yes
Menu Items: pizza, Caesar salad, various desserts, soda pop, hot chocolate, coffee, iced tea, milk, beer, sangria
Kids Menu: cheese pizza, sandwiches
Recommendation: Any of the pizzas

‡ DOCKING BAY 7 FOOD AND CARGO ❤
Star Wars: Galaxy's Edge
Description: An intergalactic canteen in a rustic, *Star Wars*-inspired building. The food here is a mix of flavors that will tickle the tastebuds of adventurous eaters.
Type: Quick-Service
Price: $$ / **Dining Plan:** Yes
Menu: breakfast items, ribs, salads, air-fried chicken, noodles, juice soda, coffee, tea, desserts
Kids Menu: air-fried chicken
Recommendation: Smoked Kaadu Ribs ❤, Oi-oi Puff (dessert) ❤, Moof Juice (sweet drink)

DOCKSIDE DINER
Echo Lake
Description: Fast food from a boat
Type: Quick-Service
Price: $$ / **Dining Plan:** Yes
Menu Items: wraps, chili-cheese hot dog, macaroni and cheese, various desserts, soda pop, hot chocolate, coffee, iced tea, beer, wine
Kids Menu: turkey sandwich
Recommendations: Seasonal Milkshake

EPIC EATS
Echo Lake

Description: *Indiana Jones*-themed dessert outpost
Type: Quick-Service
Price: $ / **Dining Plan:** No
Menu Items: funnel cakes, soda floats, beer
Recommendation: Funnel Cake with Strawberry Topping and Soft-serve Vanilla Ice Cream (drizzled with chocolate sauce)

‡ FAIRFAX FARE
Sunset Boulevard
Description: American favorites shack
Type: Quick-Service
Price: $$ / **Dining Plan:** Yes
Menu Items: ribs, sandwiches, salads, chicken, chili-cheese dog, baked potatoes, various desserts, soda pop, hot chocolate, coffee, iced tea, milk, beer
Kids: sandwiches
Recommendation: ½ Slab of Spareribs

THE HOLLYWOOD BROWN DERBY
Hollywood Boulevard
Description: Replica of the Brown Derby restaurant in the Golden Age of Hollywood
Type: Signature Dining / Table Service
Dress Code: Park attire
Price: $$$$ / **Dining Plan:** Yes
Menu Items: steak, lamb, pork chops, pho, salmon, chicken, salad, fish, burger, lobster, various desserts, soda pop, hot chocolate, coffee, iced tea, milk, beer, wine
Kids Menu: sandwiches, chicken noodle soup, chicken, fish, pasta
Recommendations: Premium American Kobe Beef and Double Vanilla Bean Crème Brulee
Why We Skip It: The Hollywood Brown Derby is a top choice for many fine diners at Walt Disney World, but the food isn't that remarkable for the price you're paying. We'd much rather go to the 50's Prime Time Café.

THE HOLLYWOOD BROWN DERBY LOUNGE
Hollywood Boulevard
Description: Lounge in the iconic Brown Derby
Type: Lounge Dining
Dress Code: Park attire
Price: $$ / **Dining Plan:** Yes

Menu Items: shrimp, corn bisque, cheese boards, sliders, salad, various desserts, soda pop, hot chocolate, coffee, iced tea, milk, beer, extensive wine list, specialty cocktails
Recommendations: Artisanal Cheeses and Charcuterie Board

HOLLYWOOD SCOOPS
Sunset Boulevard
Description: Ice Cream Parlor
Type: Lounge Dining
Price: $ / **Dining Plan:** No
Menu Items: ice cream, sundaes, apple crisp, root beer float
Recommendations: Brownie Sundae, Hard Root Beer Float

HOLLYWOOD & VINE
Echo Lake
Description: Character Breakfast / Lunch & Dinner Diner
Type: Character Dining / Table Service
Price: $$$ / **Dining Plan:** Yes
Menu Items:
*Breakfast Buffe*t: Mickey waffles, pancakes, "potato" tots, custom omelets, fruit, cereal, pastries, scrambled eggs, bacon, sausage
Lunch & Dinner Buffet: salad, baked chicken, pork, pasta, lobster and shrimp macaroni and cheese, vegetables, desserts, ice cream
Recommendation: If your young kids are early risers, book breakfast for Disney Junior Play n' Dine. They can meet their favorite Disney characters before heading into the park.

> **· Magic Tips ·**
> Hollywood & Vine has reservations well before normal park hours. If you finish eating before park guests arrive, you can be one of the first to enter Toy Story Land and Star Wars: Galaxy's Edge!

KAT SAKA'S KETTLE ❤
Description: Sweet and spicy kettle-cooked popcorn
Type: Snack
Price: $ / **Dining Plan:** Yes
Menu Items: mixed drinks, bar snacks
Recommendations: Outpost Popcorn Mix. We recommend eating the many flavors of popcorn together for the best taste!

> **· Magic Tips ·**
> Get a specially designed Star Wars soda bottle when you order a Coke or Sprite product at Kat Saka's Kettle.

KRNR THE ROCK STATION
Sunset Boulevard
Description: Concert-style Food Truck
Type: Quick-Service
Price: $ / **Dining Plan:** Yes
Menu Items: chili-cheese hot dog, all-beef hot dogs, nachos, chips, cookies, soda floats, soda pop, Jack & Coke (adult beverage)
Recommendations: Chili-Cheese Beef Hot Dog

MAMA MELROSE'S RISTORANTE ITALIANO
Grand Avenue
Description: Italian Restaurant
Type: Table Service
Price: $$$ / **Dining Plan:** Yes
Menu Items: steak, calamari, mussels, salad, flatbread, pasta, chicken, fish, lasagna, gelato, various desserts, soda pop, hot chocolate, coffee, iced tea, milk, beer, wine
Kids Menu: sandwiches, spaghetti, chicken, fish, penne pasta
Recommendation: Flatbreads

‡ MILK STAND
Star Wars: Galaxy's Edge
Description: Plant-based smoothies
Type: Snack
Price: $ / **Dining Plan:** No
Menu Items: Blue Milk (berry smoothie), Green Milk (melon smoothie), Alcoholic Blue Milk (rum), Alcoholic Green Milk (tequila)
Recommendations: Blue Milk

NEIGHBORHOOD BAKERY
Pixar Place
Description: *Incredibles*-themed snacking spot
Type: Snack
Price: $ / **Dining Plan:** No
Menu Items: pretzel, cookies, popcorn, ice cream, drinks
Recommendation: Num Num Cookie

OGA'S CANTINA ❤

Star Wars: Galaxy's Edge
Description: A lively *Star Wars*-themed bar
Type: Lounge
Price: $$ / **Dining Plan:** Yes
Menu Items: mixed drinks, bar snacks
Recommendations: T-16 Skyhopper (vodka, melon, and kiwi blend) and the non-alcoholic Hyperdrive (Punch It!), a blend of berry flavors and Sprite.

‡ PIZZERIZZO

Grand Avenue (may only run seasonally)
Description: *Muppets*-themed Pizza Diner
Type: Quick-Service
Price: $$ / **Dining Plan:** Yes
Menu Items: pizzas, pasta salad, cannoli, tiramisu, soda pop
Kids Menu: kid-sized pizzas, macaroni and cheese
Skip: The burgers and nuggets are bland.

‡ RONTO ROASTERS ❤

Star Wars: Galaxy's Edge
Description: *Star Wars*-themed snacks
Type: Quick-Service
Price: $$ / **Dining Plan:** Yes
Menu Items: sausage wraps, turkey jerky, mixed drinks, sodas
Recommendations: Ronto Wrap and the Coruscant Cooler (fruit juices and bourbon)

> **· Magic Tips ·**
> Outside of Ronto Roasters, cranking the spit of meat, is a lesser-known droid named 8D-J8. In the folklore of Galaxy's Edge, this bot was once a smelter droid who has since been reprogrammed for his meat-cooking post. The simulated roaster he's cranking under is a podracer engine reworked into a grill!

ROUNDUP RODEO BBQ

Toy Story Land
Description: *Toy Story*-themed dining
Type: Table Service
Price: $$$ / **Dining Plan:** Yes
Menu Items: American barbecue favorites for all ages

‡ ROSIE'S ALL-AMERICAN CAFE
Sunset Boulevard
Description: American favorites shack
Type: Quick-Service
Price: $$ / **Dining Plan:** Yes
Menu Items: burgers, chicken nuggets, sandwiches, various desserts, soda pop, hot chocolate, coffee, iced tea, beer, sangria
Kids: chicken nuggets, sandwich
Skip: The burgers and nuggets are bland.

SCI-FI DINE-IN THEATER RESTAURANT ❤
Commissary Lane
Description: Drive-in theater
Type: Table Service
Price: $$ / **Dining Plan:** Yes
Menu Items: steak, pasta, shepherd's pie, burgers, chicken nuggets, sandwiches, ribs, salad, various desserts, soda pop, hot chocolate, coffee, iced tea, beer, sangria
Kids Menu: penne pasta, chicken breast, salmon, salad, chicken noodle soup
Recommendation: We love this place! Sit in cars while you watch classic cheesy sci-fi film clips and eat '50s style diner food! Try any of their burgers.

> **· Magic Tips ·**
> The Sci-Fi Dine-In Theater has a complimentary popcorn machine for waiting guests—just like at the movies!

THE TROLLEY CAR CAFE (STARBUCKS)
Hollywood Boulevard
Description: Starbucks coffee and pastries
Type: Quick-Service
Price: $ / **Dining Plan:** Yes
Menu Items: Starbucks brand coffees and specialty drinks, smoothies, Teavana iced teas, hot chocolate

TUNE-IN LOUNGE ❤
Echo Lake
Description: Swanky '50s lounge
Type: Snacks
Price: $$ / **Dining Plan:** No

Menu Items: pot pie, pork chops, lasagna, pot roast, salad, fried chicken, fish, meatloaf, fries, onion rings, shakes, ice cream, various desserts, soda pop, hot chocolate, coffee, iced tea, milk, wine, beer, specialty cocktails

Kids Menu: salad, soup, salmon, spaghetti, meatloaf, chicken

Recommendation: Beer-battered Onion Rings, Aunt Liz's Golden Fried Chicken ❤, Dad's Electric Lemonade ❤

‡ WOODY'S LUNCH BOX ❤

Toy Story Land
Description: *Toy Story*-themed dining
Type: Quick-Service
Price: $$ / **Dining Plan:** Yes
Menu Items:
Breakfast: specialty pastries, breakfast sandwiches, specialty drinks, soda pop
Lunch & Dinner: specialty pastries, sandwiches, specialty drinks, potato barrels, soda pop, adult mixed drinks, beer, and hard cider
Kids Lunch & Dinner: Grilled cheese sandwich, turkey sandwich
Recommendation: S'more French Toast Sandwich for breakfast, and the Grilled Three-Cheese Sandwich with a side of tomato-basil soup for lunch. The "Totchos" are great to try, too (nachos made with fried potato barrels instead of chips).

ANIMAL KINGDOM DINING

ANANDAPUR ICE CREAM TRUCK

Asia
Description: Decorative ice cream truck
Type: Snacks
Price: $ / **Dining Plan:** No
Menu Items: ice cream, float, bottled water, soda pop
Recommendations: Float

CARAVAN ROAD

Asia
Description: Asian snack hut
Type: Snacks
Price: $ / **Dining Plan:** No

Menu Items: Teriyaki beef sliders, edamame, soda pop, water

CREATURE COMFORTS (STARBUCKS)
Discovery Island
Description: Starbucks coffee and pastries
Type: Quick-Service
Price: $ / **Dining Plan:** Yes
Menu Items: Starbucks brand coffees and specialty drinks, smoothies, Teavana iced teas, hot chocolate

DAWA BAR ❤
Africa
Description: African outdoor wine bar
Type: Lounge
Price: $ / **Dining Plan:** No
Menu Items: margarita, mojito, alcoholic punch, domestic and specialty beer, wines
Recommendation: Lost on Safari ❤

> **· Magic Tips ·**
> Not many guests realize that Animal Kingdom has full bars in nearly every themed land! Those 21+ can enjoy cocktails, beers, or their own requested creation from the bartender.

DINO-BITE SNACK
DinoLand U.S.A.
Description: Dinosaur-themed Ice Cream Parlor
Type: Ice Cream Shack
Price: $ / **Dining Plan:** No
Menu Items: ice cream, floats, sundaes, pretzels, cheese dip, chips, cookies, beer, coffee, hot chocolate
Recommendations: Bugs Sundae

DINO DINER
DinoLand U.S.A.
Description: Dinosaur-themed snack and treat truck
Type: Snacks
Price: $ / **Dining Plan:** Yes
Menu Items: sausage hoagie, churros, cupcakes, soda pop, beer, frozen lemonade with rum
Recommendations: Churro with Chocolate Sauce

DRINKWALLAH
Asia
Description: To-go snack shack
Type: Snacks
Price: $ / **Dining Plan:** No
Menu Items: chips, nuts, soda pop, and rum cocktails

EIGHT SPOON CAFE
Discovery Island
Description: Snack shack
Type: Quick-Service
Price: $ / **Dining Plan:** Yes
Menu Items: Mac and Cheese, Mickey pretzel, cheese dip, chips, soda pop, bottled water
Recommendation: Macaroni and Cheese with Pulled Pork

‡ FLAME TREE BARBECUE ❤
Discovery Island
Description: Barbecue
Type: Quick-Service
Price: $$ / **Dining Plan:** Yes
Menu Items: ribs, chicken, sandwiches, salad, French Fries, mousse desserts, soda pop, coffee, hot chocolate, hot tea, iced tea, beer, wine
Kids Menu: hot dog, drumstick, sandwiches
Recommendations: Ribs and Chicken Combo ❤, french fries with Pulled Pork and Cheese

HARAMBE FRUIT MARKET
Africa
Description: Fruit Cart
Type: Quick-Service
Price: $ / **Dining Plan:** No
Menu Items: fruit, yogurt, crackers, chips, soda pop, coffee

‡ HARAMBE MARKET
Africa
Description: African-themed worldly cuisine
Type: Quick-Service
Price: $$ / **Dining Plan:** Yes
Menu Items: ribs, skewers, sausage, soda pop, coffee, hot chocolate, iced tea, beer, wine, sangria, bottled water
Recommendation: Grilled Chicken Skewer

ISLE OF JAVA
Discovery Island
Description: Coffee shack
Type: Quick-Service
Price: $ / **Dining Plan:** No
Menu Items: cappuccino, espresso, pastries, coffee, hot chocolate, iced tea, beer, rum and Coke
Recommendation: Island Cappuccino

KUSAFIRI COFFEE SHOP AND BAKERY
Africa
Description: Coffee shack
Type: Quick-Service
Price: $ / **Dining Plan:** No
Menu Items:
Breakfast: breakfast wrap, cinnamon roll, pastries, yogurt, fruit, cappuccino, espresso, coffee, iced coffee, hot chocolate, tea
Lunch: panini, sandwiches, cinnamon roll, pastries, yogurt, fruit, cappuccino, espresso, coffee, iced coffee, hot chocolate, tea
Recommendation: Ham and Cheese Panini

MAHINDI
Africa
Description: Popcorn Hut
Type: Quick-Service
Price: $ / **Dining Plan:** No
Menu Items: popcorn, nuts, chips, slushy, soda pop, beer
Recommendation: Jungle Juice Slushy

MR. KAMAL'S ❤
Asia
Description: A snack cart with some tasty bites
Type: Quick-Service
Price: $ / **Dining Plan:** Yes
Menu Items: dumplings, hummus, fries, soda pop
Recommendation: Chicken Dumplings ❤

NOMAD LOUNGE ❤
Africa
Description: African Safari lounge
Type: Lounge
Price: $$ / **Dining Plan:** No
Menu Items: chicken wings, tapas, ribs, specialty non-alcoholic and alcoholic drinks, domestic and specialty beer, wines

Recommendation: The menu frequently changes, but we always recommend trying at least two plates.

‡ PIZZAFARI
Africa
Description: Pizza Restaurant
Type: Quick-Service
Price: $$ / **Dining Plan:** Yes
Menu Items: flatbread, pizza, salad, subs, pasta, soups, various desserts, hot tea, cold tea, coffee, hot chocolate, beer, vodka lemonade
Kids Menu: cheese pizza, macaroni and cheese, sandwich, pasta with marinara
Recommendation: Mediterranean Flatbread

PONGU PONGU
Pandora—The World of Avatar
Description: Lounge Bar
Type: Lounge
Price: $$ / **Dining Plan:** Yes
Menu Items: specialty beverages, dessert lumpia
Recommendations: The Night Blossom drink ❤

RAINFOREST CAFE
Main Entrance
Description: Jungle-themed restaurant
Type: Table Service
Price: $$ / **Dining Plan:** Yes
Menu Items:
Breakfast: omelets, bacon, sausage, eggs benedict, French toast, waffle, breakfast pizza, breakfast slider, specialty drinks
Kids Menu: waffle, oatmeal, toast, cereal
Lunch & Dinner: burgers, sandwiches, soup, salad, steak, chicken, shrimp, pasta, french fries, onion rings, various desserts, beer, wine, hard cider, specialty cocktails
Kids Menu: chicken, popcorn shrimp, cheese pizza, macaroni and cheese, sandwich, grilled cheese
Recommendation: The Rainforest Cafe is great for families because of the wide variety of options for Kids. Adults will likely find the food forgettable—though not bad. Still, the theme is so well done, especially with the décor, that it's worth a stop with Kids.

‡ RESTAURANTOSAURUS
DinoLand U.S.A.

Description: Archeological dig restaurant
Type: Quick-Service
Price: $$ / **Dining Plan:** Yes
Menu Items: burgers, salad, sandwiches, soups, chicken nuggets, various desserts, soda pop, hot chocolate, coffee, iced tea, beer
Kids Menu: cheeseburger, sandwich, corn dog nuggets
Recommendations: Another one of Walt Disney World's typical fast food. It's not very flavorful so we recommend trying another spot.

‡ SATU'LI CANTEEN ❤

Pandora—The World of Avatar
Description: Asian fusion Lunch & Dinner bowls
Type: Quick-Service
Price: $$ / **Dining Plan:** Yes
Menu Items: rice bowls, bao buns, specialty beverages
Recommendations: Cheeseburger Steamed Pods ❤ and Blueberry Cream Cheese Mousse ❤

> · **Magic Tips** ·
> Disney may change up the restaurants that offer mobile ordering, even up to the day of your visit.

THE SMILING CROCODILE

Asia
Description: Snack Shack
Type: Quick-Service
Price: $$ / **Dining Plan:** No
Menu Items: grits, drumstick, soda pop, beer, bottled water

TAMU TAMU REFRESHMENTS ❤

Africa
Description: Dessert Hut serving Dole Whips
Type: Quick-Service
Price: $$ / **Dining Plan:** No
Menu Items: Dole Whip, sundae, chocolate waffle, ice cream sandwich, soda pop, bottled water
Recommendations: Dole Whip ❤, Dole Whip Cup with Coconut Rum ❤

TERRA TREATS

Discovery Island
Description: Healthy snack shack

Type: Quick-Service
Price: $ / **Dining Plan:** No
Menu Items: hummus, gluten-free snacks and desserts, soda pop, bottled water, soy milk, gluten-free beer

THIRSTY RIVER BAR AND TREK SNACKS
Asia
Description: Specialty Drink Hut
Type: Quick-Service
Price: $$ / **Dining Plan:** No
Menu Items: pastries, juice, fruit, chocolate twist, soda pop, bottled water, milk, hot chocolate, iced coffee

TIFFINS ❤
Discovery Island
Description: International cuisine fine dining
Type: Fine Dining
Dress Code: Park attire
Price: $$$$ / **Dining Plan:** Yes
Menu Items: chicken, lamb chop, pork tenderloin, prawns, fish, short rib, vegetable curry, duck, seafood, salad, various desserts, specialty cocktails, soda pop, beer, iced tea
Kids Menu: salad, soup, chicken, fish, pasta, short ribs
Recommendations: Just about everything you get at Tiffins is absolutely delicious. Order the Wagyu Strip Loin and Braised Short Rib ❤

TRILO-BITES
Discovery Island
Description: Dinosaur outpost shack
Type: Snacks
Price: $ / **Dining Plan:** Yes
Menu Items: chicken and waffles, waffle sundae, float, soda pop, beer, bottled water
Recommendation: Buffalo Chicken Waffle Slider

TUSKER HOUSE RESTAURANT ❤
Africa
Description: American buffet in Africa with Donald Duck and friends
Type: Character Dining
Price: $$$ / **Dining Plan:** Yes
Menu Items:

Breakfast Buffet: Mickey waffles, pancakes, potato tots, custom omelets, fruit, cereal, pastries, scrambled eggs, bacon, sausage, ham, apple turnovers
Lunch & Dinner Buffet: BBQ pork loin, chutney, salad, chicken, pork, pasta, lobster and shrimp macaroni and cheese, vegetables, corn dog nuggets, desserts, ice cream, mojito, beer

WARUNG OUTPOST
Asia
Description: Asian outdoor bar
Type: Walk-up Bar
Price: $ / **Dining Plan:** No
Menu Items: margaritas, beer, Mickey pretzel, chips, smoothies

YAK & YETI LOCAL FOODS CAFES
Asia
Description: Asian street food
Type: Quick-Service
Price: $ / **Dining Plan:** Yes
Menu Items:
Breakfast: breakfast sandwiches, breakfast burritos, hash brown bites, fruit salad, juice, coffee
Kids Breakfast: pancake and sausage stick, french toast sticks
Lunch & Dinner: teriyaki bowl, Asian honey chicken, Asian chicken wrap, ginger chicken salad, tikka masala, egg rolls, Kobe beef hot dog, mango pie, soda pop, beer
Kids Lunch & Dinner: cheeseburger, chicken strips

YAK AND YETI ❤
Asia
Description: Asian-style eatery at the base of the Himalayas
Type: Bar, Quick-Service, and Table Service Restaurant
Price: $ – $$$ / **Dining Plan:** Yes (but not for Quality Beverages bar)
Local Food Cafes Menu: beef bowl, cheeseburger, chicken, sandwich, hot dog, wrap, salad, egg rolls, various desserts, soda pop, juice, milk, beer
Kids Menu: cheeseburger, sandwich, chicken strips
Restaurant: chicken wings, egg rolls, pot stickers, lettuce cups, noodles, seafood, salad, tikka masala, wok dishes, BBQ ribs, kabobs, fried rice, desserts, specialty drinks, beer, wine, sake
Kids Menu: burger, sandwich, egg roll, mac and cheese, chicken tenders, corn dogs, teriyaki chicken breast
Recommendations: Pork Pot Stickers, Pork Egg Rolls ❤, Tempura Shrimp ❤, Chicken Tikka Masala

DISNEY WATER PARKS DINING

TYPHOON LAGOON EATS

HAPPY LANDINGS ICE CREAM
Description: Snack shack
Type: Snacks
Price: $ / **Dining Plan:** No
Menu Items: ice cream, sundae, bottled water, soda pop, all-day refillable mug for soda pop

LEANING PALMS
Description: American dining beach house
Type: Quick-Service
Price: $$ / **Dining Plan:** Yes
Menu Items: burgers, chicken nuggets, wraps, sandwiches, pizzas, hot dogs, assorted desserts, soda pop, beer, wine, sangria, hot chocolate, coffee, milk, frozen lemonade
Kids Menu: chicken nuggets, turkey sandwich

LET'S GO SLURPIN'
Description: Beach bar
Type: Lounge Bar
Price: $$ / **Dining Plan:** No
Menu Items: margarita, mai tai, rum, cocktails, beer, wine

LOWTIDE LOU'S
Description: Beach sandwich bar
Type: Snacks and drinks
Price: $ / **Dining Plan:** Yes
Menu Items: turkey pesto, sandwiches, wraps, nachos, soda pop, bottled water, margarita, piña colada, vodka mixed drinks, beer, wine, sangria
Kids Menu: sandwiches

SNACK SHACK
Description: Dining hut
Type: Quick-Service
Price: $$ / **Dining Plan:** Yes

Menu Items: turkey pesto, sandwiches, wraps, salads, soda pop, bottled water, margarita, piña colada, refillable fountain beverage mug
Kids Menu: sandwiches

TYPHOON TILLY'S
Description: Barbecue shack
Type: Quick-Service
Price: $$ / **Dining Plan:** Yes
Menu Items: sandwiches, wraps, salads, shrimp, fish, soda pop, bottled water, beer, wine, sangria
Kids Menu: turkey sandwich, corn dog nuggets

BLIZZARD BEACH EATS

ARCTIC EXPEDITIONS
Description: Food truck
Type: Snacks
Price: $$ / **Dining Plan:** No
Menu Items: gyro, cheese steak, salad, turkey leg, various desserts, beer, lemonade, bottled water

AVALUNCH
Description: Dining hut
Type: Quick-Service
Price: $$ / **Dining Plan:** Yes
Menu Items: brisket, specialty hot dogs, pretzels, various desserts, beer, sangria, soda pop, bottled water

COOLING HUT
Description: Dining hut
Type: Quick-Service
Price: $ / **Dining Plan:** Yes
Menu Items: tuna sandwich, chicken wrap, popcorn, hummus, fruit cup, pretzels, chips, yogurt, various desserts, beer, hard cider, soda pop, bottled water

FROSTBITE FREDDY'S FROZEN FRESHMENTS
Description: Snack and frozen drink shack
Type: Snacks
Price: $ / **Dining Plan:** No

Menu Items: brisket nachos, turkey leg, orange swirl cone, soda pop, beer, mixed adult beverages
Recommendation: Barbecue Brisket Nachos

I.C. EXPEDITIONS
Description: Ice Cream Truck
Type: Snacks
Price: $ / **Dining Plan:** No
Menu Items: sundaes, floats, ice cream bars, bottled water

LOTTAWATTA LODGE
Description: Ski lodge restaurant
Type: Quick-Service
Price: $$ / **Dining Plan:** Yes
Menu Items: burgers, fries, wraps, rolls, hot dog, flatbread, various desserts, ice cream, sundaes, all-day refillable mug, frozen lemonade, hot chocolate, coffee, beer, sangria, wine

MINI DONUTS ❤
Description: Donut cart
Type: Snacks
Price: $ / **Dining Plan:** No
Menu Items: mini donuts and dipping sauces, coffee, hot chocolate, hot tea, frozen lemonade
Recommendation: Mini Donuts ❤

POLAR PUB
Description: Outdoor bar
Type: Lounge
Price: $$ / **Dining Plan:** No
Menu Items: margarita, daiquiri, specialty drinks, beer, wine, bottled water, chips

WARMING HUT
Description: International food hut
Type: Quick-Service
Price: $$ / **Dining Plan:** Yes
Menu Items: teriyaki rice bowl, egg roll, empanada, chicken wrap, various desserts, soda pop, beer, all-day refillable mug, hard cider

HOTEL DINING

The Walt Disney World hotels have some of the best dining choices around. If you're not staying at that particular Resort hotel, you can still wander in and dine at a restaurant. The Quick-Service locations are often just hamburgers, sandwiches, hot dogs, and soda. These aren't that special, unfortunately, so we haven't detailed them much in this section.

ALL-STAR RESORTS

These Resorts have their own themed quick-service restaurants. The breakfasts here are pretty good!

> **· Magic Tips ·**
> The World Premiere Food Court at Disney's All-Star Movie Resort has a secret menu that uses a retro Viewfinder! You can try poutine, a bacon mac 'n' cheese dog, and also a burger made with cinnamon buns (it's aptly named the Cinnamon Bun Burger)! Just ask when you order.

ALL-STAR MOVIE RESORT
Silver Screen Spirits Pool Bar – $$ / **Dining Plan:** Yes / Quick-Service
‡ World Premiere Food Court – $$ / **Dining Plan:** Yes / Quick-Service Breakfast, Lunch, and Dinner

ALL-STAR MUSIC RESORT
‡ Intermission Food Court – $$ / **Dining Plan:** Yes / Quick-Service Breakfast, Lunch, and Dinner
Singing Spirits Pool Bar – $$ / **Dining Plan:** Yes / Quick-Service

ALL-STAR SPORTS RESORT
‡ End Zone Food Court – $$ / **Dining Plan:** Yes / Quick-Service Breakfast, Lunch, and Dinner
Grandstand Spirits – $$ / **Dining Plan:** Yes / Quick-Service Pool Bar

ANIMAL KINGDOM LODGE

BOMA – FLAVORS OF AFRICA
Jambo House
Description: African cuisine in a safari setting
Type: Table Service
Price: $$$ / **Dining Plan:** Yes
Menu Items:
Breakfast: fruit, salad, yogurt, salmon, cheeses, omelets, pancakes, bread pudding, oatmeal, ham, turkey, waffles, corned beef hash, potatoes, vegetables, coffee, tea, lemonade, juices, soda pop, milk
Dinner: soups, stews, salads, salmon, pork ribs, chicken, beef sirloin, vegetables, soda pop, coffee, tea, milk
Recommendation: Come for breakfast. The dinner is pricey, so we'd recommend just dining at Jiko instead.

JIKO – THE COOKIE PLACE ❤
Jambo House
Description: African cuisine with an extensive wine selection
Type: Fine Dining
Dress Code: Business casual / cocktail attire – though we've seen plenty of men in shorts here
Price: $$$$ / **Dining Plan:** Yes
Menu Items: steak, wild boar tenderloin, halibut, vegetables, pork shank, seafood, short rib, macaroni and cheese, lamb shank, assorted desserts, teas, liqueurs, wines, specialty cocktails, soda pop, coffee, tea, milk
Kids Menu: cheese pizza, macaroni and cheese, chicken, steak, fish, scallops
Recommendations: Crispy Bobotie Roll for the appetizer ❤, Grilled Buffalo Rib-Eye or Botswana-style Seswaa Beef Short Rib for the entrée ❤, Braai Macaroni and Cheese enhancement

‡ THE MARA ❤
Jambo House
Description: African- and American-inspired fast food
Type: Table Service
Price: $-$$ / **Dining Plan:** Yes
Menu Items:
Breakfast: scrambled eggs, breakfast potatoes, Mickey-shaped waffles, breakfast sandwiches, oatmeal, bacon, sausage, pastries, coffee

Kids Breakfast: cereal, waffles, breakfast platter with eggs and bacon or sausage

Lunch: burger, flatbreads, salads, sandwiches, soup, cupcakes, coffee, soda pop

Dinner: ribs, burger, lamb stew, chicken nuggets, flatbreads, falafel, salads, chili-cheese hot dog, soup, soda pop, coffee

Kids Lunch & Dinner: turkey sandwich, cheeseburger, chicken nuggets, salad with chicken

Late-Night Dining: flatbreads, kids' cheese pizza, desserts, soda pop, coffee

Recommendation: We like The Mara for its inexpensive, but tasty entrees. It's a great place to stop by for breakfast before heading to the parks or late-night after you play.

SANAA
Kidani Village

Description: American and African dining with an Indian flare overlooking an animal-filled Savanna

Type: Table Service

Price: $$$ / **Dining Plan:** Yes

Menu Items:

Breakfast: eggs benedict, grains and fruit, French toast, breakfast sandwich, pastries, fruit, banana bread, oatmeal, biscuits, bacon, coffee, juice, tea, bloody mary, bellini

Lunch & Dinner: tandoori chicken, salad, burger, Indian-style bread service, desserts, soda, cocktails, beer, wine (steak, fish, and chicken also available for dinner)

Kids Menu: cheese pizza, macaroni and cheese, chicken, cheeseburger, fish, shrimp

Recommendation: Sanaa's biggest perk is watching the animals while you eat! Sanaa is also better for those looking for cultural food with an Indian or African twist.

UNIQUE DINING EXPERIENCES
Reservations Required and Dining Plan Not Accepted

- **Dine with Animal Specialist** – $$$ – Dine with an animal specialist at Sanaa. You'll learn a lot about the many species of African animals while dining on a 4-course meal of bread, salad, meat, and a dessert.
- **Wanyama Safari** – $$$$ – Board a caravan safari and meet several of the Animal Kingdom Lodge's African animals like giraffes and zebras. Afterward, you'll dine at Jiko.

LOUNGES AND BARS

- **CAPE TOWN LOUNGE AND WINE BAR** (*Jambo House*) – $-$$ / **Dining:** No / Lounge
- **MAJI POOL BAR** (*Jambo House*) – $$ / **Dining:** Yes / Quick-Service
- **UZIMA SPRINGS POOL BAR** (*Jambo House*) – $$ / **Dining:** No / Quick-Service Pool Bar

ART OF ANIMATION

- **THE DROP OFF POOL BAR** – $$ / **Dining Plan:** No / Quick-Service
- **LANDSCAPE OF FLAVORS** – $$ / **Dining Plan:** Yes / Quick-Service Breakfast, Lunch, and Dinner / **Recommendations:** breakfast or build-your-own-burger for lunch or dinner.

BEACH CLUB AND YACHT CLUB

ALE & COMPASS LOUNGE
Description: New England-style restaurant
Type: Table Service
Price: $$-$$$ / **Dining Plan:** Yes
Menu Items: American breakfast buffet, salad, flatbreads, burgers, sandwiches, lobster roll, desserts, soda, wines, cocktails, beers
Kids Menu: cheeseburger, grilled chicken, pasta bolognese, fish
Recommendation: Breakfast buffet, Applewood-smoked Bacon Flatbread, Cabernet-braise Short Ribs

BEACHES & CREAM SODA SHOP ❤
Description: Seaside soda parlor and diner
Type: Table Service
Price: $$ / **Dining Plan:** Yes
Menu Items: steak, lobster, chicken, pork chop, desserts, wines, soda, juices
Kids Menu: chicken breast, fish, steak skewers, mac and cheese
Recommendations: Get a reservation because this cool little diner is popular! The food here is good, but the beach-style ambience and desserts are even better. Try a sandwich and get the huge (and

delicious) Kitchen Sink dessert (a mix of ice creams and toppings served in a small kitchen sink) ❤

· Magic Tips ·
Some items on the Disney Dining Plan can be combined to purchase items. For example, 4 people can combine their desserts to get the Kitchen Sink at Beaches & Cream Soda (it's more than enough for four adults to share)!

CAPE MAY CAFE ❤
Description: New England-style beach buffet
Type: Character Dining
Price: $$$ / **Dining Plan:** Yes
Menu Items:
Breakfast and Brunch: Mickey waffles, cheeses, cereals, pastries, yogurt, fruit, meats, coffee, mimosas, espresso, teas
Lunch & Dinner: pasta, carving station, seafood, soup, salad, cheese, bread, desserts
Recommendation: Character breakfast or brunch buffet ❤

YACHTSMAN STEAKHOUSE ❤
Description: New England-style steakhouse
Type: Signature Dining
Dress Code: Business casual / cocktail attire
Price: $$$$ / **Dining Plan:** Yes
Menu Items: steak, lobster, chicken, pork chop, desserts, wines, soda, juices
Kids Menu: chicken breast, fish, steak skewers, mac and cheese
Recommendations: Any of their steaks ❤

MORE DINING
- **Ale & Compass Lounge** ($$) – **Dining Plan:** No / **Type:** Lounge / **Description:** seafood appetizers, wines, cocktails, beers
- **Beach Club Marketplace** ($) – Dining Plan: Yes / Description: Get American breakfast, lunch, and dinner at this Quick-Service location / Type: Quick-Service
- **Crew's Cup Lounge** ($$) – **Dining Plan:** No / **Type:** Lounge / **Description:** Seafood, spirits, and American favorites served late
- **Hurricane Hanna's Waterside Bar and Grill** ($-$$) – **Dining Plan:** Yes / **Type:** Quick-Service / **Description:** Poolside drinks /

Recommendation: Great for an adult beverage and fine for a bite to eat poolside.

- **Martha's Vineyard** ($$) – **Dining Plan:** No / **Type:** Lounge / **Description:** Bar with seafood bites / **Recommendation:** Martha's Vineyard offers a full bar for alcoholic drinks. Try the Sautéed Mussels or Salt and Pepper Calamari

BOARDWALK INN

See Disney's BoardWalk in the "Dining Out" section of this chapter.

CARIBBEAN BEACH RESORT

SEBASTIAN'S BISTRO
Description: *The Little Mermaid*-inspired dining
Type: Table Service
Price: $$$ / **Dining Plan:** Yes
Menu Items:
Lunch: burgers, sandwiches, steak, grilled fish, vegetarian sandwich, jerk chicken, crab cake, rolls, chicken wings, salads, desserts, cocktails, wines, beer, coffee, soda
Dinner: pork shoulder, shrimp and tamales, fish, jerk chicken, curry, jerk butternut squash, steak, crab cake, rolls, chicken wings, salads, desserts, cocktails, wines, beer, coffee, soda
Kids Lunch & Dinner: pasta, jerk chicken, shrimp, burger, meat pie, pork shoulder
Recommendations: Caribbean Pull-Apart Rolls for appetizer and Jerk Chicken for lunch or dinner

‡ SPYGLASS GRILL
Description: Caribbean walk-up counter
Type: Quick-Service
Price: $$ / **Dining Plan:** Yes
Menu Items:
Breakfast: sandwiches, breakfast wrap, oatmeal, scrambled eggs, fruit plate, cream cheese guava-stuffed French toast, coffee, tea
Lunch & Dinner: bacon cheeseburger, chorizo burger, Cuban sandwich, Caribbean tacos, turkey sandwich, vegan taco, smoothies
Recommendations: Caribbean Tacos and a Lava Smoothie

MORE DINING

- **Banana Cabana Pool Bar** ($$) – Dining Plan: No / Pool Bar
- ‡ **Centertown Market** ($$) – Dining Plan: Yes / Quick-Service for Breakfast, Lunch, and Dinner / Recommendation: Strawberry-Guava French Toast (breakfast) or to-go wrap (lunch)

CONTEMPORARY & BAY LAKE TOWER

CALIFORNIA GRILL ❤

Description: American and Seafood Restaurant that overlooks the Magic Kingdom and Seven Seas Lagoon
Type: Fine Dining
Dress Code: Business casual / cocktail attire
Price: $$$$ / **Dining Plan:** Yes
Menu Items:
Brunch: pastries, salad, greek yogurt, fish, shrimp tempura, sushi, pancakes, chicken, grits, eggs benedict, assorted desserts, wine, cocktails
Dinner: sausage, flatbread, cheese boards, charcuteries, sushi, soup, salad, steak, pork, fish, chicken, vegetable curry, seafood ramen, various desserts, wine, cocktails, beer, ciders
Kids Dinner: chicken breast, salmon, beef tenderloin, cheese pizza, macaroni and cheese
Recommendation: A great date spot, we recommend booking here for dinner during Magic Kingdom fireworks! We highly recommend the Braised Beef Short Rib Wontons and Poulet Rouge Chicken. Their cocktails and desserts are also fantastic. Ask to be seated near the window.

CHEF MICKEY'S

Description: Buffet with Mickey and friends
Type: Character Dining
Price: $$$ / **Dining Plan:** Yes
Menu Items:
Breakfast: bagels, croissants, pastries, biscuits and gravy, pancakes, potato casserole, shrimp, frittatas, tofu scramble, oatmeal, fruit, yogurts, soda pop, coffee, tea
Brunch: fruit, salad, yogurts, soup, frittatas, pork ribs, assorted desserts
Kids Breakfast: scrambled eggs, tater tots, macaroni and cheese, chicken nuggets, mini waffles, soda pop

Dinner: mixed fruit, salad, shrimp, seafood, pasta, beef, turkey, soup, salmon, macaroni and cheese, mashed potatoes, vegetables, pastries, assorted desserts, specialty cocktails, lemonade, soda pop

Kids Dinner: chicken nuggets, mini corn dogs, vegetables, macaroni and cheese

Recommendations: Because of its lively environment and central location near the monorail, Chef Mickey's can get a bit noisy. If you're looking for a character dining experience with Mr. Mouse himself, there's no better place! Go for the breakfast buffet.

STEAKHOUSE 71 ❤

Description: A casual steakhouse named after the year Walt Disney World debuted.
Type: Table Service
Price: $$$ / **Dining Plan:** Yes
Menu Items:
Breakfast: eggs, bacon, rib hash, pancakes, omelets, steak and eggs, fruit, pastries, bloody marys, mimosas, coffee, tea, juice
Lunch & Dinner: steak, salad, mac and cheese, mashed potatoes, grilled vegetables, desserts, beer, wine, soda
Recommendation: Try a delicious Disney steak in a laidback environment. We recommend any of the steaks with a side of mac and cheese.

MORE DINING

- **CALIFORNIA GRILL LOUNGE** ($$) – Dining Plan: No / Lounge
- ‡ **CONTEMPO CAFE** ($$) – Dining Plan: Yes / Quick-Service American breakfast, lunch, and dinner
- **CONTEMPORARY GROUNDS** ($) – Dining Plan: No / Snacks and Coffee
- **COVE BAR** ($$) – Dining Plan: No / Lounge
- **OUTER RIM** ($$) – Dining Plan: No / Lounge
- **THE SAND BAR** ($) – Dining Plan: Yes / Quick-Service
- **THE WAVE LOUNGE** ($$) – Dining Plan: No / Lounge

CORONADO SPRINGS

EL MERCADO DE CORONADO
Description: American / **Type:** Quick-Service

Price: $-$$ / **Dining Plan:** Yes
Menu Items: American breakfast items, nachos, rice bowls, burgers, sandwiches, pizza, paninis, salads, beer, wine, margaritas, coffee, tea, soda pop
Recommendations: Crispy Santa Fe Chicken Sandwich

MAYA GRILL
Description: Mexican and American Cuisine / **Type:** Table Service
Price: $$$ / **Dining Plan:** Yes
Menu Items: queso, calamari, tacos, tomatillos, pork, short ribs, fish, Cornish hen, fajita, steak, assorted desserts, specialty drinks, beer, wine, margaritas, coffee, tea, soda pop
Recommendations: Maya Grill's Signature Fajita Skillet

THREE BRIDGES BAR & GRILL ❤
Description: Outdoor Spanish-American dining spot in the center of the resort's lake / **Type:** Table Service
Price: $$-$$$ / **Dining Plan:** Yes
Menu Items: sandwiches, salads, steak, burgers, tacos, churros, cocktails, beer, wine, hard cider, soda pop, tea, coffee
Recommendations: Come here for shareable appetizers and drinks. Try the Warm Manchego with Oaxaca Cheese and Fried Shrimp Corn Dogs
Secret Menu Item: Mexican Corn Dip (chips with spicy cheese and corn dipping sauce)

TOLEDO — TAPAS, STEAK, & SEAFOOD
Description: Spanish-inspired rooftop dining / **Type:** Table Service
Price: $$$ / **Dining Plan:** Yes
Menu Items: tapas, steak, chicken, seafood, desserts, cocktails, beer, wine, margaritas, coffee, tea, soda pop
Recommendations: Best for adults who might enjoy rooftop dining with sweeping views of the Walt Disney World Resort. We recommend small bites like Savory Churros (deep-fried cheese), and "Bravas" Potatoes. For a finer tapas experience, visit Jaleo in Disney Springs.

MORE DINING

- **Barcelona Lounge** ($) – Dining Plan: No / Espresso bar
- **Cafe Rix** ($) – Dining Plan: Yes / Dessert bar
- **Dahlia Lounge** ($) – Dining Plan: No / Drinks and snacks
- **Rix Sports Bar & Grill** ($-$$) – Dining Plan: Yes /

Quick-Service Spanish-American breakfast, lunch, and dinner
- **Laguna Bar** ($) – Dining Plan: No / Outdoor bar
- **Siestas Cantina** ($$) – Dining Plan: Yes / Pool bar

FORT WILDERNESS

TRAIL'S END RESTAURANT
Description: American Dining / **Type:** Table Service
Price: $$$ / **Dining Plan:** Yes
Menu Items:
Breakfast & Brunch: fruit, pastries, eggs, breakfast pizza, Mickey waffles, cheese grits, carving station, soup, chili, fried chicken, desserts, bacon, sausage, coffee, tea, milk, juices
Lunch & Dinner: chicken breast, shrimp, salad, flatbread, sandwiches, chicken and waffles, steak, grits, assorted desserts, beer
Kids Lunch & Dinner: baked chicken, grilled salmon, cheeseburger, macaroni and cheese, chicken nuggets, grilled cheese
Recommendations: Breakfast or Brunch Buffet, Chicken and Waffles

MORE DINING
- **Crockett's Tavern** ($) – Dining Plan: No / Quick-Service pizzas, wings, nachos and lounge
- **P and J's Southern Takeout** ($$) – Dining Plan: Yes / Quick-Service Western favorites

GRAND FLORIDIAN

1900 PARK FARE
Description: American Buffet and Tea Party
Type: Character Dining Buffet
Price: $$$ / **Dining Plan:** Yes
Menu Items:
Brunch: salads, bacon, bagels, soup, rice, potato puffs, sausage, eggs, French toast, shrimp, fruit, croissants, Mickey waffles, assorted pastries, tea, coffee, soda pop
Dinner: salad, greens, soup, chicken, salmon, fried catfish, stir fry, shrimp, mashed potatoes, pork, ravioli, assorted desserts, tea, coffee, soda pop

Kids Dinner: macaroni and cheese, cheese ravioli, hot dog, pizza, chicken tenders, vegetables, taco bar
Recommendation: Dine any time for delicious meals and many characters.

CITRICOS
Description: *Mary Poppins*-themed dining
Type: Table Service
Price: $$$-$$$$ / **Dining Plan:** Yes
Menu Items: steak, short rib, rigatoni, fish, chicken, salad, mac and cheese, desserts, beer, wine, cocktails
Kids Menu: steak, chicken, pizza, mac and cheese, shrimp, pasta
Recommendations: Dinner is served in courses. We recommend the Strawberry Salad (first course), Short Ribs or Smoked Duck Breast (Second Course), and the Blackberry Tartelette for dessert.

GRAND FLORIDIAN CAFE
Description: American dining
Type: Table Service
Price: $$$ / **Dining Plan:** Yes
Menu Items:
Breakfast: omelets, eggs, steak, bacon, sausage, breakfast potatoes, French toast, pancakes, Mickey waffles, salads, yogurt, oatmeal, pastries, morning mixed drinks, wines, beer, soda pop, tea
Kids Breakfast: omelet, eggs, Mickey waffles, pancakes with sprinkles
Lunch: shrimp, soup, salad, sandwiches, fish, chicken, wraps, burgers, assorted desserts, mixed drinks, wines, beer, soda pop, tea
Kids: chicken, salmon, chicken wrap, meaty macaroni, cheese pizza, chicken nuggets
Dinner: salad, soup, shrimp, chicken, fish, steak, pork chops, burgers, grits, ravioli, assorted desserts, mixed drinks, wines, beer, soda pop, tea
Kids Dinner: chicken, salmon, chicken wrap, meaty macaroni, cheese pizza, chicken nuggets
Recommendations: Artisan-made Spinach-Ricotta Ravioli, The Café Sandwich (open faced with ham, turkey, bacon, cheese, and fried onion), or the Lobster "Thermidor" Burger

NARCOOSSEE'S ❤
Description: American and Seafood Restaurant
Type: Fine Dining
Dress Code: Business Casual
Price: $$$-$$$$ / **Dining Plan:** Yes

Menu Items: soups, salads, shellfish, fish, cheeses, pasta, steak, chicken, pork, lobster, vegetables, assorted desserts, wines, soda pop, tea

Kids Menu: steak, cheeseburger, hamburger, mac and cheese, fried chicken tenders, shrimp, pasta, veggie burger

Recommendations: St. Augustine Soft-shell Crab, Grass Fed Filet Mignon ❤, Chocolate Crème Brulee ❤

VICTORIA & ALBERT'S ❤
Description: Victorian dining
Type: Fine Dining
Dress Code: Men – dinner jackets and slacks with shoes / Women – dress, pant suit, or skirt and blouse. This dress code is strictly enforced.
Price: $$$$-$$$$$ / **Dining Plan:** Yes
Menu Items: caviar, shrimp, fish, scallops, duck, pork, lasagna, lamb, beef, cheeses, various desserts, soda pop, coffee, tea, wines
Recommendation: The finest dining in all of Walt Disney World with perfect Victorian décor and service. There are options for Kids, but this is mostly an adult affair. Note that the menu changes from time to time, so we don't provide recommendations other than the food here is exquisite.

MORE DINING
- **Beaches Pool Bar and Grill** ($$) – Dining Plan: Yes / Pool bar
- **Citricos Lounge** ($$) – Dining Plan: No / Lounge
- **Courtyard Pool Bar** ($$) – Dining Plan: No / Pool bar
- **Enchanted Rose** ($$-$$$) – Dining Plan: No / A lounge with decor and drinks inspired by Disney's *Beauty and the Beast*.
- **Garden View Tea Room** ($$) – Dining Plan: No / Tea lounge
- ‡ **Gasparilla Island Grill** ($$) – Dining Plan: Yes / American quick-service pool bar

OLD KEY WEST

OLIVIA'S CAFE
Description: American Cuisine
Type: Table Service
Price: $$$ / **Dining Plan:** Yes
Menu Items:

Breakfast: biscuits and gravy, omelets, eggs, chorizo, French toast, pancakes, waffles, cereal, bacon, sausage, ham, potatoes, coffee, tea, milk, morning cocktails, bottled water

Kids Breakfast: mini pancakes, waffles, eggs and breakfast potatoes

Lunch & Dinner: corn fritters, onion rings, crab cakes, soup, salads, burger, pork ribs, chicken, pasta, sandwiches, chicken, fish, assorted desserts, specialty drinks, beer, coffee, tea, soda pop

Kids Lunch & Dinner: chicken, grilled cheese

Recommendations: Island Barbecue Pork Ribs, Olivia's Potatoes for a side

MORE DINING

- **Good's Food to Go** – $ / Dining Plan: Yes / Burger and hot dog quick-service
- **Gurgling Suitcase** – $ / Dining Plan: No / Pool bar
- **Turtle Shack Poolside** – $ / Dining Plan: Yes / Pool bar

POLYNESIAN VILLAGE

KONA CAFE

Description: American and Seafood Restaurant / **Type:** Table Service

Price: $$ / **Dining Plan:** Yes

Menu Items:

Breakfast: French toast, steak and eggs, ham, bacon, sausage, pancakes, omelets, eggs, fruit, oatmeal, assorted pastries, tea, coffee, soda pop, juices

Kids Breakfast: oatmeal, fruit, eggs, pancakes, French toast, toast

Lunch: crab cakes, beef, pork, pot stickers, salad, soup, tacos, Asian noodles, sandwiches, burgers, assorted desserts, tea, coffee, soda pop, milk

Kids Lunch: salad, chicken, shrimp skewers, cheeseburger, cheese tortellini, hot dog

Dinner: crab cakes, beef, pork, pot stickers, sushi, salad, soup, duck, pork, lamb, assorted desserts, tea, coffee, soda pop, milk

Kids Dinner: salad, chicken, shrimp skewers, cheeseburger, cheese tortellini

Recommendations: Big Kahuna for breakfast, fish tacos for lunch, any of the pan noodles for dinner

'OHANA ❤

Description: Polynesian Character Dining

Type: Character Dining / Buffet
Price: $$$-$$$$ / **Dining Plan:** Yes
Menu Items:
Breakfast Buffet: scrambled eggs, fried potatoes, pork, Mickey-shaped waffles, assorted pastries, tea, coffee, soda pop, juices, milk
Dinner Buffet: breads, salads, dumplings, chicken wings, Asian chicken, steak, shrimp, stir fry, desserts, tea, coffee, soda pop, milk
Recommendations: We recommend coming for dinner for some unique dishes served family style (shareable plates). 'Ohana is also very popular, so book your reservation as far in advance as possible!

· **Magic Tips** ·
'Ohana offers a little-known Twilight Feast room service option. Get several plates delivered to your room for around $50/person. Adults with small to moderate appetites may find that splitting this meal is a great option, too. It's cheaper than the dinner price tag of 'Ohana and you can order late into the night!

TRADER SAM'S GROG GROTTO ♥
Description: Island Dive Bar
Type: Lounge
Price: $$ / **Dining Plan:** No
Menu Items: mixed drinks, wines, beer, sushi, lettuce cups, tacos, fish, sliders, sausages, dumplings, soda pop
Recommendation: Disney fans love Trader Sam's! The room is a bit secret and stowed away behind a metal door. Open it to discover a hidden gem in the Walt Disney World Resort. The room and the waiters react to different ordered drinks. Watch the volcanoes erupt, the room storm, and bartenders transform into zombies looking for brains! Okay, it's more funny than scary, but Trader Sam's is not to be missed! Order any of their delicious mixed drinks and Kalua Pork Tacos. After 8pm, it's 21+ only.

MORE DINING
- **Barefoot Pool Bar** – $ / Dining Plan: No / Pool Bar
- **‡ Capt. Cook's** – $$ / Dining Plan: Yes / Quick-Service Breakfast, Lunch, and Dinner
- **Kona Island** – $ / Dining Plan: No / Quick-Service treats and drinks

- **Oasis Bar and Grill** – $$ / Dining Plan: Yes / Quick-Service and Pool Bar
- **Pineapple Lanai** ❤ – $$ / Dining Plan: Yes / Dole Whip Station
- **Tambu Lounge** – $$ / Dining Plan: No / Lounge
- **Trader Sam's Tiki Terrace** – $$ / Dining Plan: No / Lounge / Go to Trader Sam's Grog Grotto instead for a better theme and experience

POP CENTURY

- **‡ Everything POP Shopping and Dining** ($$) – Dining Plan: Yes / Quick-Service
- **Pedals Pool Bar** ($$) – Dining Plan: No / Pool Bar

PORT ORLEANS - FRENCH QUARTER

‡ SASSAGOULA FLOATWORKS & FOOD FACTORY ❤
Description: Southern American Boat Restaurant
Type: Quick-Service
Price: $$ / **Dining Plan:** Yes
Menu Items:
Breakfast: pancakes, waffles, scrambled eggs, omelets, breakfast sandwich, bacon, biscuits and gravy, tea, coffee, juice
Lunch: shrimp & grits, gumbo, jambalaya, burgers, sandwiches, chicken strips, wraps, salads, soda, tea, beer, wine
Dinner: ribs, fried chicken, shrimp & grits, gumbo, jambalaya, burgers, sandwiches, chicken strips, pizza, pasta, salads, soda, tea, beer, wine
Kids (lunch & dinner): pasta, ribs, chicken strips, pizza, mac n cheese, grilled cheese
Dessert: Beignets
Recommendations: If you want to try a sweet and savory favorite, get the Beignet Cheeseburger—it uses beignets as the buns! More beignets are found next door at the Scat Cat's Club.

MORE DINING
- **Mardi Grogs** – $ / Dining Plan: No / Quick-Service Bar
- **Scat Cat's Club** – $$ / Dining Plan: No / Lounge / Get the beignets

> **· Magic Tips ·**
> Scat Cat's Club is known for its Baton Rouge Beignets—
> with your choice of alcohol (Baileys, Kahlua, or RumChata).
> You can also ask for the secret menu item: Chocolate Baton
> Rouge Beignets (we recommend these with RumChata)!

PORT ORLEANS - RIVERSIDE

BOATWRIGHT'S DINING HALL
Description: Southern American Boat Restaurant
Type: Table Service
Price: $$$ / **Dining Plan:** Yes
Menu Items: seafood, salad, fritters, gumbo, meat and cheese board, prime rib, steak, catfish, pork chop, pasta, jambalaya, chicken, vegetables, assorted desserts, tea, coffee, soda pop, juices, beer, mixed drinks
Kids Menu: turkey, pasta, fish, beef skewers, macaroni and cheese, cheeseburger, cheese pizza, jambalaya
Recommendations: Cajun Bayou Catfish, Crawfish Mac and Cheese, Red Velvet Cheesecake

MORE DINING
- **Muddy Rivers** ($) – Dining Plan: No / Bar
- **River Roost** ($$) – Dining Plan: No / Yehaa Bob Jackson performs a wacky, high-energy show here, twice a night, Wednesday through Saturday (8:30pm and 10:30pm).
- **‡ Riverside Mill Food Court** ($$) – Dining Plan: Yes / New Orleans-style Quick-Service

RIVIERA RESORT

‡ PRIMO PIATTO ❤
Description: American and European Dining
Type: Quick-Service
Price: $$ / **Dining Plan:** Yes
Menu Items:
Breakfast: croque madame, pancakes, waffles, eggs, oatmeal, pastries, fruit, coffee, tea, juice, breakfast cocktails

Lunch & Dinner: sandwiches, burger, pizza, salad, fries, desserts, pastries, soda, coffee, tea, beer, wine, cocktails
Kids (Lunch & Dinner): cheeseburger, pizza, chicken strips
Recommendations: One of the best quick-service restaurants in Walt Disney World! If you want to dine here, but aren't staying at the Riviera, just take the Skyliner over from Epcot. You'll be able to walk the grounds of the Riviera and dine at Primo Piatto. We highly recommend the Grilled Chicken Sandwich with a side of Romano & Herb Fries.

TOPOLINO'S TERRACE
Description: French and Italian dining
Type: Character Dining / Dinner
Price: $$$-$$$$ / **Dining Plan:** Yes
Menu Items:
Breakfast: character breakfast with omelets, smoked salmons, steak, waffles, quiche, pastries, cocktails, juice, tea, coffee
Dinner: pasta, seafood, steak, cocktails, wines, European beers, soda pop, juice
Recommendations: This restaurant has a fantastic rooftop view while you dine! Kids love seeing classic Disney characters during breakfast.

MORE DINING
- **Bar Riva** ($$) – Dining Plan: No / Poolside bar with drinks and bites
- **Le Petit Cafe** ($) – Dining Plan: No / Pastries and coffee

SARATOGA SPRINGS

THE TURF CLUB BAR AND GRILL
Description: American Dining
Type: Table Service
Price: $$$ / **Dining Plan:** Yes
Menu Items: calamari, mussels, soups, onion rings, salad, shrimp, prime rib, lamb chops, pasta, fish, chicken, steak, vegetables, assorted desserts, tea, coffee, soda pop, juices, beer, mixed drinks, soda pop
Kids Menu: grilled fish, pasta, chicken breasts, cheeseburger, hot dog, pizza
Recommendations: Onion Rings with dips, Grilled New York Strip

MORE DINING
- ‡ **The Artist's Palette** ($) – Dining Plan: Yes / Quick-Service sandwiches while painting
- **Backstretch Pool Bar** ($$) – Dining Plan: Yes / Pool Bar
- **On the Rocks** ($) – Dining Plan: Yes / Lounge
- **The Paddock Grill** ($) – Dining Plan: Yes / Lounge
- **The Turf Club Lounge** ($) – Dining Plan: No / Lounge

WILDERNESS LODGE

STORY BOOK DINING AT ARTIST POINT ❤
Description: *Snow White*-themed dinner event
Type: Character Dining
Price: $$$$ / **Dining Plan:** Yes—a great value!
Menu Items: prime rib roast, chicken, gnocchi, snapper, veal shank, desserts, cocktails
Kids Menu: grilled chicken, pasta, prim rib, chicken tenders
Recommendations: Dine with characters from *Snow White and the Seven Dwarfs* in an enchanted setting! This fun-filled evening has characters from the classic animated film including Snow White, some of the Seven Dwarfs (usually Dopey and another), and the Evil Queen! Guests interact with these characters while they dine under twinkling indoor trees. The meal is served in courses and we recommend the entree Brother's Grimm Roasted Chicken (served with herb-crusted potatoes and squash).

WHISPERING CANYON CAFE
Description: American Dining with rowdy waiters! The Whispering Canyon Cafe has quieted down in contrast to its early years.
Type: Table Service
Price: $$$ / **Dining Plan:** Yes
Menu Items:
Breakfast: all-you-can-eat skillets, omelets, benedicts, eggs, waffles, pancakes, breakfast sides, juice, tea, coffee
Kids Breakfast: all-you-can-at skillets, omelets, Mickey waffles, breakfast sides
Lunch & Dinner: nachos, all-you-can-eat skillets, sandwiches, burgers, salad, desserts, cocktails, wines, beers, soda pop, juice
Kids Lunch & Dinner: all-you-can-eat skillets, quesadilla, cheeseburger, chicken nuggets, mac and cheese, fish
Recommendation: All-You-Care-To-Enjoy Skillet

MORE DINING

- **‡ Roaring Fork** – $ / Dining Plan: Yes / Quick-Service breakfast and sandwiches
- **Territory Lounge** – $$ / Dining Plan: No / Bar and Lounge / Recommendation: Great for adults
- **Trout Pass Pool Bar** – $ / Dining Plan: No / Pool Bar

DOLPHIN AND SWAN

Note: Disney Dining Plans are not accepted at these hotels.

THE FOUNTAIN
Description: American Dining
Type: Table Service
Price: $$$ / **Location:** Dolphin
Menu Items:
Breakfast and Brunch: fruit, pastries, eggs, breakfast pizza, Mickey waffles, cheese grits, carving station, soup, chili, fried chicken, desserts, bacon, sausage, coffee, tea, milk, juices
Lunch & Dinner: chicken breast, shrimp, salad, flatbread, sandwiches, chicken and waffles, steak, grits, assorted desserts, beer
Kids Lunch & Dinner: baked chicken, grilled salmon, cheeseburger, macaroni and cheese, chicken nuggets, grilled cheese
Recommendations: We're not very impressed with this menu. For the price, you may as well boat over to Disney's BoardWalk.

FRESH MEDITERRANEAN MARKET
Description: American and Mediterranean Dining
Type: Table Service / **Location:** Dolphin
Price: $$$
Menu Items:
Breakfast and Brunch: French toast, grits, eggs, cereal, yogurt, pancakes, omelets, bacon, sausage, coffee, tea, milk, juices, breakfast mixed drinks
Lunch: salads, wine
Recommendations: "Monkey Puzzle" French Toast

GARDEN GROVE
Description: American and Seafood Dining
Type: Character Dining

Price: $$$ / **Location:** Swan
Menu Items: clam chowder, soups, salads, meat and seafood buffet, assorted desserts, soda pop, wine, sangria, beer
Kids Menu: pasta, fish tacos, chicken fingers, turkey sliders, tuna salad sandwich, Margherita pizza
Recommendation: Dinner Buffet

IL MULINO
Description: Italian Restaurant / **Type:** Table Service
Price: $$$ / **Location:** Swan
Menu Items: shrimp, calamari, steaks, mussels, clams, insalate, beef, soup, pizza, risotto, pasta, fish, assorted desserts, soda pop, wine, sangria, beer
Kids Menu: pizzas, fettuccini alfredo
Recommendation: Rustica Pizza

KIMONOS ❤
Description: Sushi Bar with Karaoke / **Type:** Table Service
Price: $$$ / **Location:** Swan
Menu Items: sushi, salad, kimchee, tempura, miso soup
Recommendations: The best sushi in Orlando—and a great place to sing some karaoke in the evenings. Try the Gyoza or Tempura Platter and a Shrimp Tempura Roll for the entrée.

SHULA'S STEAK HOUSE
Description: American Steakhouse designed to celebrate the Miami Dolphins football team.
Type: Fine Dining
Price: $$$$ / **Location:** Dolphin
Menu Items: steak, seafood, soup, salad, mashed potatoes, vegetables, assorted desserts, wines, soda pop
Kids Menu: chicken, cheeseburger
Recommendation: Try any of their savory steaks.

TODD ENGLISH'S BLUEZOO
Description: Stylish Seafood Restaurant
Type: Fine Dining
Price: $$$$ / **Location:** Dolphin
Menu Items: fish, steak, chicken, lobster, Bolognese, fries, vegetables, assorted desserts, soda pop, cocktails, wines, cider, beer
Kids Menu: beef tenderloin, chicken, fish fillets, spaghetti, cheese pizza, clam chowder, shrimp

Recommendations: Maine Lobster Pot Pie, Lobster Broccoli Stuffed Cheddar Potato

MORE DINING (SWAN)
- **Il Mulino Lounge** – $$$ / Type: Lounge
- **Java Bar** – $$ / Type: Lounge
- **Kimonos Lounge** – $$ / Type: Lounge
- **Splash** – $$ / Type: Quick-Service / Menu: wraps, burgers, pizza

MORE DINING (DOLPHIN)
- **Todd English bluezoo Lounge** – $$ / Type: Lounge / Menu: burgers and nachos
- **Cabana Bar and Beach Club** – $ / Type: Poolside tacos and salads
- **Lobby Lounge** – $ / Type: Lounge
- **Picabu** – $$ / Type: Quick-Service / Menu: American Favorites
- **Shula's Lounge** – $$ / Type: Lounge

> **· Magic Tips ·**
> Guests can order pizza to their resort from popular chains like Pizza Hut and Dominos. However, you'll need to meet the delivery person in the lobby.

DINING OUT

Disney Springs and Disney's BoardWalk have several delicious dining options. Their spaces are ever-evolving, so we've included the best choices.

DISNEY SPRINGS

THE BOATHOUSE ❤
Description: American Seafood Dining
Type: Table Service
Price: $$$ / **Dining Plan:** Yes

Menu Items: steak, fish, lobster, shrimp, salad, burger, sandwiches, seafood small plates, fries, macaroni and cheese, cocktails, wines, beer, assorted desserts, soda pop
Kids Menu: fish, chicken, popcorn shrimp, pig in a blanket, cheese burger, macaroni and cheese, chicken tenders
Recommendations: We love the presentation of this restaurant. It's classy but fun and the food is fantastic. Their steaks are great and you can make a surf and turf combo by adding Main Lobster.

CHEF ART SMITH'S HOMECOMIN' ❤

Description: Southern Florida comfort food
Type: Table Service
Price: $$-$$$ / **Dining Plan:** Yes
Menu Items:
Brunch: biscuits, eggs, doughnuts, hush puppies, breakfast cocktails, bacon, coffee, tea, juice
Lunch & Dinner: fried chicken, fried catfish, pork chop, seafood, short rib, burgers, sandwiches, biscuits, moonshine, beers, cocktails, wines, soda pop, sweet tea
Kids Menu: quesadillas, tacos, enchiladas
Recommendations: One of the best restaurants in Walt Disney World! Come for lunch or dinner and try Art's Famous Fried Chicken (comes with the restaurant's signature cheddar drop biscuit) or the Fried Chicken & Doughnuts ❤

‡ CHICKEN GUY

Description: Chicken by celebrity chef Guy Fieri
Type: Quick-Service
Price: $ / **Dining Plan:** Yes
Menu Items: Chicken tenders, chicken sandwich, mac and cheese, salad bowls, shakes, soda, beer, some wines
Recommendations: It's all about the sauce! Try some of the Tenders with Special Sauce or Ranchero Sauce. Skip the mac and cheese.

CITY WORKS EATERY & POUR HOUSE

Description: American Food and Beer
Type: Table Service
Price: $$-$$$ / **Dining Plan:** Yes
Menu Items:
Brunch: French toast, hash, grits, eggs, salad, burger, wraps, sandwiches, bacon, sausage, fruit, bloody mary, mimosas, juice, tea, coffee, soda
Lunch & Dinner: burgers, wraps, salads, mac n cheese, ribs, rigatoni, pork chop, tacos, fries, cocktails, beer, wine, soda, juice, coffee, tea

Kids Menu: pizza, tacos, grilled cheese, mac and cheese, ribs, fish and chips, chicken sandwich
Recommendations: mac and cheese, tacos, or wraps

‡ D-LUXE BURGER ❤

Description: Burger Joint
Type: Quick-Service
Price: $ / **Dining Plan:** Yes
Menu Items: burgers, fries, macaron, soda pop, beer, wine, alcoholic sodas, shakes, floats
Kids Menu: cheeseburger, chicken burger
Recommendations: The burgers are some of best in Disney World. Try the Barbecue Classic Burger and a Red Velvet Burger Macaron for dessert.

EARL OF SANDWICH ❤

Description: Sandwich Shop
Type: Quick-Service
Price: $ / **Dining Plan:** Yes
Menu Items: hot sandwiches, soups, wraps, macaroni and cheese, salad, various desserts, soda pop, hot tea, coffee, wine, beer, hot chocolate, milk
Recommendation: The best hot sandwiches in all of Walt Disney World! We recommend The Holiday Turkey (tastes like Thanksgiving!) ❤

THE EDISON

Description: A gothic-style restaurant with American favorites
Type: Table Service
Price: $$ / **Dining Plan:** Yes
Menu Items: burgers, ribs, salmon, salad, desserts, wines, beer
Kids Menu: chicken tenders, burgers, grilled cheese
Recommendations: Organic Tomato Soup and Gooey Grilled Cheese sandwich

FRONTERA COCINA

Description: Mexican dishes crafted by celebrity chef Rick Bayless
Type: Table Service
Price: $$ / **Dining Plan:** Yes
Menu Items: tacos, carnitas, carne asada, enchiladas, tortas, queso, chips and guacamole, desserts, soda pop, margaritas, cocktails, sangria, tequila flights, wines, beer
Kids Menu: quesadillas, tacos, enchiladas
Recommendations: One of the enchiladas

· **Magic Tips** ·
Many restaurants in Disney Springs also use the Open Table app for reservations. Sometimes Open Table will have availability for seating when DisneyWorld.com does not. Cancellation policies are also more lenient with this app.

GIDEON'S BAKEHOUSE ❤

Description: A gothic-style cookie store
Type: Quick Service
Price: $$ / **Dining Plan:** No
Menu Items: gourmet cookies, cakes, cold brew, soda, milk
Recommendations: Original Chocolate Chip Cookie

JALEO ❤

Description: Tapas Restaurant and Lounge
Type: Signature Dining / Table Service
Price: $$$-$$$$ / **Dining Plan:** Yes
Menu Items: Spanish-style tapas, queso, cocktails, beers, wines, juice, tea, coffee, desserts
Kids Menu: tapas including chicken, fish, and pork
Recommendations: Jaleo is ideal for large parties, dates, and foodies. We highly recommend ordering off of the Chef's Tasting Menu for the full experience. These come with a series of tapas perfect for sharing!

MARIA & ENZO'S RISTORANTE

Description: Southern Italian Cuisine / **Type:** Table Service
Price: $ **Dining Plan:** Yes
Menu Items: pasta, salad, ricotta, parmigiana, steak, ahi tuna, Italian desserts
Kids Menu: pasta, chicken finger parmesan
Recommendations: Come hungry and order a three-course meal! Perfect for date nights. Try the Sicilian Lasagna.
Hideaway: Check out Enzo's Hideaway, a Prohibition-style speakeasy next to the restaurant. Adults can score some tasty drinks here!

MORIMOTO ASIA

Description: Modern Asian Cuisine
Type: Signature Dining / Table Service

Price: $$$ / **Dining Plan:** Yes
Menu Items: sushi, shrimp tempura, edamame, miso soup, salad, calamari, dumplings, egg rolls, noodles, fried rice, fish, vegetable dishes, assorted desserts, sake, cocktails, beer, wine
Kids Menu: macaroni and cheese, lo mein, orange chicken, menchi katsu, hot dogs, fried chicken
Recommendations: The sushi is great! We recommend the Shrimp Tempura roll and the Sake Sangria (21+). There are also less-expensive, to-go options at Morimoto Asia Street Food next door.

THE POLITE PIG ❤
Description: One of Disney Springs' best dining spots! New American BBQ favorites and beer with excellent service.
Type: Quick-Service
Price: $$ / **Dining Plan:** Yes
Menu Items: baby back ribs, chicken, salmon, sausage, brisket, sandwiches, salads, fries, macaroni and cheese, soda pop, beer, wine, bourbon
Kids Menu: chicken tenders, macaroni and cheese, pork slider, smoked chicken
Recommendations: Sweet Potato Tots, Crispy Brussels Sprouts, the Southern Pig (pulled pork sandwich)

RAGLAN ROAD
Description: Irish Pub and Restaurant often with live music
Type: Table Service
Price: $$-$$$ / **Dining Plan:** Yes
Menu Items: bangers and mash, shepherd's pie, burger, fish and chips, steak, chicken, salad, desserts, beer, whisky, wine
Kids Menu: chicken, fish, mac n cheese
Recommendations: Fish and Chips or Shepherd's Pie

T-REX
Description: Dinosaur-themed Restaurant
Type: Table Service
Price: $$$ / **Dining Plan:** Yes
Menu Items: nachos, quesadilla, salad, soup, burgers, sandwiches, shrimp, fish, fries, pasta, chicken, steak, various desserts, cocktails, beer, wine, soda pop
Kids Menu: grilled chicken, corn dog, sliders, popcorn shrimp, chicken nuggets, pork ribs, pasta, pizza, macaroni and cheese
Recommendations: Like the Rainforest Cafe, T-REX is more about the theme than the food. Kids will love it, but adults will find it just okay, and nothing to write home about. Still, it's worth seeing the

enormous dinosaurs and prehistoric scenery while you eat. Order a burger.

TERRALINA CRAFTED ITALIAN
Description: Home-cooked Italian
Type: Table Service
Price: $$$ / **Dining Plan:** No
Menu Items: antipasta, calamari, meatballs, salad, wood-fired pizza, sandwiches (crispy chicken, roasted pork, grilled vegetable), chicken, beef short rib, porchetta, pasta (wide variety), parmesan burger, swordfish peperonata, ribeye, pork chop, gelato, wines
Kids Menu: spaghetti, mac and cheese, chicken fingers, grilled chicken, hamburger, hot dog, grilled fish

MORE DISNEY SPRINGS DINING
- **AMC Disney Springs** ($$) – Eat dinner while you watch a movie!
- **AristoCrepes** ($) – Grab a gourmet crepe to go!
- **Blaze Fast-Fire'd Pizza** ($$) – Build your own pizza dinner
- **Coca-Cola Store Rooftop Beverage Bar** ($) – Try sodas and mixed drinks from around the world! Guests can also try the infamously bitter Italian soda, The Beverly!
- **The Daily Poutine** ($) – Fries with gravy and cheese curds!
- **Everglazed Donuts** ($) ❤ – Fan-favorite gourmet donuts!
- **Jock Lindsey's Hangar Bar** ($$) ❤ – An *Indiana Jones*-themed bar with tasty bites and plenty of specialty drinks!
- **Pizza Point** ($-$$) – Delicious pizza slices and sandwiches.
- **Paradiso 37** ($$) – While the outside looks fun and inviting, the Latin American food is less than savory and the seating is very close together.
- **Sprinkles** ($) – Delicious cupcakes! Get their famous Red Velvet Cupcake.

DISNEY'S BOARDWALK

FLYING FISH ❤
Description: American Seafood Dining
Type: Fine Dining
Dress Code: Business casual / cocktail attire
Price: $$$$ / **Dining Plan:** Yes
Menu Items: fish, crab, salad, steak, chicken, shellfish, assorted desserts, specialty cocktails, wine, beer, cider

Kids Menu: fish, chicken breast, pasta
Recommendations: Easily one of the Walt Disney World Resort's best and well-themed dining experiences. There aren't as many options for kids, but adults will love this seafood culinary experience.

TRATTORIA AL FORNO
Description: Old World Italian
Type: Table Service and Character Breakfast
Price: $$$ / **Dining Plan:** Yes
Menu Items:
Breakfast: Buffet with breakfast calzone, eggs, pastries, pancakes, frittata, cheese torte, omelets, and kids' items
Dinner: pizza, steak, gnocchi, pasta, salad, calamari, mussels
Kids Menu: pasta with meatballs, pizza, and steak
Recommendation: Character dining at the Bon Voyage Adventure Breakfast to meet Rapunzel!

MORE DINING

- **AbracadaBar** – $$ / Dining Plan: No / Lounge / Recommendation: Try one of several delicious mixed drinks, beers, or wines. There are also non-alcoholic choices for kids.
- **Boardwalk Ice Cream** ($-$$) – Ice cream and an assortment of delicious sundaes.
- **Boardwalk Joe's Marvelous Margaritas** ($-$$) – Delicious margaritas and other tropical drinks.
- **Belle Vue Lounge** – $$ / Dining Plan: Yes / Quick-Service
- **Funnel Cake Cart** ($) – Try one of Walt Disney World's famous funnel cakes. They are fried and dusted with powdered sugar to perfection.
- **Leaping Horse Libations** ($$) – Dining Plan: Yes / Quick-Service
- **Pizza Window** ($) – Dining Plan: Yes / Quick-Service / Recommendation: Grab a full-sized pizza here

FOUR SEASONS ORLANDO

CAPA
Description: Stylish steakhouse and bar
Type: Fine Dining / Lounge
Dress Code: Business casual / cocktail attire
Price: $$$$ / **Dining Plan:** No
Menu Items: steak, tapas, sushi, pork chop, lobster, seafood, cocktails, beer, wine, soda, juice, desserts

Kids Menu: chicken fingers, steak, mac and cheese, grilled cheese
Recommendations: You don't need to be a guest at the Four Seasons to enjoy this fine dining experience. The steaks and seafood at Capa are highly recommended.

> **· Magic Tips ·**
> Capa has a great view of the Magic Kingdom fireworks! They are a bit far away, but you'll have an excellent view of the resort from the rooftop.

VISITING WITH KIDS

INTRODUCTION

If you're planning a vacation to Walt Disney World, there's a huge chance that you'll be visiting with children (if not, you might want to skip this chapter and head straight to the next one). Walt Disney World feels like a haven for families with kids—and, for the most part, it is! There are hundreds of attractions, dozens of Disney-themed places to stay, pools with waterslides, and, of course, the enchanting magic of the parks.

If your kids know that they're visiting Disney World, they are likely bursting at the seams and counting down the days. After all, it's one of the happiest places they can be! That's not to assume there won't be a snag or two... or *six* on your vacation. Kids have their limitations, even on fun. Unfortunately for adults, the not-so-fun times can be difficult to deal with outside of the home. Fortunately, however, there are ways that you can limit the problems and also cut them short when they arise.

We haven't forgotten the tweens and teens! This chapter covers their favorites as well. Maybe you're looking for the best places to stay, eat, or play—we've got it covered. Now we'll review the best of everything designed for kids of all ages at Walt Disney World.

TIPS FOR VISITING WITH KIDS

1. **Get to the Theme Parks Early** – This may be the most valuable piece of information that we can give you when traveling to the Walt Disney World theme parks. Kids aren't fans of long lines (but who is?), and the best way to keep them happy is to avoid waiting. Getting to the parks early on will help you.

2. **Don't Over-Do It** – Kids get tired. Ride after ride. Show after show. From morning until night. The Young Kids likely won't make it and the Teens will be groaning for some pool time. Plan for about 4-5 hours on the rides with Kids and Young Kids (Tweens and Teens can generally last longer). After that, take a break and see what everyone is in the mood for afterward. We also recommend spacing out your days. If you know that everyone loves the Magic Kingdom Park and Epcot is not as important, get a Park Hopper and return to the Magic Kingdom later in your trip for more of what they love.

3. **Take Breaks** – In order to not "over-do it" you'll need to take breaks. Plan to head back to the hotel for lunch or right after. Keep them cool, hydrated, and ready for more once their batteries have charged. It's common to walk up to 12 miles a day in a single park! After all that walking, both you and the kids might be craving naps.

4. **Have Backup Plans** – Bad weather or tantrums can wreck an otherwise perfect day. Plan to have something else fun to do. Maybe bring a board game for the hotel room or change your time slot for lunch or dinner. Like temper tantrums, Florida showers tend to last under a half hour, but if you're faced with longer poor weather or fits, having a backup is a lifesaver.

5. **Consider Giving *Yourself* a Break** – In a perfect world, being around our kids 24/7 would bring us endless joy. However, this is not a perfect world. We invite you to review our next chapter that's all about adults. It'll give you tips on what to do with your kids while you save some time for the spa, dining out, or just visiting the parks without them.

BABIES & TODDLERS

We hear a lot of parents asking if they should bring their baby to Walt Disney World. The answer is YES! Many parents love bringing their babies to the parks! You're bringing your baby to the Resort, here is a list of what to bring, need to know, and all about the Baby Care Centers.

WHAT TO BRING

- **Stroller** – Kids can get tired and Walt Disney World has zones to park strollers with attendants that watch them while you ride. All strollers must be within the limits of 31" (79cm) wide and 52" (132cm) long. Rental locations are near the entrance of the theme parks and start at $15 a day ($13/day for longer stays). Double Strollers are also available for $31 a day or $27 for multi-day lengths. Stroller parks are located around many of the kid-friendly areas. Cast Members patrol these areas for safety.
- **Protection from the Sun** – We recommend sunscreen, hats, blankets, and a covered stroller to keep your little one comfortable.
- **Blankets and Warm Clothes** – These items are essential for cooler days (or at night when the temperatures drop).
- **Diapers, Wipes, and a Change of Clothes** – Just in case of a mess, a change of clothes can be a lifesaver.
- **Bottles and Formula** – Don't forget the liners!
- **Baby Food** – Walt Disney World will allow small glass jars as long as they contain baby food.
- **Backpack** – Carry your baby's necessities in the bag. We also recommend a backpack that you can easily hook onto a stroller.

> **· Magic Tips ·**
> If you're unable to travel with a stroller or other items, it may be best to order them. Target and Amazon sell single and double strollers at a fraction of the rental cost. Have one delivered to your hotel room or purchase one at a nearby Target store. You can get other necessary supplies this way, too!

BABY CARE CENTERS

Just in case you forget something, the Walt Disney World Resort parks are equipped with nannies that are there to help. They offer nursing rooms, rocking chairs, changing tables, highchairs for feeding, a microwave, and fresh water. You can also purchase items like clothing, medications (over-the-counter), formula, baby food, diapers, and wipes.

LOCATIONS
Magic Kingdom Park – Next to First Aid, between Main Street, U.S.A. and Adventureland
Epcot – In the World Showcase, at the Odyssey Center building, next to the Mexican Pavilion

Disney's Hollywood Studios – Hollywood Boulevard, to the left as you enter through the main gate
Disney's Animal Kingdom – Discovery Island, near the bridge to Africa
Changing Rooms – These are found in most restrooms (men and women)
Breastfeeding – Feeding your baby is a top priority and you shouldn't be nervous to do so at Walt Disney World. If you want privacy (or quiet), head to the Baby Care Centers in the parks.
First Aid – Located next to the Baby Care Center in the Magic Kingdom on Main Street, U.S.A.

ATTRACTIONS WITH BABIES & TODDLERS
- **See a Show or Parade** – With wonderful music and dancing characters, your baby or toddler will be delighted. Check the map for a schedule of shows and parades.
- **Space Out Rides** – Space out rides and times waiting in line for simple joys like looking at the baby ducks in the many ponds or eating a snack under some shade.

RIDER SWITCH

Do you have a Young Kid with you, but all of the adults in your party want to ride? Many Walt Disney World Resort rides give you the option to wait and switch places when finished. This especially helps when a kid turns out not to be tall enough to ride or they become too scared. To use the Rider Switch, ask a Cast Member at the start of the queue. You will be assigned a Rider Switch pass and moved to a special area as people from your party ride the attraction.

ATTRACTIONS WITH RIDER SWITCH

Magic Kingdom Park
- The Barnstormer
- Big Thunder Mountain Railroad
- Space Mountain
- Splash Mountain
- Tomorrowland Speedway

Epcot
- Frozen Ever After
- Mission: SPACE
- Soarin'
- Test Track

Disney's Hollywood Studios
- Rock 'n' Roller Coaster Starring Aerosmith
- Star Tours – The Adventures Continue
- The Twilight Zone Tower of Terror
- Millennium Falcon: Smugglers Run

Disney's Animal Kingdom Park
- Avatar Flight of Passage
- DINOSAUR
- Expedition Everest
- Kali River Rapids

KIDS AGES 3-9

Taking Kids this age is fun because their excitement is unparalleled. They will be *itching* to ride attractions, see parades, and meet their favorite characters. You'll be busy keeping them busy, but planning everything ahead is what makes things go a lot smoother.

1. **Make Time for the Pool** – One of the best vacation memories for kids will likely be the hotel pool. A couple of hours in the pool can be the recharge that everyone needs. If you're staying for a while, you may want to reserve an entire day for the pool.

2. **Budget to Shop** – Kids love to buy things at the parks. Disney knows this so they place gift shops with dazzling trinkets *everywhere*. Sometimes getting pre-filled Disney gift cards is the best way to go. Your kids can manage their own budget without expecting you to fork out more money. This will save you a lot of no's and negotiating.

3. **Book Character Dining** – If your kids are going to want to meet characters, there's no better way. These are buffets where characters hang out, take pictures, sign autographs, and joke around with your family. A dozen characters can show up to a Character breakfast. We recommend booking one of these experiences early in your trip so that the kids are burnt out on attempting to get autographs. This will save you *tons* of time waiting in long lines for character meetups in the parks.

· **Magic Tips** ·

If you're staying at a Walt Disney World Resort hotel, select a character wake up call! These are phone calls by Disney characters (usually Mickey) that kids will love to hear from in the morning. Character calls are free and can be accessed from a button on hotel room phones.

TWEENS AGES 10-12

Tweens can be both a very fun and very challenging group to visit Walt Disney World with. They call them "Tweens" because they're in between being a Kid and a Teen. Because of this, you might be dealing with an array of emotions. They might want to be a diehard

Frozen fan with you as well as be in a "leave me alone" mood, all at the same time. There are ways to avoid the latter. Here are a few tips to planning a trip with Tweens:

1. **Plan with Them** – You'll need to make the final choices, but ask your Tween what their interests are. Which Parks are most important? What rides are they itching to jump on? Do the water parks sound fun to them? If you're having trouble picking a hotel, you might also narrow it down to a few and have your Tween help you decide. They are often very good at expressing themselves emotionally and logically. That's the perfect combination for planning a trip to Walt Disney World!

2. **Tween-Only Time** – It's completely up to you, but you might opt to let your Tween explore in a group. A group of responsible thirteen year olds can often explore the water parks and some of the parks by themselves. You're the adult, so you set the rules. Maybe give them a few hours alone. Check in with them on a phone. Have them meet you promptly at a certain location. They'll be happy they had their independence and extremely excited to share their experiences with you. Also keep in mind that not every Tween will want to go off on his or her own. Sometimes you are their comfort zone. In that case, embrace it, and take turns picking the rides.

3. **Try Something New** – If you've been to the parks before with your Tweens, maybe it's time for them to try something you like. Have them explore the foods of Epcot with you or sit and watch a fireworks display. They'll appreciate you treating them as older, even though you also allow them to be a kid at the resort.

TEENS AGES 13-17

We recommend all of the Tween activities for Teens as well. Because Teens are much more decisive and independent, they'll often want more wiggle room to be themselves. There are a few other options that Teens will crave:

1. **Get Some Sleep** – Don't plan early with Teens. Most of the time, they'd rather be at the theme parks until closing and not have a bright and early agenda.

2. **Disney Springs** – Shopping at Disney Springs is a blast for Teens. There are so many amazing stores for them to look at, clothes to try on, and unique items to buy. Teens will also love the movie theatre with dine-in seating.

3. **The Spa** – Perhaps have a mother/daughter or father/son spa day. Take them out for their first bit of relaxation at the spa. Being pampered can sometimes feel very adult and like a rite of passage. Let them indulge with you! The Grand Floridian and Saratoga Springs resorts both have spas. You don't need to stay there to book.

4. **Caring for Giants** (Animal Kingdom admission required) – Go beyond the atmosphere of a zoo with this up-close encounter with elephants at Animal Kingdom! This 1-hour experience shows you how the elephants are cared for at the park. It's an unforgettable and breathtaking opportunity that animal-loving teens will never forget. Reserve over the phone for $30 / person: (407) 939-7529

5. **Time for Selfies** – While vacations are a great time for families to relax and enjoy each other's company, individual expression shouldn't be ignored. If your teen wants to take a selfie—or *ten*— we recommend being supportive of this. For many teens, sharing their vacation updates with friends is all part of the fun! Of course, while excessive selfies are never a healthy choice, the right amount of sharing will make your teen feel more appreciative of the trip.

6. **Disney Genie** – Allow your teen to be in control of the Disney Genie for a day. They might love using a phone to find out the lowest wait times and other tips. You may also consider splurging on a day with Genie+ as an option. Allow your teen to book the next Lightning Lane slot and plan out the day based on their interests.

CHAPTER SEVENTEEN

WALT DISNEY WORLD FOR ADULTS

INTRODUCTION

The Walt Disney World Resort may have been originally built with families in mind, but that doesn't mean it hasn't also become an adult retreat. After all, Walt Disney himself was an adult when he came up with the idea for the parks, and he knew that also the kids at heart would come there for enjoyment.

Over the decades, Walt Disney World has done a fantastic job catering to adults. With the previous Pleasure Island in the former Downtown Disney, they created an adult playground with sweeping sights and delicious food and beverages. They've since revamped it with Disney Springs, and the adult-aimed entertainment has never been better. With bountiful places to shop and eat all around the resort, adults have an abundance of choices. From dive bars to thrill rides to fine-dining and golf courses, the Walt Disney World Resort has something for every grown-up. In this section, we outline adult activities from the best places to drink to avoiding families with children.

PARENTS' EVENING OUT

If you're an adult with children, part of your perfect Walt Disney World Resort vacation might be a night without them. If you're interested in heading back to the parks, many are often open until midnight. Our top choice is Epcot for its beautiful views, fine dining, and variety of adult beverages. Then again, you might just feel like hitting the parks late at night, utilizing those extended park hours for Magic Kingdom.

Whatever you choose to do with your time, there are great options for kids without their parents inside the resort. We recommend planning the night ahead of time to ensure you have an easy transition into your night alone.

CHILDREN'S CENTERS

A place just for kids—without the parents! Kids make arts and crafts, watch movies, and eat while parents can enjoy an evening at the resort. This is a perfect time for your kids to make new friends as they enjoy Disney-themed fun under the supervision of Disney's professional caregivers. Guests don't have to stay at that particular hotel to book:

REQUIREMENTS:
1. Make a reservation in advance.
2. Your child must be potty-trained (without using pull-up diapers).

BEACH CLUB RESORT
Captain Hook's Pirate Crew
A dinner event for kids with Captain Hook! They'll learn to act like a pirate before dining on pasta and dessert.
Location & Hours: Seaside Retreat in Beach Club / 5:00pm – 8:30pm
Cost: $55 flat rate per child (ages 4-12 years old). Dinner is included with this cost.
Reservations: (407) 824-5437

> · **Magic Tips** ·
> Some Children's Centers and activities may be unavailable in 2022.

DOLPHIN HOTEL
Camp Dolphin
This might be our least favorite because of the fewer activities, but older kids might enjoy their Xbox 360. For just a couple of hours, it's perfect for any kid.
Location: On the first floor of the Dolphin hotel
Hours: 5pm – Midnight
Ages: 4 - 12

Cost: $12/hour per child. You can get 2 hours free if you book a spa package at the Mandara Spa or a dining reservation at Shula's Steak House, Todd English's bluezoo, or Mulino New York Trattoria. Dinner is an additional $10 per child.
Reservations (required): (407) 934-4241

BABYSITTERS

The Walt Disney World works with a third-party service for babysitting. This service is call Kid's Nite Out and it's perfect if you'd rather have a babysitter in the room than take your child to an Activity Center.

SERVICES
- Professional assistance in-room.
- Professional assistance at the parks. If you desire, the babysitter will accompany your family around the resort.
- Provides for Kids ages 6 months to 12 years old.
- Offers arts and crafts, bedtime reading, and games to play.

RATES
- Per hour: 1 Child - $18 / 2 Children - $21 / 3 Children - $24 / 4 Children - $26
- An extra $2 per hour charge occurs for every hour after 9pm.
- $10 babysitter travel fee (one-time only)

Reservations: (800) 696-8105
Website: http://www.kidsniteout.com

TOP ADULT DINING & BARS

If you're looking for an evening out, there are plenty of choices around the Walt Disney World Resort. However, you might have a difficult choice deciding. Should you just stay at your hotel? Should you go off-property? Maybe you just want to try something different, but don't know where to begin. In this section, we review all of the best bars, restaurants, and activities that we highly recommend for adults looking for a delicious evening by themselves.

1.   **TRADER SAM'S GROG GROTTO**
      Location: Disney's Polynesian Village Resort
      Theme: Island-themed tiki bar inspired by the character in the Jungle Cruise ride
      Price: $$ / Dining Plan: No

Why We Recommend It: Dim lighting, air conditioning, and scraggly bartenders serve excellent drinks and bar food in this unique setting. Try a specialty cocktail or order a beer on draft. Certain drinks cause the room's volcanoes to erupt or a storm to brew! Trader Sam's is also known for its excellent tacos. After 8pm, Trader Sam's is 21 and older only.

2. **TEPPAN EDO**
   Location: Epcot World Showcase, Japan
   Theme: Teppanyaki grill with live chefs
   Price: $$$ / Dining Plan: Yes
   Why We Recommend It: Very similar to Benihana. Watch talented Japanese chefs make your choice of course right before your eyes! They are like ninjas with their knives and create delicious masterpieces on a hot grill. If you've never been to a Teppanyaki-style restaurant, you can't miss this one!

3. **VICTORIA & ALBERT'S**
   Location: Disney's Grand Floridian Resort
   Theme: Elegant, Victorian-style fine dining
   Price: $$$$ / **Dining Plan:** Yes
   Why We Recommend It: A 5-Diamond culinary experience. If you're craving a perfectly prepared meal for a special occasion, look no further than Victoria and Albert's.
   Dress Code: This restaurant is only open for dinner and has a strict dress code. It's required for men to wear dinner jackets, slacks, and shoes. Women must wear a dress, pant suit, or skirt and blouse.

4. **CALIFORNIA GRILL**
   Location: Disney's Contemporary Resort
   Theme: California upscale restaurant atop Disney's Contemporary Resort tower
   Price: $$$$ / **Dining Plan:** Yes
   Why We Recommend It: Some of the best sushi, steaks, and drinks on property!
   Dress Code: This has a "business casual" dress code.

5. **KIMONOS**
   Location: Walt Disney World Swan Hotel
   Theme: Freshly made sushi house
   Price: $$ / **Dining Plan:** No
   Why We Recommend It: The best sushi and sake in Orlando! At night, Kimonos offers karaoke and hosts a sake bar.

6. **JIKO**
   Location: Disney's Animal Kingdom Lodge
   Theme: African cuisine
   Price: $$$$ / **Dining Plan:** Yes
   Why We Recommend It: Get a taste for Africa in a unique, wild setting. Try an African wine or specially marinated chicken or vegetables. When you're done eating, you can roam the hotel and see some of the exotic animals on site.
   Dress Code: This restaurant is only open for dinner and has a dress code, though it's not as strict as Victoria & Albert's. It's requested that men wear collared shirts, slacks or jeans, and close-toed shoes. Women may wear a dress, jeans or capris, dress shorts or skirts. Dinner jackets are not required. Hats, tank tops, swimming gear, and cut-off clothing are not permitted.

7. **ROSE & CROWN DINING ROOM**
   Location: Epcot World Showcase, United Kingdom
   Theme: British Pub
   Price: $$$ / **Dining Plan:** Yes, but not for alcohol
   Why We Recommend It: A cool environment with great beer, cocktails, and tasty fish and chips. Book a reservation to see the Epcot fireworks from the patio.

8. **LA CAVA DEL TEQUILA** – Epcot World Showcase, Mexico
   Theme: Tequila cellar with authentic Mexican flare
   Price: $$ / **Dining Plan:** No
   Why We Recommend It: Dim lighting, air conditioning, and delicious margaritas! Need we say more?

9. **ENZO'S HIDEAWAY** – Disney Springs
   Theme: Prohibition-Era Speakeasy
   Price: $$ / **Dining Plan:** Yes
   Why We Recommend It: Head underground for this surprising, rustic bar. It's a lot of fun "discovering" Enzo's Hideaway before you dine on light bites and drink cocktails.

10. **YACHTSMAN STEAKHOUSE**
    Location: Yacht Club Resort
    Theme: New England steakhouse
    Price: $$$$ / **Dining Plan:** Yes
    Why We Recommend It: Savory steaks and wines made better here than anywhere else in Walt Disney World.

Dress Code: This restaurant is only open for dinner and has a "business casual" dress code.

11. **JOCK LINDSEY'S HANGAR BAR** – Disney Springs
    Theme: An *Indiana Jones*-themed bar set inside of an old 1940s airplane hangar.
    Price: $$ / **Dining Plan:** No
    Why We Recommend It: Open from the afternoon into the evening, this is a well-themed hangout for *Indiana Jones* fans. The drinks and bites are great, too!

12. **JELLYROLLS**
    Location: BoardWalk Resort
    Theme: Boardwalk-style dueling piano bar for those 21+
    Price: $$ / **Dining Plan:** No
    Why We Recommend It: If you are into loud, fun piano music, this is the place to be. Everyone laughs and sings along to the performers.

UNIQUE FINE DINING

HIGHWAY IN THE SKY DINE AROUND
Theme: Unique monorail dining experience for adults 21+
Price: $170 per person / **Dining Plan:** No
Why We Recommend It: If you're craving something different, adventurous, romantic, and unforgettable, look no further than Highway in the Sky! Check in at the Contemporary hotel and hop aboard Disney's monorail system to start your tasting journey. You'll be served 5 courses in several different locations like the Grand Floridian and Polynesian. The menu varies but is filled with American-fusion cuisine and alcoholic beverages to please the most discerning tastebuds!
Reservations Required: disneyworld.disney.go.com/dining/contemporary-resort/highway-in-the-sky-dine-around/

AVOIDING CHILDREN

It's impossible to absolutely avoid *all* children at the Walt Disney World Resort. But you can avoid being around the bulk of them.

We've listed some great tips on how to stay clear of families with small children at the Resort.

RESORTS WITH THE FEWEST CHILDREN

1. **Disney's Grand Floridian Resort** – It's expensive, so many families won't want to spend their budget on this.
2. **Disney's Yacht Club** – Families typically prefer Beach Club, so the Yacht Club pools generally remain kid-free.
3. **Coronado Springs** – Not our favorite hotel, but on a budget, this is a great choice to avoid kids.

MORE TIPS

1. **The Right Place, the Right Time** – No one under 21 is allowed in Trader Sam's after 8pm. Jelly Rolls is also 21+ only.
2. **Stick to Epcot's World Showcase** – You'll have plenty of adult activities that will simply bore children.
3. **Avoid the Water Parks** – These are often wall-to-wall with families with kids.
4. **Stay Away from Pools with Water Slides** – Even at night the children play in these. The simple pools without water slides have by far the fewest children.
5. **Avoid "Kids Lands"** – Fantasyland in the Magic Kingdom Park, Toy Story Land in Hollywood Studios, and Rafiki's Planet Watch in Animal Kingdom are all spots filled with kid attractions. Avoid them.
6. **Ride the Thrills** – Attractions with height requirements will weed out the littlest ones.
7. **Go at Night** – The parks are often open late during the peak seasons of summer and winter. It'll be less common to see children at those times.
8. **Avoid Parades and Shows** – These attractions are like magnets for small children. You've been warned! Instead, plan to ride attractions during the shows and parades to avoid the families with children.
9. **Dine at a Bar** – Pick from one of the places we've mention in the previous section of this chapter.
10. **Forget the Characters** – You might be *dying* to meet Ariel from *The Little Mermaid*, but if you're looking to avoid the kids, you'll have to make some sacrifices. Bye, Ariel!

ADULT EXPERIENCES

1. **Get a Massage** – Traveling can be stressful. Navigating around the parks can be stressful. Dealing with your kids... well, you get it. Take some time for yourself and schedule a massage with your resort hotel. They are world-class and unforgettable:

    + Animal Kingdom Lodge – Zahanati Massage & Fitness Center
    + BoardWalk Villas – Muscles & Bustles Health Club
    + Contemporary Resort – Olympiad Fitness Center
    + Coronado Springs – La Vida Health Club
    + Dolphin Hotel – Mandara Spa
    + Saratoga Springs – Senses
    + Wilderness Lodge Villas – Sturdy Branches
    + Yacht Club – Ship Shape Massage Salon
    Mandara Spa Reservations: (407) 934-4772
    Reservations for all other Spas: (407) 939-7727

2. **See a Concert** – The House of Blues in Disney Springs offers a wide variety of live music shows. We always recommend pre-booking tickets for these events: houseofblues.com/orlando

3. **Catch a Movie** – AMC Disney Springs 24 offers a wide selection of films. They also have an amazing Dine-In experience where you can sit and eat while you watch a movie. We highly recommend the two-story Dolby Cinema showings with enhanced sound, reserved seating, and comfortable loungers. We recommend booking on the lower level for the best views of the screen. Showtimes and purchase: **www.amctheatres.com**.

4. **Golf** – Walt Disney World has some world-class golfing at Saratoga Springs!

5. **Go Shopping** – Disney Springs is home to 100 shops you can explore during the afternoon and early evening.

NON-RIDER GUIDE

INTRODUCTION

Typically, the first thing that comes to mind when people think about Walt Disney World is Mickey Mouse. The second thought is usually the rides that fill the Resort's parks. But what if you or your guest don't enjoy the drops, turns, and twists? Are there things for you to do? Would you enjoy yourself? Would it be worth the money to plan a vacation around a set of theme parks? In short, is the Walt Disney World Resort for you?

The answer is *yes*! There are about 150 attractions all around the Walt Disney World Resort—and the best part for non-riders is that most of them aren't rides. These attractions are found in every park, whether you'd like to see exotic tigers in Disney's Animal Kingdom, watch a stunning fireworks display at the Magic Kingdom, see a Broadway-style musical at Disney's Hollywood Studios, sunbathe at the water parks, or sample an array of worldly cuisine at Epcot.

In this chapter, we explore the dozens of options in each park and give non-riders the opportunity to discover the best that Walt Disney World has to offer without the craze of the heart-racing rides.

TOP RECOMMENDATIONS

1. **Photograph the Sights** – The Walt Disney World Resort is truly a feast for the eyes. The parks offer intricate architecture, well-planned lands, and lush, meticulously manicured foliage. There are unlimited things to take photos of!

2. **Try Gourmet Food** – Dazzle your senses with savory meals and sweet treats all around the parks, hotels, and Disney Springs. Epcot offers some of the best samplings from all over the globe!

3. **Meet Famous Characters** – Take a photo with your favorite Disney character.

4. **See a Music Group** – Watch one of the many musical bands playing around the park. We recommend seeing the barbershop quartet, the Dapper Dans, on Main Street in the Magic Kingdom Park.

5. **Hop on a Slow Ride** – Some rides don't have drops or move fast, many of them can be perfect for your speed as you experience the magnificent stories these rides have to offer. Epcot has over a dozen slow-moving boat rides perfect for everyone.

6. **See Stunning Shows** – The Walt Disney World Resort is known for magnificent shows. Every park has a huge list of attractions.

MOST RECOMMENDED SHOWS (in order):

1. Festival of the Lion King (Animal Kingdom)
2. *Finding Nemo* – The Musical (Animal Kingdom)
3. Magic Kingdom Fireworks (Magic Kingdom)
4. Fantasmic! (Hollywood Studios)
5. Indiana Jones Stunt Spectacular! (Hollywood Studios)

BEST SLOW RIDES AND OTHER ATTRACTIONS (not in order):

✦   **Epcot** – This theme park is *filled* with slow-moving rides. Journey into Imagination with Figment is a great start, especially for kids.

- **Jungle Cruise** (Magic Kingdom) – A humorous tour guide takes you on a riverboat through the Amazon and Africa.
- **Peter Pan's Flight** (Magic Kingdom) – See the story of *Peter Pan* while flying in a slow-moving pirate ship.
- **The Little Mermaid – Ariel's Undersea Adventure** (Magic Kingdom) – a slow-moving "dark ride" that explores the story of Disney's *The Little Mermaid*.
- **Haunted Mansion** (Magic Kingdom) – A slow-moving dark ride through a haunted house. Might be too scary for Young Kids.
- **"it's a small world"** (Magic Kingdom) – The classic, slow-paced boat ride around the world.
- **Tomorrowland Transit Authority PeopleMover** (Magic Kingdom) – Another classic Walt Disney World attraction that travels slowly through Tomorrowland. It's also a great way to beat the heat!
- **The Walt Disney World Railroad** (Magic Kingdom) – Travel at a slow-paced speed around the Magic Kingdom.
- **Go Shopping** – There are stores on every corner of the Resort. Disney Springs is loaded with them. You can find gifts for yourself or souvenirs to being back home.
- **Get a Princess Makeover at the Bibbidi Bobbidi Boutique** – Perfect for kids who want to dress as their favorite Disney Princess. The Boutiques are located in Disney Springs, the Magic Kingdom Park, and the Grand Floridian Resort.
- **People Watch** – This will either sound fun or creepy to you, but Walt Disney World has some unique visitors in creative outfits and style. Or just sit by a ride like Splash Mountain in the Magic Kingdom Park and watch them plummet!
- **Look for Hidden Mickeys!** – We have a list of elusive, Mickey Mouse-shaped hidden marks found all over the resort. Read the Hidden Mickey chapter later in this guide.

MORE TO DO

The ESPN Wide World of Sports Complex – Get your game on in this massive 220-acre hub for athletics located in the Walt Disney World Resort, close to Disney's All-Star Resorts. There are baseball fields, softball diamonds, basketball courts, cross country courses, track and field, and so much more. The base fee for entry is $17.50 for Adults and $12.50 for Children ages 3-9.

For more information, visit: https://www.espnwwos.com

Disney Mini Golf – The Walt Disney World Resort is home to a few fantastic, Disney-themed mini golf courses. Not only are these inexpensive, but they are stunning. The price is $14.00 for adults and $12.00 for children ages 3-9. The golf courses include the magical Fantasia Gardens by the Walt Disney World Swan hotel and the snowy Winter Summerland near Blizzard Beach.

· **Magic Tips** ·
Some of these experiences, including the ESPN Wide World of Sports Complex, could remain closed for part of 2022.

Disney Golf – Disney has enormous golf courses located just outside the Magic Kingdom near the Grand Floridian and Disney's Polynesian Resort Village. There are strict dress codes and reservations are a must.
For more information, visit: http://golfwdw.com

EVEN MORE

Most of the hotels will come with volleyball, tennis, or basketball courts to play games. Many of the resorts based on water have fishing and boat rentals for extra fun. Always check out the Times Guide brochure when arriving to your hotel.

FINDING CHARACTERS

Disney is known for its iconic, heartwarming, and even villainous characters. That is why they bring them to life inside the Walt Disney World Resort. You can meet most of your favorite Disney characters throughout the parks and hotels. They are always happy to sign autographs, interact, and take a photo with guests. Aren't sure if you should meet a character? We recommend it! After getting a hug from Mickey, Goofy, or a Disney Princess, people of all ages will get a smile that won't go away! Sadly, not every character comes out each day. Here, we offer some invaluable tips to easily find your favorite characters.

HOW TO EASILY FIND CHARACTERS

1. **Get the App** – Download the Walt Disney World App on your mobile device to track the characters! Simply search by park or character name to find them.
2. **Grab a Map** – Many of the characters have "show times" in certain locations. Be sure to check the character times on the park maps early in the day.
3. **Book a Character Dining Buffet** – The Resort parks and hotels have many characters who will interact with you while you eat. Sometimes you can meet 6 or more in one meal!
4. **Pick the Perfect Dining Spot** – If you are looking to meet several Disney Princesses, get a reservation at the Akershus Royal Banquet Hall in Epcot.
5. **Keep Your Eyes Peeled** – You may also see Disney characters unexpectedly walking around the parks, and in the shows and parades.

MORE TIPS

1. Kids will love the character autograph books sold on Main Street.
2. During the holidays, characters are often dressed in seasonal outfits (Halloween, Christmas, and other special days).
3. If you love villains, come during Halloween (mid-August through October 31st) to see more of them roaming the parks. You can also take photos with them in several character meeting spots!
4. Sadly, not every character comes out each day—though one of your favorites is sure to be there!

· **Magic Tips** ·
Character experiences may be modified in 2022. Meaning, you may be able to pose for a photo but not receive a hug or an autograph.

CHAPTER NINETEEN

HIDDEN MICKEY LOCATIONS

INTRODUCTION

You know that famous logo of the Mickey ears? It's just three circles; a large one for the face and two smaller ones for the ears. Well, these show up *everywhere* from the bubbles while Cinderella scrubbed the floors during her labors to a quick scene where Jasmine's pet tiger, Raja, changes briefly into a Mickey-like head. Even *Frozen* has a Mickey doll in a bookcase in one of the scenes.

But like we said, Mickey doesn't just show up in the films— he's also all over the parks. These often hard-to-spot images of him are called "Hidden Mickeys" because, well, they're hidden! Who does this? Is it on purpose? It's hard to say because Disney rarely confirms hidden Mickey locations, but we believe they are the work of Disney Imagineers. After all, they are the people responsible for the creation of the rides and attractions inside and outside of the parks. Since they make every detail from the structure to the paint, they often ensure that the Mouse leaves his mark.

But why? Think of Hidden Mickeys as a nod to Walt, the spirit of the parks, and as a special treat for the guests. Finding Hidden Mickeys is a fun way to pass the time while waiting in the decorated queues. Discovering the Mickeys is fun for everyone of all ages—especially tweens and teens. Even if you know where one is, it's always exciting when you see one for the first time. As we've discovered, once you find one, you start seeing them everywhere! In this exciting chapter, we reveal dozens of Hidden Mickeys from the parks to the Resort hotels and Disney Springs!

THE MAGIC KINGDOM

1. Adventureland – Look for the Jungle Cruise sign. There are some bumps on the wood below the curve of the "J" that reveal a small Hidden Mickey.
2. Adventureland – Look for a wooden tiki near the entrance. The paint reveals a mousy shape.
3. Fantasyland – The Be Our Guest Restaurant has a few Hidden Mickeys. The first is along the walls where the corner craftwork twists together to form a Mickey Mouse head (this may be easier to spot in back of the knight armor).
4. Fantasyland – Still in the Be Our Best Restaurant, this Hidden Mickey is located at the top where the axes point between silk banners. Check out the steel on one of the axes to see a shape punctured through the middle of the blade.
5. Fantasyland – Still in the Be Our Best Restaurant, the soap suds of the Mrs. Potts and Chip mural reveal a Mickey!
6. Fantasyland – Naturally, the Cinderella Castle has a Hidden Mickey, but it's hard to see. Look near the roof canopy to see a Mickey Mouse head (it's right above a vent-like piece).
7. Fantasyland – In the pond with the ducks and frogs during The Little Mermaid–Ariel's Undersea Adventure, look for three lily pads in the shape of Mickey's head.
8. Frontierland – Look inside of the Mercantile store to see the shapes of the ropes on the cashier wall.
9. Frontierland – In the grass near the station in Big Thunder Mountain are three gears covered in rust. They come together to make a Hidden Mickey.
10. Frontierland – Splash Mountain has a clever Hidden Mickey that's very rewarding once you find it. Look for Brer Frog and his fishing pole. The red and white bobber is an unmistakable shape.
11. Liberty Square – Check out the shape of the three charts on a wall in the Harbour House.
12. Liberty Square – Enter the Hall of Presidents to spot George Washington holding a gold sword. You might have to squint for this one, but the Hidden Mickey is located at the tip of his sword.
13. Liberty Square – There's a fancy, rustic Hidden Mickey on the hinges of the Haunted Mansion gates.
14. Main Street, U.S.A – One of our favorite Hidden Mickeys is also one of the loveliest of all. Located in Tony's Town Square restaurant, there's a bouquet of flowers near some book on a high shelf. Three red roses make the shape of a Hidden Mickey.
15. Tomorrowland – Buzz Lightyear's Space Ranger Spin ride has a couple of great Hidden Mickeys. The first is a bit hard to spot. Right after loading

onto the ride, look on the glowing wall paint to see a pile of batteries. On the left side is a Mickey Mouse-shaped head with a blue face and orange ears.

16. Tomorrowland – Another great Buzz Lightyear Space Ranger Spin Mickey is in the gift shop where the exit is. One of the monitors in the mural with the aliens has a Mickey.

17. Tomorrowland – This one is a little hard to spot. Look for a sign for the Recreational Rocket Vehicle Show on a dark blue wall. There's a moon on the sign with craters that make a Hidden Mickey.

18. Tomorrowland – The Mickey's Star Traders store naturally has a row of Hidden Mickeys. They are side-by-side, lining the walls with characters inside their portholes.

19. Tomorrowland – Stay inside Mickey's Star Traders to see the murals on the walls. One is an expressway filled with cars. The tracks make up a hidden Mickey.

20. Tomorrowland – There's another one in the same mural! Look at the satellite tower windows!

21. Tomorrowland – Yet another Hidden Mickey in Mickey's Star Traders! Look above to the front of the train painting. You'll see the sideways shape of Mickey's head in the chrome.

Epcot

22. Canada Pavilion – Look for a spotted wooden trout in the décor of the Northwest Mercantile store. Some of its spots form a very familiar shape!

23. China Pavilion – The white posts at the entrance to China have Mickey heads carved into them.

24. France Pavilion – The painting of Vincent Van Gogh has a Hidden Mickey in the sky near his left shoulder (his left, not yours).

25. Germany Pavilion – When roaming this section, look for the clock tower in the Biergarten. There is a bell held onto the stone wall with an iron hoist. Look at the shape of the iron to reveal a Hidden Mickey.

26. Mexico Pavilion – Look for the erupting volcano in the back of the pyramid. The smoke is in a cloudy, familiar shape.

27. Morocco Pavilion – The Moroccan Souk has metal plates on the red store door. Three of them come together for that famous shape.

28. United Kingdom Pavilion – The Sportsman's Shoppe sign just outside of the door has several sports items that make a peculiar shape.

29. The American Adventure Pavilion – There's a painting called "Building a Future Together" where construction workers do their job high in the sky. The man in the center is standing on a crane. The metal hooks at his feet appear to make a Mickey Head.

30. World Celebration – Imagination the ride has a small, glittery Hidden Mickey just below the dragon's mouth as he blows air. It's hard to spot as it's printed in one of the pink clouds.

31. World Discovery – Test Track has a couple of cool Mickeys. The first is in the queue where a few bolts on the table of tools from the shape.

32. World Discovery – The second Test Track Hidden Mickey we've seen is also in the queue. Look for the depiction of the artist drawing on the wall with a dry erase pen. He's recently outlined a small Mickey Head.

33. World Nature – Living with the Land has one in the last fish tank on the right. It's made of mesh.

34. World Nature – Living with the Land has a second Mickey in the green house. Look for the chocolate vine curling around the familiar shape.

35. World Nature – The Land's Soarin' Around the World has a great Hidden Mickey that you'll never miss once you see it. During the ride there is a fireworks display right behind Epcot's Spaceship Earth. Two bursts of light come behind the globe to reveal a massive Hidden Mickey.

36. World Nature – There's yet another Hidden Mickey in Soarin' Around the World. Look for three hot air balloons that come together to make a Hidden Mickey.

HOLLYWOOD STUDIOS

37. Echo Lake – Look for a Mickey Mouse-shaped piece under the lightsaber builder of the Star Tours gift shop. It's a bit hard to find, but there are black markings to make the ears look like they might have been made by laser blasts.

38. Grand Avenue – During the Muppet*Vision 3D ride, look for the 3D character changing into Mickey Mouse.

39. Grand Avenue – In the waiting area, look for a set of pressure gauges in the shape of a Mickey head.

40. Grand Avenue – On the fountain with Ms. Piggy as Lady Liberty, look for a Muppet standing on a rubber ducky with a Mickey-shaped head.

41. Grand Avenue – This is one of the trickiest to find. In the Company Store, look up to see cables on the lighting fixtures that form a Hidden Mickey with looped wire ears.

42. Sunset Boulevard – The Rock 'n' Roller Coaster Starring Aerosmith has a couple of Hidden Mickeys. The first is lead singer Steven Tyler's blouse which is covered in Mickey print.

43. Sunset Boulevard – The second from the Rock 'n' Roller Coaster is in the groovy-looking carpet. The warped swirls make out Mickey heads.

44. Sunset Boulevard – The Hollywood Tower of Terror has one located in the cobweb-covered office at the ride's exit. Look for a drawer with a Hidden Mickey popping out of it.

45. Toy Story Land – In the queue for Toy Story Mania! look for a red sign that reads "Circus Fun!" The dot of the exclamation point is a Hidden Mickey!

46. Toy Story Land – While in the queue for Alien Swirling Saucers, look at the Space Ranger control panel mural. Three buttons make a Hidden Mickey!

47. Toy Story Land – While boarding the Slink Dog Dash coaster, look for Andy's hand-drawn mural. You'll notice that one of the clouds looks very familiar.

48. Star Wars: Galaxy's Edge – The back of Docking Bay 7 Food & Cargo has a Hidden Mickey blasted into the wall. Look for three laser hits in the shape of the famous mouse!

49. Star Wars: Galaxy's Edge – In the queue for the Millennium Falcon: Smugglers Run ride, look for a monitor with Hondo Onaka giving you flight instructions. On the side of the monitor are bolts in the shape of a Hidden Mickey!

50. Star Wars: Galaxy's Edge – In the Millennium Falcon: Smugglers Run ride, look at the top of the cockpit in the center of the space to see a Hidden Mickey!

51. Star Wars: Galaxy's Edge – In Oga's Cantina, look directly at DJ R-3X's face and you'll see that his mouth and eyes looks like Hidden Mickey!

ANIMAL KINGDOM

52. Africa – The flamingo island on the Kilimanjaro Safari is made to look like a Mickey head.

53. Asia – There are three very cool Hidden Mickeys around Expedition Everest. The first is in the queue for the ride where a Mickey-shaped head is behind some wires in the initial supply area.

54. Asia – Expedition Everest's second Hidden Mickey is a rustic Mickey head at the top of the pillars in the queue.

55. Asia – The third from Expedition Everest is hard to find and located near the restrooms. The posts have metal wires that reach near the top to form a Mickey.

56. DinoLand U.S.A. – A few of the scales on the triceratops head on TriceraTop Spin appear to make a Hidden Mickey.

57. DinoLand U.S.A. – There's a blue dinosaur on the left side of Chester & Hester's Dino-Rama! sign. Look on his arm and you'll see a Hidden Mickey made up of his scales.

58. Pandora – Look at the ground in front of Windtraders to see a familiar shape in the rust.

59. Pandora – When you exit the Flight of Passage ride and head toward Windtraders, look in the tree to see a fruit in the shape of Mickey's head!

DISNEY RESORT HOTELS

60. Disney's All-Star Sports Resort – Look for a Mickey head made of a baseball in the gift shop.

61. Disney's Animal Kingdom Lodge – In the grand center of the lodge, look for a Mickey in the many pieces of art. One depicts a monkey with orange and red swirls.

62. Disney's Animal Kingdom Lodge – The Jiko restaurant has carpet with cheetah spots—some that look like Mickey heads.

63. Disney's Animal Kingdom Lodge – In fact, most of the spotted flooring has Mickey heads, even in the hallways leading to the rooms and on the rugs.

64. Disney's Art of Animation – They are everywhere here! Look for one in the spots of the fish outside of the Finding Nemo building.
65. Disney's BoardWalk Inn – Mickeys decoratively appear in the wooden carvings on the TV stands in the rooms.
66. Disney's BoardWalk Inn – The lobby has a Hidden Mickey located on the floral rug.
67. Disney's Coronado Springs – In the Gran Destino Tower, look for Hidden Mickeys in the light-up pillars around the lobby.
68. Disney's Grand Floridian Resort & Spa – Look for an entire Mickey Mouse (and Minnie) in the tile work in the grand lobby.
69. Disney's Grand Floridian Resort & Spa – The M. Mouse Mercantile has a Hidden Mickey on its sign.
70. Disney's Port Orleans Resort – Look for Hidden Mickeys on the chair designs in the rooms.
71. Disney's Polynesian Village Resort – In the gift shop, look for netting filled with certain round items that make a Mickey head.
72. Disney's Riviera Resort – There are Hidden Mickeys swirled in the design of the Skyliner Gondola stations.
73. Disney's Riviera Resort – Look for golden Mickey shapes in the carpets of the hotel's hallways.
74. Disney's Riviera Resort – In Bar Riva, look for a mural with a Disney Cruise Line Ship. There's a Hidden Mickey on the front of the boat!
75. Disney's Yacht Club Resort – In the rooms, look for Hidden Mickeys made of knotted ropes between the boats on the shower curtains.

DISNEY SPRINGS

76. Pin Traders – There's a large Hidden Mickey (maybe it's not so hidden) located in the concrete just outside of this store.
77. Once Upon a Toy – Check out the build-your-own Mr. Potato Head section. The sandals have little Hidden Mickeys on them (there's also a Mickey Mouse hat he can wear).
78. T-Rex Café – Look for the truck in front of the sign. Inside of the truck, there is a lot of dirt—except in one area. Look closely and you'll see that the missing dirt is in fact a Hidden Mickey.
79. Tren-D – Look for a mannequin with short blonde hair. Under her left eye is a very familiar black design.

DID YOU FIND THEM ALL?

Now keep your eyes peeled around the parks, stores, and Resort hotels for Mickey Mouse's iconic look. There are hundreds (maybe thousands) of more Hidden Mickeys to find around the parks!

CHAPTER TWENTY

WALT DISNEY WORLD SECRETS

INTRODUCTION

We've uncovered hundreds of tips, tricks, and other insider insights to help plan your Walt Disney World vacation. In this chapter, we reveal some of the Resort's hidden secrets and history in order to expand your knowledge of the parks. These are some of Disney's best-kept secrets, so we hope you enjoy!

MAGIC KINGDOM

1. **Above All Things** – The Magic Kingdom is actually built above a secret building. Beneath the theme park are tunnels for costumed characters and Cast Members to roam!

2. **Opening Day Tickets** – The Magic Kingdom opened on October 1, 1971. Admission for an adult was $3.50 (for those 18 and older), $2.50 for juniors (those ages 12-17), and only $1 for a child (ages 3-11)!

3. **What's in This?** – Guests can visit City Hall on Main Street and ask for recipes and ingredients to meals served at the Magic Kingdom!

4. **Is This Code for Something?** – Visit the Main Street Railroad Station and keep your senses alert. You can hear the beeping of Morse code, but not just any code. It's the actual translated speech that Walt Disney gave when he opened Disneyland in 1955!

5. **Romantic Dinner for Two** – Also outside of Tony's Town Square Restaurant, you'll find paw prints of a couple of spaghetti-loving dogs—Lady and the Tramp!

6. **A Timely Tower** – Cinderella Castle only took about a year and a half to construct!

7. **The Golden Touch** – The dazzling spires on the castle were made with real gold!

8. **Make Her Royal** – There's a fountain behind the castle with Cinderella placed perfectly in the center. Notice the pink backdrop with a gold crown. If you position yourself just right, the crown will look placed on Cinderella's head!

9. **Watch Yer Step** – After riding Pirates of the Caribbean, look for yellow footprints as you exit the attraction. You'll see a peg-legged stamp from a pirate missing a foot!

10. **Eight-Legged Creature** – In the queue of the Jungle Cruise, you'll see a tarantula in a cage. If you get too close, though, you might rattle him!

11. **Stinky Streets** – The brown-colored concrete walkway through Liberty Square is designed after the colonial method for the disposing sewage. Yuck!

12. **Mr. Memory of...** – When the classic Mr. Toad's Wild Ride closed in 1998, Mr. Toad's tombstone was placed in the lawn of the Haunted Mansion.

13. **The Death Count** – The Haunted Mansion is said to be haunted by 999 ghosts—spooky!

14. **Stretching Out** – Both Disneyland and the Magic Kingdom's versions of the Haunted Mansion feature a stretching room. The

biggest difference is that, in the Magic Kingdom, the walls pull up, and at Disneyland, the guests are lowered like an elevator.

15. **You Dropped Something** – When waiting in the queue for the Haunted Mansion, look for a wedding ring stuck in the pavement. It belongs to the corpse bride who haunts the mansion!

16. **Lucky 13** – The 13 Lanterns hanging from the Liberty Tree represent the 13 original colonies of the United States.

17. **Out Dated** – The numbers at the top of the buildings in Frontierland aren't street addresses. They represent the time period in which they were modeled after!

18. **Legacy Bears** – The Country Bear Jamboree was one of the final attractions developed by Walt Disney before he passed away.

19. **Five-Story Splash** – The total drop of Splash Mountain is 50 feet — or five stories!

20. **Wait for Longer** – Splash Mountain's line grows longer in the heat, but it's worth the wait. At nearly 11-minutes in length, Splash Mountain is one of Walt Disney World's longest attractions (Space Mountain runs only 2.5 minutes)!

21. **Experimental Prototype PeopleMover of Tomorrow** – The PeopleMover was originally designed by Disney to fit in Epcot. This, of course, was during the days when Epcot also had a real neighborhood where residents could use the PeopleMover to go everywhere from the theme parks to the grocery store and back home!

22. **Million Mover** – About half of the people who visit the Magic Kingdom ride the PeopleMover attraction!

EPCOT

23. **Home Is Where the Golf Ball Is** – Walt Disney's original concept for Epcot was an actual town where thousands of people could

live. They would shop, work, and also travel by monorail and the PeopleMover!

24. **When It Rains...** – To keep the giant orb dry, Spaceship Earth was built with a special drainage system. Therefore, when it rains, the water funnels through the system and eventually runs into the lagoon!

25. **Now That's a Lot of Fish!** – The Aquarium of the Seas is the second largest aquarium in the United States!

26. **Ride-Sized** – With its 5.7 million gallons of water, The Aquarium of the Seas is big enough to hold all of Spaceship Earth!

27. **A Popular Innovation** – After opening in 1999, Test Track was so popular that it became one of Disney's first attractions to be issued a Single Rider Line! Test Track is an ideal attraction for single riders since its odd number of seats per rows (three with a total of six riders per car) would otherwise not be fully filled!

28. **Free Drink!** – Walking around Epcot might work up a thirst! To quench this, head over to Club Cool where Coca Cola beverages from around the world are available to sample for free!

29. **Rush Hour** – The walkways in the China pavilion were designed close together so that crowds cluster like in Beijing!

30. **Northern Influence** – The huge troll statue in The Puffin's Roost store in the Norway Pavilion was inspired by the statues found in Voss, Norway!

31. **The Next Chapter** – Instead of a retelling of the Frozen film, Imagineers decided to tell a continuation story involving beloved characters like Elsa, Anna, and Olaf. In Frozen Ever After's storyline, Elsa uses her magic to bring a snow day during summer!

32. **Get It Strait** – Between the France and Morocco pavilions, there is a section of pavement that becomes gradually darker. This area represents the Strait of Gibraltar, a body of water that separates Europe from Africa!

33. **United Nations** – What are some of the countries that may be added? Spain, Israel, and Equatorial Africa were announced to

join, but never came to be. Brazil has been rumored to be Epcot's next added country!

DISNEY'S HOLLYWOOD STUDIOS

34. **Mickey to the Rescue!** – The Crossroads of the World tower at the park's entrance has a metal Mickey Mouse on top that works as a lightning rod—just in case!

35. **Good Boy (and Girl)** – There are two foo dog statues outside of the Chinese Theater (these look like small lions). The right is a male dog and the left is a female. How do we know? Well, the female dog has a pup under her paw while the male has an orb!

36. **Inside Was Out** – The Rock 'n' Roller Coaster was first built outside before having the building constructed around it! Some guests also have photos of the former outdoor coaster before the walls went up!

37. **Second Choice** – Though Aerosmith received a big welcome for their placement on the Rock 'n' Roller Coaster, Disney originally wanted U2. Eventually the band declined and so Aerosmith was asked—we prefer Aerosmith anyway!

38. **Plates of Vanity** – The cars for the Rock 'n' Roller Coaster are shaped like limos. Check out the funny sayings on their license plates before you ride!

39. **Matching Plates** – The car you get chooses the song. For instance, the limo coaster with the "2FAST4U" license plate plays "Sweet Emotion" and "UGOBABE" plays "Walk This Way" and "Love in an Elevator."

40. **The Same Scream** – From below the Tower of Terror, you'll hear guests screaming as they plummet. Much of the sound that you're hearing is actually "canned," meaning Disney uses pre-recorded sound effects to make your hair stand on end.

41. **Stay Tuned!** – When designing the Hollywood Tower Hotel, Imagineers watched over 150 episodes of "The Twilight Zone" to get ideas

for the attraction.

42. **Always Halloween** – In true "Twilight Zone" fashion, the Hollywood Tower Hotel ride dates October 31, 1939!

43. **A Dubbing Recast** – Since Rod Serling passed away in 1975, nearly 20 years before the ride opened, voice actor Mark Silverman dubbed over the clips. Rod Serling's widow, Carol Serling, was heavily involved in the casting process for her husband's iconic voice.

44. **Icon-"neck"** – Echo Lake's famous prehistoric resident, Gertie the Dinosaur, is based on the world's first keyframe animation. The cartoon clip was first released in 1914!

45. **Star Traders** – Like in the *Star Wars* films, Jawas will trade you for interesting objects! When you meet one, offer it a pen or a Disney pin and get something cool in return!

46. **Mouseketeer in Here** – In the waiting area for Muppet*Vision 3D, look for a hanging net with Jell-O cubes. This is a nod to the late Annette Funicello from the Mickey Mouse Club (a net full of Jell-O)!

47. **Muppet in Training** – Sweetums comes to life during the Muppet*Vision 3D show. The Cast Members playing him go through a lot of schooling from muppeteers to get the movements just right!

48. **LEGO Foot** – Toy Story Land has over 400 toy blocks scattered around it!

49. **The Forbidden Instrument** – Andy's crayons line the walkways of Toy Story Mania. Most of them have dull or partly dull heads. Only one goes unused—pink!

50. **Robots Say What?** – While Star Wars: Galaxy's Edge takes place on the fictional planet of Batuu, the trading outpost is known as Black Spire Outpost. This name was first mentioned in the Star Wars film *Solo* by Lando's robot, L3.

51. **Mini-lennium Falcon** – There's a smaller version of the Millennium Falcon built into the actual ship. It's a bit hard to

describe its exact location, but it's on the bottom of the cockpit beneath an oil-greased bar. Can you spot it?

52. **Crash Site** – At the Toy Story Land entrance to Galaxy's Edge, look for a crater with some spaceship parts. While many people believe that this is the crash site of Oga Cantina's DJ R-3X, it's actually one of a probe droid (which can be found in a net near the restrooms in back of Droid Depot).

DISNEY'S ANIMAL KINGDOM

53. **Moldy Steps** – To create an authentic feel of Asia, Africa, and also the ancient past, Disney's Imagineers made molds of actual ground in foreign countries. They then used these molds to print the pavement all over Animal Kingdom!

54. **Plant Planet** – To create the lush environment in the park, Disney planted over 400 million plants in Animal Kingdom!

55. **A Mountain of Stone** – Animal Kingdom's natural look goes beyond plants and animals. The rocks give the park the rough and wild edge of the wilderness. There's more than double the stone in Animal Kingdom than in all of Mount Rushmore's sculptures!

56. **Lion King Is Cool** – To get the lions to hang out on Pride Rock (and in public view), the rock has air conditioning to keep the cats cool.

57. **Memories Above** – While the Forbidden Mountain is the most striking landmark in Animal Kingdom's Asia, the many colorful square flags easily catch the eye. You'll notice them strung from above and even on the Expedition Everest roller coaster—but what are they? These are prayer flags, based on the Himalayan culture in India. Each waving flag is said to bring good fortune as the wind blows. The flags in Animal Kingdom are printed with animals and other designs that don't have as much meaning.

58. **What's in a Name?** – The DINOSAUR ride was originally named Countdown to Extinction. However, after initial tests, the ride was deemed too scary. Instead, Disney re-themed it to DINOSAUR after the kid-friendly CGI film of the same name.

59. **Eastern Influence** – Imagineers used the Wulingyuan historical site in China as inspiration for Pandora. The green-topped mountains in Wulingyuan appear to float when dense fog crawls between them!

60. **Nearly Mythical** – Disney originally wanted Animal Kingdom to incorporate mythological creatures. A land called Beastly Kingdom was designed to hold dragons, unicorns, and more. However, this land was never built and now Pandora occupies the expansion spot. Nevertheless, you can still spot a dragon's head at the park's entrance!

CHAPTER TWENTY-ONE

UNIVERSAL STUDIOS
ORLANDO

INTRODUCTION

If you're planning an extended stay at the Walt Disney World Resort, we highly recommend visiting the Universal Studios Orlando Resort. With three world-class theme parks—Universal Studios Florida, Universal's Islands of Adventure, and the new water park, Volcano Bay —there is plenty to do. Even if you just have one extra day to spend at Universal, we highly recommend getting a park-to-park ticket to see  the Harry Potter attractions at both parks. In other words, there is plenty of magic to experience outside of Disney!

In this chapter, we review Universal Studios Orlando from the rides to the shows and also our choice dining spots!

TRAVELING TO UNIVERSAL

There are many ways to visit Universal Orlando from the Walt Disney World Resort or anywhere else in Orlando. While Walt Disney World doesn't offer transport to Universal, many other hotels do.

Shuttle – Staying outside of the Walt Disney World Resort? Check with your hotel about their shuttle services that might take you for free to Universal for the day!

Ride Share – We prefer using Lyft to get to Universal Orlando. This way, we can go and return as we choose, fairly inexpensively. Rides start at around $20 each way for a standard car and it takes about 30 minutes to drive there.

Rental or Your Own Car – You can also drive to Universal Studios yourself and pay $26 for the entire day to park.

WHICH PARK SHOULD I VISIT?

If you can't decide which park to visit, we *highly* recommend both—especially if you are only visiting for one day! The Harry Potter attractions are in both parks (Hogsmeade Village is in Islands of Adventure and Diagon Alley is in Universal Studios Florida) and you can only ride the Hogwarts Express if you have a park-to-park ticket, which connects the two theme parks by a gentle and fun *Harry Potter*-themed train! Though Hogsmeade is stunning and home to many more rides, Diagon Alley is somehow even more breathtaking. You'll magically enter the area—we won't tell you how, as it's a surprise for when you get there—and visit shops, dark back alleys, and Gringotts bank. The centerpiece of Diagon Alley is a life-size fire-breathing dragon. Yes, *real* fire!

Universal Studios Florida uses a lot of motion simulation for its rides while Islands of Adventure sticks mostly to immersive dark rides and roller coasters. If you get motion sickness from motion simulation rides like Star Tours, you might want to skip Universal Studios and just do Islands of Adventure. Overall, we believe that Islands of Adventure is one of the best theme parks is the world. The immersive lands and unique rides will impress any theme park fan!

UNIVERSAL STUDIOS FLORIDA

In 1986, after the success of Universal Studios Hollywood and Walt Disney World, Universal broke ground on a new world-class theme park. Utilizing Florida's warm, tropical weather and abundance of land, the movie studio, along with co-founder Steven Spielberg, began designing attractions for a new set of tourists. While its Hollywood sister park brought guests inside actual film studios, Universal Studios Florida would focus on "riding the movies." The park feels like you're stepping into a Hollywood studio backlot before you plunge into worlds like Springfield from *The Simpsons* and the super-popular Diagon Alley from *Harry Potter*.

RIDES

DESPICABLE ME MINION MAYHEM
Description: A motion simulation ride with moving seats that follows characters of the *Despicable Me* film series.
Type: Motion Simulation Ride
Perfect for: Kids, Tweens, Family
Height Restriction: 40"
Review: This ride is a lot of fun with its comedy and large screen surprises. Even if you're not a fan of *Despicable Me*, put this zany attraction on your list.

SHREK 4-D
Description: A 4D theater show starring the characters from the *Shrek* franchise.
Type: 3D Theater Show (with "4D" effects)
Perfect for: Kids, Tweens, Family
Height Restriction: None
Review: Children 12 and under will likely enjoy this attraction very much. Filled with hilarious characters and 3D effects, Shrek gives lots of enjoyment. Adults and Teens may find the attraction a little too silly and wish for more. However, the 4D effects like water spritzes and moving seats keep everyone on their toes.

Note: Non-moving seats are available on Shrek 4-D.

HOLLYWOOD RIP RIDE ROCKIT

Description: A high-speed steel roller coaster set to your choice of music.

Perfect for: Thrill Riders

Height Restriction: 51" minimum and 79" maximum

Review: The Rip Ride Rockit has a very cool feature of selecting your own soundtrack. Pick from around 30 different songs from pop and rock to country and dance before you ride. Then you'll soar over 16 stories in the sky before dropping nearly straight down at up to 65 miles per hour.

TRANSFORMERS: THE RIDE-3D

Description: An explosive, 3D motion simulation ride starring the robots from Transformers.

Perfect for: Kids, Tweens, Teens, Adults, Thrill Riders

Height Restriction: 40"

Review: Battle the Decepticons in a city as you ride along with the Autobots. The ride is very similar to The Amazing Adventures of Spider-Man ride at Islands of Adventure. Though Transformers has much crisper and newer special effects and action sequences.

REVENGE OF THE MUMMY

Description: An Egyptian-themed indoor roller coaster.

Perfect for: Tweens, Teens, Adults, Thrill Riders

Height Restriction: 48"

Review: Face everything from darkness to pyrotechnic effects as you face the wrath of an ancient mummy. This lengthy roller coaster moves through several rooms before reaching 45 miles per hour just before the climax.

FAST AND FURIOUS: SUPERCHARGED

Description: A 3D high-speed race simulator starring the characters from the *Fast and Furious* franchise.

Perfect for: Kids, Tweens, Teens, Adults, Thrill Riders
Height Restriction: TBA
Review: This action-packed ride includes concept cars, an original storyline from *Fast and the Furious*, and 3D motion simulation and additional "4D" effects.

RACE THROUGH NEW YORK STARRING JIMMY FALLON
Description: 3-D Motion Simulator
Perfect for: Kids, Tweens, Teens, Adults
Height Restriction: 40"
Review: Enter a façade of NBC's New York building and race through New York City along with Tonight Show host, Jimmy Fallon. The ride is set up theatre style with a large screen in front. It's a little bit cheesy with the jokes, but tweens and fans of Jimmy Fallon will enjoy this ride the most.

MEN IN BLACK: ALIEN ATTACK
Description: A laser-guided shooting ride.
Perfect for: Young Kids, Kids, Tweens, Teens
Height Restriction: 42"
Review: Start your training as an MIB agent by blasting as many aliens as you can with your laser gun.

THE SIMPSONS RIDE
Description: Motion simulation ride starring characters from The Simpsons.
Perfect for: Tweens, Teens, Adults
Height Restriction: 40"
Review: One of the funniest rides ever, The Simpsons delivers edgy, top-quality amusement. Join Homer, Bart, Marge, Lisa, Maggie, Grampa, and the rest of Springfield as Sideshow Bob threatens to destroy Krustyland.

KANG AND KODOS' TWIRL N' HURL
Description: A spinning kids' ride starring aliens from *The Simpsons*.
Perfect for: Young Kids and Kids
Height Restriction: None
Review: The Simpsons meets Dumbo the Flying Elephant ride in this classic spin-around kiddie attraction. Despite the ride's name, this attraction is rather slow-paced and aimed at families with young kids.

E.T. ADVENTURE

Description: Ride flying bikes to help save E.T. and his home planet.
Perfect for: Families
Height Restriction: None
Review: The magic of E.T. is brought to life with animatronics and also sends you soaring on a flying bicycle. If you've experienced Peter Pan's Flight at Disney, it's a bit like that. While we enjoy E.T., you'll either love the nostalgia of the ride or wish that Universal would tear E.T. down to make room for an updated attraction.

WOODY WOODPECKER NUTHOUSE COASTER

Description: An outdoor "junior coaster" designed for families with kids.
Perfect for: Families
Height Restriction: None
Review: Ride around on Woody Woodpecker's train coaster. It's slow-paced and a lot of fun for kids looking for something thrilling to experience.

SHOWS

THE BOURNE STUNTACULAR

Description: A Hollywood stunt show based on *The Bourne Identity*.
Perfect for: Tweens, Teens, Adults
Length: 25 min
Review: A jaw-dropping indoor stunt show based on *The Bourne Identity* film series. Unlike any other stunt show before it, *The Bourne Stuntacular* uses a massive screen and amazing technical effects to bring the action to life!

ANIMAL ACTORS ON LOCATION!

Description: A stage show starring talented animals.
Perfect for: Families
Length: 20 Minutes
Review: Live animals take over a stage and show audiences their natural talents. There are tons of laughs for families with kids. Watch birds soar, dogs perform tricks, and maybe also hear a pig snort. At the end of the show, the animal trainers may allow audience members to pet some of the animals.

UNIVERSAL ORLANDO'S CINEMATIC CELEBRATION

Description: A superb nighttime water show with special effects and themes from *Jurassic World*, *Harry Potter*, *Despicable Me*, and more.

Perfect for: Everyone

Review: This stunning, 20-minute water show brings movies alive with music and projections on water fountains in the center lagoon. Scenes from popular film franchises are projected onto the water with music and colors. This effect looks a bit like the Bellagio Fountains in Las Vegas or the World of Color show at the Disneyland Resort in California. Cinematic Celebration brings to life the best experiences in the parks with thrilling *Harry Potter* sequences, hilarious *Despicable Me* vignettes, and a roaring *Jurassic Park* segment. We highly recommend planning this show as a conclusion to your day.

> **· Magic Tips ·**
>
> Showtimes vary throughout the year and depend on park hours and sunset times. We recommend showing up at least 40 minutes before showtime for a better view of the water features. The key is to sit back far enough in the seating section to see all of the projections around the theme park, but close enough for the best view of the water features. The best viewings are in the center of the tiered seating area, but the show can be viewed from anywhere around the lagoon.

MORE ATTRACTIONS

FIEVEL'S PLAYLAND

Shrink down to enjoy massive scenery and water fun designed after the *An American Tail* and *Fievel Goes West* animated films. Kids might not know the stories, but they'll love the water slide!

CURIOUS GEORGE GOES TO TOWN

A brightly colored playground straight out of the *Curious George* book series. It's famous for splash areas and things to climb. Perfect for parents who need a break and kids who have a lot of energy.

HORROR MAKE-UP SHOW

Horror movies come to life in this unique Hollywood make-up show. Where there are more laughs than screams, audience members will love the informative make-up effects and creepy monsters that arise from them. It may be too scary for young kids.

DIAGON ALLEY
THE WIZARDING WORLD OF HARRY POTTER

RIDES

HARRY POTTER & THE ESCAPE FROM GRINGOTTS
Description: A 3-D steel roller coaster starring characters from the *Harry Potter* film series
Perfect for: Kids, Tweens, Teens, Adults, Thrill Riders
Height Restriction: 42"
Review: Enter the cavernous vaults of Gringotts Bank and ride an enchanted mine cart as you face Lord Voldemort and his Death Eaters. The visuals are stunning, from the elevator that takes your deep into the depths of the bank to the cave-like start of the coaster. 3D glasses add to the magic as magical creatures and dark wizards attack, unleashing fury until Harry Potter arrives to save the day! Escape from Gringotts is a great first ride, even from just the details in the queue. While Thrill Riders will wish the coaster was a bit more intense, families with children will find the speed just right.

HOGWARTS EXPRESS
Description: A steam engine train that takes visitors from Universal Orlando to Islands of Adventure.
Perfect for: Everyone
Required: A Park-to-Park admission ticket
Review: Zip through the wall of Platform 9 ¾ to board the Hogwarts Express. You'll see famous characters from *Harry Potter* outside the window and face danger in this slow moving, yet exciting attraction. We highly recommend this ride for every Harry Potter fan. Since the train links both parks, you will need a Park-to-Park admission in order to ride.

SHOWS

OLLIVANDERS

Located next to the famous Ollivanders—where Harry Potter gets his wand—this show isn't to be missed by any Wizarding World fan. Garrick Ollivander, or one of his assistants, chooses one lucky person to discover their wand. Sadly, you don't get to keep the wands, but they are available for purchase in the next room.

· Magic Tips ·

There isn't a precise way to get chosen for Ollivanders, but from what we've noticed, participants usually near the front and to his right get chosen. Though there are always exceptions, he mostly chooses someone under the age of 21 and above the age of 8.

UKRAINIAN IRONBELLY DRAGON

A massive dragon that roosts on Gringotts Bank and periodically blows flames over Diagon Alley! The dragon doesn't run on a set schedule so you may need to wait a few minutes before it breathes fire again.

ISLANDS OF ADVENTURE

Universal Studios Florida continued its legacy of world-class entertainment when it broke ground in May 1999 with Islands of Adventure. The theme is a set of eight islands placed across a massive lagoon. All pulling from popular franchises like *Harry Potter*, *Jurassic Park*, Marvel Comics, and Dr. Seuss, every island is captivating. While Universal Studios makes you feel immersed in a Hollywood backlot, Islands of Adventure brings fictional worlds to life. Jurassic Park Island is filled with palm trees and dinos while Hogsmeade Village plunges guests into the magical, snow-covered world of Harry Potter.

RIDES

THE INCREDIBLE HULK
Description: A fast-launching steel roller coaster with loops.
Type: Roller Coaster
Perfect for: Thrill Riders
Height Restriction: 54"
Review: The Incredible Hulk roller coaster was revamped in 2016 to include a new storyline and special effects. Prepare for 7 loops, high speeds, and a lot of thrilling fun! In our opinion, The Hulk Coaster is one of the best.

Note: Many roller coasters will make you store your belongings in a locker before riding. You may need to pay a few dollars for larger bags as the lockers are designed for cellphones and wallets.

STORM FORCE ACCELATRON
Description: A spinning ride similar to Disney's tea cups.
Perfect for: Kids, Tweens
Height Restriction: None
Review: Battle Magneto alongside Storm from X-Men. Designed like the spinning Tea Cups at the Magic Kingdom, Storm Force is dizzying fun for families with kids—and strong stomachs. The cups spin as fast as you turn the wheel, so you're in control of how dizzy you want to feel.

THE AMAZING ADVENTURES OF SPIDER-MAN
Description: A 3-D motion simulation ride with a moving car.
Perfect for: Kids, Tweens, Teens, Adults, Thrill Riders
Height Restriction: 40"
Review: Grab your 3D glasses for this motion simulator based around the many adventures of Spider-Man. Combat villains like Dr. Octopus and Hobgoblin as you race through New York City. This ride is great fun for everyone with its unique style of large screens and a moving vehicle—only the Transformers ride feels similar. Families will leave Spider-Man's ride with a smile.

DR. DOOM'S FALL
Description: An 18-story freefall ride.

Perfect for: Thrill Riders
Height Restriction: 52"
Review: Calm your nerves before facing Dr. Doom's revenge for you and The Fantastic Four. Smoke, lights, and a massive drop will make any heart race! At least while you're at the top, there's an amazing view of the park. But what goes up must come down. We only recommend this scary ride for Thrill Riders.

THE CAT IN THE HAT
Description: A slow-paced ride starring The Cat in the Hat.
Type: Dark Ride
Perfect for: Kids
Height Restriction: 36"
Review: Hop aboard a slow-moving car that takes you through the storyline of *The Cat in the Hat*. Families with kids under 10 will love the colorful scenes and crazy animatronics. Actually, any Dr. Seuss fan will find this ride completely charming.

THE HIGH IN THE SKY SEUSS TROLLEY TRAIN RIDE
Description: A slow-moving train that winds around Seuss Landing.
Perfect for: Families
Height Restriction: 40"
Review: Travel over the low buildings of Seuss Landing on this vivid train. It's a nice time if you're looking for a break, as the lines are rarely long.

CARO-SEUSS-EL
Description: A Dr. Seuss-themed carousel.
Perfect for: Young Kids
Height Restriction: None
Review: Hop on bobbing yaks, elephants, and other Seuss-drawn creatures. Another well-detailed ride designed for families with young kids.

ONE FISH, TWO FISH, RED FISH, BLUE FISH
Description: A fish-themed ride like Dumbo the Flying Elephant at Disneyland and the Magic Kingdom.
Perfect for: Young Kids and Kids
Height Restriction: None
Review: Gently soar above the water on your choice of primary-colored fish. Control how high—or how low—your fish goes! Young kids will especially love this attraction.

POPEYE AND BLUTO'S BILGE-RAT BARGES
Description: A water rapids raft ride with the characters from *Popeye* cartoons.
Type: River rapids raft ride
Perfect for: Kids, Tweens, Teens, Adults
Height Restriction: 42"
Car: 12 riders per raft with seats in pairs of 2
Review: Rush down a raging rapid on rafts as Popeye and Bluto battle for Olive Oyl's attention. This is one of the best rapid rides we've ever experienced with its comical humor and cartoon design. You will get wet and you may get soaked! Prepare for laughs and sopping clothes.

DUDLEY DO-RIGHT'S RIPSAW FALLS
Description: A log water ride starring characters from Rocky and Bullwinkle's *Dudley Do-Right* cartoon
Perfect for: Kids, Tweens, Teens, Adults
Height Restriction: 44"
Review: Journey through the wacky tale of Canada's cartoon Mountie on a log raft fit for 5. At the end, you'll plunge down a 7-story waterfall. We love Dudley Do-Right's Ripsaw Falls for the beautiful decorations, comedy, and excellently made water ride. This attraction is especially popular in the summer, so visit just before noon to avoid the longer lines. You will get wet, but likely not nearly as soaked as Popeye and Bluto's Bilge-Rat Barges.

Note: If you're worried about your belongings getting soaked on the water rides, store them in a free locker near the queues.

SKULL INSLAND: REIGN OF KONG
Description: A 3D journey into the island ruled by the giant gorilla King Kong.
Type: 3D simulation ride
Perfect for: Tweens, Teens, and Adults
Height Restriction: 36"
Review: Step into a dark, forbidden temple that houses a fierce, massive gorilla. A safari truck takes you into Kong's world where dinosaurs and massive spiders might attack at any moment. The ride is divided into segments including a 360° 3-D screen that domes over the caravan. In the queue, there are a few spooky surprises as well. At the end, prepare to face Kong himself. This ride may be too terrifying for young kids.

JURASSIC PARK RIVER ADVENTURE

Description: A water-based boat ride with dinosaurs and an 85-foot drop!
Type: Boat ride
Perfect for: Thrill Riders
Height Restriction: 42"
Review: A ride that begins with gentle, animatronic giants ends up just like the movies with attacking carnivores. Drift calmly at first until the raptors and T-Rex show their teeth, then get ready for the big, 8-story fall! You'll likely get wet, but it'll be worth it because Jurassic Park River Adventure is one of the best rides in Islands of Adventure!

JURASSIC WORLD VELOCICOASTER

Description: High-speed roller coaster.
Type: Roller Coaster
Perfect for: Thrill Riders
Height Restriction: 51"
Review: The wildest ride in the park! The Jurassic World VelociCoaster is a smooth, high-speed coaster with several inversions—and airtime! Yes, you will lift out of your seat on this ride! Designed for those looking for thrills, the VelociCoaster also has a great queue filled with *Jurassic* movie easter Eggs and animatronics.

PTERANODON FLYERS

Description: High-flying kids' gliders on a track.
Type: Glider coaster
Perfect for: Thrill Riders
Height Restriction: Since this attraction is designed for kids, adults must have a child between 36" and 48" with them to ride.
Review: Kids soar around Jurassic Park island on these high-up tracked gliders. This ride's loading system is a bit slow, so lines often back up. Luckily, Universal started a Virtual Line for this attraction. A kiosk in front of the ride distributes return times so your kids can have fun in the playground instead of waiting in a long line!

SHOWS

POSEIDON'S FURY

Review: The Olympian God Poseidon unleashes his aquatic wrath on all those who intrude his ruins. Hokey comedy and special effects make this 15-minute show a cool first watch. Kids and tweens will likely love it and teens will find it fine.

RAPTOR ENCOUNTER

Meet "Blue" the Velociraptor from the *Jurassic World* film series. This giant costumed character can be a bit intimidating for younger kids. Still, brave kids will love to take photos with her!

HOGSMEADE VILLAGE
THE WIZARDING WORLD OF HARRY POTTER

RIDES

HAGRID'S MAGICAL CREATURES MOTORBIKE ADVENTURE

Description: Wind through the Forbidden Forest on this story-based rollercoaster with cinematic scenes, animatronic magical creatures, and beautiful forested scenery.

Type: Roller coaster

Perfect for: Kids, Tweens, Teens, Adults, Thrill Riders

Height Restriction: 48" (122 cm)

Car: 2 riders per row with motorbike and sidecar seats

Single Rider Available

Review: Hagrid's Magical Creatures Motorbike Adventure is a nearly 3-minute long journey of fantastic Harry Potter storytelling. Hagrid's has animatronics, stop-and-go zips, and

also surprising drops! There are two different seats here, one that feels like you're riding a motorcycle and another similar to a standard coaster. Both are fun in their own way!

> · **Magic Tips** ·
> Some popular rides may use a Virtual Line Pass to access the ride. Check availably and grab your spot for free via the Universal Orlando app.

HARRY POTTER AND THE FORBIDDEN JOURNEY

Description: An adventure ride starring the characters of the *Harry Potter* films.

Type: Simulation dark ride

Perfect for: Kids, Tweens, Teens, and Adults

Height Restriction: 48"

Review: Enter the magnificent Hogwarts castle and meet Harry Potter characters in the various rooms. Look for enchanted portraits, magic spells, a winding garden, and stunning artwork. The queue is just as entertaining as the ride. You'll fly through Hogwarts to encounter a game of Quidditch, a run-away dragon, spitting spiders, and soul-sucking Dementors. Harry Potter and the Forbidden Journey is one of the most unique rides in the world, and not to be missed!

Note: If you're worried about your comfort on Harry Potter and the Forbidden Journey, a test seat is available before the queue. Also, those with motion sickness may feel it the most on this attraction.

FLIGHT OF THE HIPPOGRIFF

Description: An outdoor, family-friendly roller coaster.

Type: Junior Roller coaster

Perfect for: Young Kids, Kids, Tweens

Height Restriction: 36"

Review: A hippogriff is half eagle, half horse and very snappy. Hagrid, the groundskeeper at Hogwarts castle, once had a hippogriff named Buckbeak who befriended Harry Potter. This ride revolves around that creature. Flight of the Hippogriff is a perfectly gentle introductory roller coaster for kids who need a stepping stone to the bigger coasters. Though the ride is just over a minute in length, it is fun for the whole family. The seats on this ride are designed for kids, so taller and larger guests may not fit comfortably in the seats. Unfortunately, Flight of the Hippogriff does not offer a test seat.

VOLCANO BAY

Looking for another water park outside of Disney? Volcano Bay is the newest and greatest family-friendly aquatic theme park to hit Orlando! Based around a towering volcano, this tropical theme park offers everything from gentle pools to extreme water slides! Adults can ride with the kids or sip cocktails on lounge chairs. Meanwhile, kids of all ages will wear themselves out riding all of the popular slides throughout the park. Even better is Volcano Bay's "queue-less" line system. Guests receive a free water-proof wristband pager for the most popular slides and only go when pinged. Then you can select another attraction from your wristband to try after you ride!

TOP CITYWALK DINING

Within walking distance of the parks is Universal CityWalk. Designed like a mall focused on entertainment and dining experiences, CityWalk delivers some tasty bites! In this section, discover our most-recommended dining locations for food and ambience.

ANTOJITOS AUTHENTIC MEXICAN FOOD
Price: $$ – $$$ / **Type:** Table Service / **Open:** Lunch and Dinner
Description: Mexican dining with live music.
Review: Antojitos is certainly one of the better restaurants in Universal Orlando. We love the south-of-the-border ambiance with colorful décor, friendly staff, and mariachi music playing around the restaurant.
Menu Overview: chips and guacamole, nachos, beans, quesadillas, taco salad, enchiladas, fajitas, tacos, carnitas, burritos, chimichangas, tortilla soup, margaritas, tequila, cocktails, soda
Kids Menu: tacos, quesadillas, empanadas, grilled chicken breast
Recommendations: Chimichanga, Fajitas, Margarita (21+)

BUBBA GUMP SHRIMP CO.
Price: $$ / **Type:** Table Service / **Open:** Lunch and Dinner
Description: *Forest Gump*-themed seafood and American dining.
Review: This restaurant from *Forest Gump* comes to life with some very delicious fried seafood and American favorites! Prepare for your waiter to ask you Forest Gump trivia—it's a lot of fun, even if you haven't seen the movie in years.

Menu Overview: burger, shrimp, salad, clam chowder, sandwiches, fried chicken, cocktails, beer, wine, soda
Kids Menu: hamburger, hot dog, chicken fingers
Recommendations: Shrimper's Heaven, Mama's Southern Fried Chicken

THE COWFISH

Price: $$–$$$ / **Type:** Table Service / **Open:** Lunch and Dinner
Description: A clever name! The Cow stands for burgers and the Fish stands for sushi. Grab either at this trendy dining joint.
Review: Cowfish is sort of genius because there's something for everyone. The sushi lovers will get their fill and those just craving a great burger will feel satisfied. Known for decent-size portions in this multi-level building, you'll certainly get your fill. We love sushi and burgers, but their signature Burgushi—where they mix sushi and hamburgers—sounded strange. However, the rolls were extremely delicious and a must try. Even if you don't like sushi, the Burgushi's powerful blend will be tasty (and don't worry, they skip the seaweed).
Menu Overview: Sushi, burgers, salads, calamari, edamame, sandwiches, cocktails, wine, beer, shakes, soda, desserts
Recommendations: The All-American Bacon Double Cheeseburgooshi

BIGFIRE

Price: $$$ / **Type:** Table Service / **Open:** Dinner
Description: American favorites cooked over a massive wood-burning fire.
Review: A fun concept for diners looking for something a little different. Get steaks, burgers, and more cooked over a giant "bigfire" grill in the restaurant. Each meal is placed on a piece of wood—cherry, pecan, and oak—to give added flavor to the dish being cooked. The menu is a bit like one you'd find at a steakhouse, but the theatrics of the big fire make it something much more fun.
Menu Overview: Steaks, seafood, fried chicken, burgers, fish, lamb chops, salads, desserts, wine, beer, sodas
Kids Menu: chicken fingers, sliders, mac and cheese, steak, chicken and beef skewers, juice, chocolate milk, milk, root beer
Recommendation: Steak, Bison Burger, S'mores (dessert), and the Smoked Maple drink (sweet Bourbon for 21+)

PRE-PLANNED ATTRACTION LISTS

INTRODUCTION

With so many choices of things to do in Walt Disney World, it's impossible to get everything done in one day without a plan. However, with our pre-made ride and attraction lists, you can enjoy the very best that Walt Disney World has to offer. These are proven to work using multiple tests, and we recommend following one of these in order to save yourself the hassle of hustling through enormous crowds. That's right, these pre-made lists work on even the busiest days!

TIME-SAVING TIPS

1. Choose one of our pre-made ride and attraction lists to follow.
2. Pre-book any dining reservations before your trip.
3. Get boarding passes for attractions that require a Virtual Queue.
4. Get to the park before it opens.
5. If you're staying at a Disney Resort, take advantage of Early Theme Park Entry.
6. Grab a map at the entrance to help guide you around.
7. Prepare to take a break when you need to in between rides.
8. Don't rush. Keep calm, enjoy the sights, and take in the magical feelings on your unforgettable vacation!

9. Also keep in mind that your boarding group time may not align with our pre-planned list. So go in order and head to your Virtual Queue experience when called.

LIGHTNING LANE TIPS

Our pre-planned attraction lists are designed to both save you time waiting in line and money. Though Disney Genie+ can help you pay to skip the lines, it's not always necessary. As we said before, there are cons to the paid feature, as it doesn't work nearly as well on busy days. In addition, guests may find Genie+ a waste of money on slower and even moderately busy days.

There's also the option to skip Genie+ but pay for select Lightning Lane reservations. Generally, if you get to the parks early enough, buying Lightning Lane access isn't necessary. Popular rides like Avatar Flight of Passage and Frozen Ever After have much shorter wait times earlier in the morning. Keep in mind that many other guests know this and could rush to these attractions right after opening. So you could end up with a bit of a line, but typically not nearly as long as later in the morning.

As you browse our attraction lists in this chapter, take note of the symbols next to the rides. The checkmarks √ are for those who opt to pay for Disney Genie+ and signify attractions that we most recommend booking. However, there are several other rides and attractions on these lists that use Genie+, so why not book them all? On slower days, you can easily book Lightning Lanes for every attraction. But during busier days, you may find it difficult to snag reservations one after another. In this event, we highly recommend following our list and selecting the checkmarks in order.

· **Magic Tips** ·

Walt Disney World will likely add more attractions to the Genie+ Lightning Lane list. We expect Frozen Ever After at Epcot and Space Mountain in Magic Kingdom to find their way to the Disney Genie+ list. In addition, character meets and shows like *Fantasmic!* could be added to Genie+. These are just guesses but you may want to double check the list of attractions on the Walt Disney World app before visiting.

MUST-SEE ATTRACTIONS

THE MAGIC KINGDOM
MUST-SEE ATTRACTIONS PLAN

1. **Seven Dwarfs Mine Train** * (Fantasyland)
2. **Space Mountain** (Tomorrowland)
3. **Peter Pan's Flight** √ (Fantasyland)
4. **"it's a small world"** (Fantasyland)
5. **Haunted Mansion** (Liberty Square)
6. **Transit Authority PeopleMover** (Tomorrowland)
7. **Pirates of the Caribbean** (Adventureland)
8. **Splash Mountain** √ (Frontierland)

LUNCH: Be Our Guest Restaurant or Columbia Harbour House

9. **Under the Sea~Journey of the Little Mermaid** (Fantasyland)
10. **Walt Disney World Railroad** (Fantasyland to Frontierland)
11. **Big Thunder Mountain Railroad** √ (Frontierland)
12. **Jungle Cruise** √ (Adventureland)
13. **Mad Tea Party** (Fantasyland)
14. **The Many Adventures of Winnie the Pooh** (Fantasyland)
15. **Magic Kingdom Fireworks** (Main Street, U.S.A.)

BONUS (OR SUBSTITUTIONS)
16. **Buzz Lightyear's Space Ranger Spin** √ (Tomorrowland)
17. **The Barnstormer** (Fantasyland)

> ** Once TRON Lightcycle Run opens, we recommend heading to Tron first. However, Tron may require a boarding pass from the Virtual Queue.*
>
> *√ Recommended Disney Genie+ Lightning Lane selections.*

EPCOT
MUST-SEE ATTRACTIONS PLAN

1. **Remy's Ratatouille Adventure** * ◊ (France)
2. **Frozen Ever After** (Norway)
3. **Test Track** √ (World Discovery East)
4. **Mission: SPACE** √ (World Discovery)
5. **Spaceship Earth** (World Celebration)
6. **The Seas with Nemo & Friends** (World Nature)
7. **SeaBase Aquarium** (World Nature)

LUNCH: Space 220, Via Napoli, or Les Halles Boulangerie-Patisserie

8. **Soarin' Around the World** √ (World Nature)
9. **Living with the Land** (World Nature)
10. **Journey into Imagination with Figment** (World Celebration)
11. **Explore World Showcase Country Pavilions**
12. **Gran Fiesta Tour** (Mexico)
13. **Harmonious (fireworks)**

BONUS (OR SUBSTITUTIONS)
14. **Disney & Pixar Short Film Festival** (World Celebration)

> * Once Guardians of the Galaxy: Cosmic Rewind opens, we recommend heading to Cosmic Rewind first. The upcoming ride may also require a boarding pass from the Virtual Queue.
>
> ◊ May use Virtual Queue.
>
> √ Recommended Disney Genie+ Lightning Lane selections.

DISNEY'S HOLLYWOOD STUDIOS
MUST-SEE ATTRACTIONS PLAN

1. **Star Wars: Rise of the Resistance** ◊ (Star Wars: Galaxy's Edge)
2. **Mickey & Minnie's Runaway Railway** (Hollywood Boulevard)
3. **Slinky Dog Dash** √ (Toy Story Land)
4. **Toy Story Mania!** (Toy Story Land)
5. **Twilight Zone Tower of Terror** √ (Sunset Boulevard)
6. **Alien Swirling Saucers** (Toy Story Land)
7. **Millennium Falcon: Smugglers Run** √ (Star Wars: Galaxy's Edge)
8. **Explore Star Wars: Galaxy's Edg**e

LUNCH: Sci-Fi Dine-In Theater Restaurant or Docking Bay 7

9. **Muppet*Vision 3D** (Grand Avenue)
10. **Indiana Jones Epic Stunt Spectacular!** (Echo Lake)
11. **Star Tours – The Adventures Continue** (Echo Lake)
12. **Rock 'n' Roller Coaster** √ (Sunset Boulevard)
13. **Fantasmic!** (Sunset Boulevard)

BONUS (OR SUBSTITUTIONS)
14. **Mickey Shorts Theater** (Echo Lake)
15. **Walt Disney Presents** (Animation Courtyard)
16. **Lightning McQueen's Racing Academy** (Sunset Boulevard)

◊ *May use Virtual Queue.*

√ *Recommended Disney Genie+ Lightning Lane selections.*

DISNEY'S ANIMAL KINGDOM
MUST-SEE ATTRACTIONS PLAN

1. **Avatar Flight of Passage** (Pandora)
2. **DINOSAUR** √ (DinoLand U.S.A.)
3. **Expedition Everest** (Asia)
4. **Maharajah Jungle Trek** (Asia)
5. **Kilimanjaro Safaris** √ (Africa)
6. **Gorilla Falls Exploration Trail** (Africa)
7. **Kali River Rapids** (Asia)

LUNCH: Yak & Yeti Restaurant or Satu'li Canteen

8. **Festival of the Lion King** (Asia)
9. **Na'vi River Journey** √ (Pandora)
10. **It's Tough to Be a Bug!** (Discovery Island)
11. **Finding Nemo – The Musical** (DinoLand U.S.A.)

BONUS (OR SUBSTITUTIONS)
12. **Wildlife Express Train** (Africa)
13. **The Animation Experience** (Rafiki's Planet Watch)

√ Recommended Disney Genie+ Lightning Lane selections.

VISITING WITH KIDS

MAGIC KINGDOM
VISITING WITH KIDS PLAN

1. **Seven Dwarfs Mine Train** (Fantasyland)
2. **Peter Pan's Flight** Δ √ (Fantasyland)
3. **"it's a small world"** Δ (Fantasyland)
4. **Haunted Mansion** Ø (Liberty Square)
5. **Pirates of the Caribbean** Ø √ (Adventureland)
6. **Swiss Family Treehouse** (Adventureland)

LUNCH: Be Our Guest Restaurant or Casey's Corner

7. **Princess Fairytale Hall** Δ (Fantasyland)
8. **Mickey's PhilharMagic** (Fantasyland)
9. **Festival of Fantasy Parade** Δ (Fantasyland)
10. **Under the Sea ~ Journey of the Little Mermaid** Δ (Fantasyland)
11. **Dumbo the Flying Elephant** Δ (Fantasyland)
12. **Mad Tea Party** (Fantasyland)
13. **Tomorrowland Speedway** √ (Tomorrowland)
14. **Buzz Lightyear's Space Ranger Spin** √ (Tomorrowland)
15. **The Many Adventures of Winnie the Pooh** Δ (Fantasyland)
16. **Jungle Cruise*** √ (Adventureland)
17. **Magic Kingdom Fireworks** (Main Street, U.S.A.)

BONUS (OR SUBSTITUTIONS)
18. **Walt Disney World Railroad** (Fantasyland to Frontierland)
19. **The Barnstormer (junior roller coaster)** Ø (Fantasyland)

Δ *Attractions recommended for ages 3-5.*

√ *Recommended Disney Genie+ Lightning Lane selections.*

Ø *May not be suitable for kids under 8 years old.*

EPCOT
VISITING WITH KIDS PLAN

1. **Remy's Ratatouille Adventure** ◊ (France)
2. **Frozen Ever After** (Norway)
3. **Test Track** Ø √ (World Discovery East)
4. **Spaceship Earth** (World Celebration)
5. **The Seas with Nemo & Friends** Δ (World Nature)
6. **SeaBase Aquarium** Δ (World Nature)

LUNCH: Space 220, Via Napoli, or Garden Grill

7. **Soarin' Around the World** √ (World Nature)
8. **Journey into Imagination with Figment** Δ (World Celebration)
9. **Disney & Pixar Short Film Festival** Δ (World Celebration)
10. **Harmonious (fireworks)**

BONUS (OR SUBSTITUTIONS)
11. **Gran Fiesta Tour** (Mexico)

◊ *May use Virtual Queue.*

Ø *May not be suitable for kids under 8 years old.*

Δ *Attractions recommended for Ages 3-5.*

√ *Recommended Disney Genie+ Lightning Lane selections.*

Note: *The Guardians of the Galaxy: Cosmic Rewind coaster is described as "family friendly." Some kids who are tall enough to ride this roller coaster may love it! Check the Disney World app for height restrictions if the attraction opens in 2022.*

DISNEY'S HOLLYWOOD STUDIOS
VISITING WITH KIDS PLAN

1. **Star Wars: Rise of the Resistance** ◊ Ø (Star Wars: Galaxy's Edge)
2. **Mickey & Minnie's Runaway Railway** Δ (Hollywood Boulevard)
3. **Slinky Dog Dash** Ø √ (Toy Story Land)
4. **Toy Story Mania!** Δ √ (Toy Story Land)
5. **Star Tours – The Adventures Continue** (Echo Lake)
6. **Millennium Falcon: Smugglers Run** √ (Star Wars: Galaxy's Edge)
7. **Explore Star Wars: Galaxy's Edge**

LUNCH: Sci-Fi Dine-In Theater Restaurant or Woody's Lunchbox

8. **Muppet*Vision 3D** Δ (Grand Avenue)
9. **Indiana Jones Epic Stunt Spectacular!** (Echo Lake)
10. **For the First Time in Forever:** A Frozen Sing-Along Celebration Δ (Echo Lake)
11. **Lightning McQueen's Racing Academy** (Sunset Boulevard)
12. **Alien Swirling Saucers** Δ (Toy Story Land)
13. **Fantasmic!** (Sunset Boulevard)

BONUS (OR SUBSTITUTIONS)
14. **Walt Disney Presents** (Animation Courtyard)
15. **Mickey Shorts Theater** (Echo Lake)

◊ *May use Virtual Queue.*

Ø May not be suitable for kids under 8 years old.

Δ *Attractions recommended for Ages 3-5.*

√ *Recommended Disney Genie+ Lightning Lane selections.*

DISNEY'S ANIMAL KINGDOM
VISITING WITH KIDS PLAN

1. **Avatar Flight of Passage** Ø (Pandora)
2. **Na'vi River Journey** Δ √ (Pandora)
3. **Kilimanjaro Safaris** Δ √ (Africa)
4. **Gorilla Falls Exploration Trail** Δ (Africa)
5. **Festival of the Lion King** (Asia)

LUNCH: Yak & Yeti Restaurant or Satu'li Canteen

6. **Wildlife Express Train** Δ (Africa)
7. **The Animation Experience** (Rafiki's Planet Watch)
8. **Habitat Habit!** Δ (Rafiki's Planet Watch)
9. **UP! A Great Bird Adventure** Δ (Asia)
10. **Maharajah Jungle Trek** Δ (Asia)
11. **Finding Nemo – The Musical** Δ (DinoLand U.S.A.)
12. **It's Tough to Be a Bug!** Δ (Discovery Island)

BONUS (OR SUBSTITUTIONS)
13. **Kali River Rapids** Ø (Asia)
14. **DINOSAUR** Ø (DinoLand U.S.A.)

Ø May not be suitable for kids under 8 years old.

Δ *Attractions recommended for ages 3-5.*

√ *Recommended Disney Genie+ Lightning Lane selections.*

THRILL RIDES

MAGIC KINGDOM
THRILL RIDE ATTRACTION PLAN

> **Recommended Lightning Lane Selections:**
> Splash Mountain, Seven Dwarfs Mine Train, Space Mountain

1. **Seven Dwarfs Mine Train** * (Fantasyland)
2. **Space Mountain** (Tomorrowland)
3. **Big Thunder Mountain Railroad** √ (Frontierland)
4. **Pirates of the Caribbean** (Adventureland)
5. **Splash Mountain** √ (Frontierland)
6. **Haunted Mansion** (Liberty Square)

LUNCH: Be Our Guest Restaurant or Columbia Harbour House

7. **Peter Pan's Flight** √ (Fantasyland)
8. **Mad Tea Party** (Fantasyland)
9. **The Barnstormer** (Fantasyland)
10. **Astro Orbitor** (Tomorrowland)
11. **Transit Authority PeopleMover** (Tomorrowland)
12. **Jungle Cruise** √ (Adventureland)
13. **Magic Kingdom Fireworks** (Main Street, U.S.A.)

BONUS (OR SUBSTITUTIONS)
14. **Buzz Lightyear's Space Ranger Spin** (Tomorrowland)

> * *Once TRON Lightcycle Run opens, we recommend heading to this attraction first. However, Tron may require a boarding pass from the Virtual Queue.*

> √ *Recommended Disney Genie+ Lightning Lane selections.*

ANIMAL KINGDOM & EPCOT
THRILL RIDE ATTRACTION PLAN

Note: There aren't enough thrill rides in each of these parks to fill an entire list. For this reason, we recommend starting at Disney's Animal Kingdom and later hopping to Epcot for the rest of the day. However, with these plans you may not be able to experience Remy's Ratatouille Adventure without paying for an Individual Lightning Lane. The only reason we recommend starting with Animal Kingdom is because its hours are typically shorter and Epcot stays open late.

DISNEY'S ANIMAL KINGDOM
1. **Avatar Flight of Passage** (Pandora)
2. **DINOSAUR** √ (DinoLand U.S.A.)
3. **Expedition Everest** (Asia)
4. **Kali River Rapids** (Asia)
5. **Kilimanjaro Safaris** √ (Africa)

LUNCH: Yak & Yeti Restaurant or Satu'li Canteen

EPCOT
6. **Test Track** √ (World Discovery East)
7. **Mission: SPACE** (World Discovery)
8. **Soarin' Around the World** (World Nature)
9. **Frozen Ever After** √ (Norway)
10. **Remy's Ratatouille Adventure** ∑ ◊ (France)
11. **Harmonious** √ **(fireworks)**

BONUS (OR SUBSTITUTIONS)
12. **Na'vi River Journey** (Disney's Animal Kingdom - Pandora)

√ *Recommended Disney Genie+ Lightning Lane selections.*

∑ *May have to use paid Lightning Lane to experience.*

◊ *May use Virtual Queue.*

Note: *The Guardians of the Galaxy: Cosmic Rewind roller coaster may open with a Virtual Queue.*

HOLLYWOOD STUDIOS
THRILL RIDE ATTRACTION PLAN

Recommended Lightning Lane Selections:
Tower of Terror, Rock 'n' Roller Coaster,
Mickey & Minnie's Runaway Railway

---

1. **Star Wars: Rise of the Resistance** ◊ (Star Wars: Galaxy's Edge)
2. **Mickey & Minnie's Runaway Railway** (Hollywood Boulevard)
3. **Slinky Dog Dash** √ (Toy Story Land)
4. **Twilight Zone Tower of Terror** √ (Sunset Boulevard)
5. **Star Tours – The Adventures Continue** √ (Echo Lake)
6. **Millennium Falcon: Smugglers Run** √ (Star Wars: Galaxy's Edge)
7. **Explore Star Wars: Galaxy's Edge**

LUNCH: Sci-Fi Dine-In Theater Restaurant or Docking Bay 7

8. **Rock 'n' Roller Coaster** √ (Sunset Boulevard)
9. **Indiana Jones Epic Stunt Spectacular!** (Echo Lake)
10. **Toy Story Mania!** √ (Toy Story Land)
11. **Alien Swirling Saucers** (Toy Story Land)
12. **Fantasmic!** (Sunset Boulevard)

BONUS (OR SUBSTITUTIONS)
13. **Muppet*Vision 3D** (Grand Avenue)

◊ *May use Virtual Queue.*

√ *Recommended Disney Genie+ Lightning Lane selections.*

CUSTOM RIDE LIST

Theme Park: _____

Names: _____   _____

_____   _____

_____   _____

1. _____
2. _____
3. _____
4. _____
5. _____
6. _____
7. _____
8. _____
9. _____
10. _____
11. _____
12. _____
13. _____
14. _____
15. _____
16. _____
17. _____
18. _____
19. _____
20. _____
21. _____
22. _____
23. _____
24. _____

CUSTOM RIDE LIST

Theme Park: _____

Names: _____   _____

_____   _____

_____   _____

1. _____
2. _____
3. _____
4. _____
5. _____
6. _____
7. _____
8. _____
9. _____
10. _____
11. _____
12. _____
13. _____
14. _____
15. _____
16. _____
17. _____
18. _____
19. _____
20. _____
21. _____
22. _____
23. _____
24. _____

CUSTOM RIDE LIST

Theme Park: _____

Names: _____   _____

_____   _____

_____   _____

1. _____
2. _____
3. _____
4. _____
5. _____
6. _____
7. _____
8. _____
9. _____
10. _____
11. _____
12. _____
13. _____
14. _____
15. _____
16. _____
17. _____
18. _____
19. _____
20. _____
21. _____
22. _____
23. _____
24. _____

CUSTOM RIDE LIST

Theme Park: _____

Names: _____ _____

_____ _____

_____ _____

1. _____
2. _____
3. _____
4. _____
5. _____
6. _____
7. _____
8. _____
9. _____
10. _____
11. _____
12. _____
13. _____
14. _____
15. _____
16. _____
17. _____
18. _____
19. _____
20. _____
21. _____
22. _____
23. _____
24. _____

VACATION CHECKLIST

❏ Park tickets
❏ Ride list
❏ ID
❏ Credit card / cash
❏ Hotel address
❏ Phone (and charging cable)
❏ Sunscreen
❏ Toiletries: toothbrush, toothpaste, etc.
❏ Swimsuit
❏ Jacket
❏ Comfortable shoes
❏ Plastic bag for cellphone (water rides)
❏ Snacks
❏ Water bottles (if you aren't flying)
❏ Backpack or bag
❏ Restaurant reservations
❏ Walt Disney World 2022 by Magic Guidebooks
❏ _____
❏ _____
❏ _____
❏ _____
❏ _____
❏ _____
❏ _____
❏ _____
❏ _____
❏ _____

CONCLUSION
AND THE FUTURE OF THE
WALT DISNEY WORLD RESORT

The Walt Disney World Resort is always changing and so will this guide throughout the years. As noted at the beginning, we are Disney World fans and we've created this book from our firsthand knowledge and research. We sincerely hope that our tips have been a valuable resource for your vacation.

With Walt Disney World's 50th anniversary running through 2022, it's entirely possible that we'll see the 18-month long celebration get extended. In addition, Epcot turns 40 in October of 2022. So we expect to see several commemorative events to celebrate the theme park's milestone.

We're often asked what we'd like from the Walt Disney World Resort and our answer is always: more! Disney is committed to bringing its beloved franchises to its theme parks, including Star Wars, Marvel, and Pixar. So keep an eye out for even more changes —including the *Princess and the Frog* ride at the Magic Kingdom!

In closing, we'd like to invite you to stay connected with us. Our website, **magicguidebooks.com**, is packed with new information and details about Walt Disney World, Disneyland, and the Universal Studios theme parks! Small parts of this book may need updating due to Walt Disney World's constant changes, however, we keep you up to speed to improve your vacation experience.

Happy and safe travels!
Magic Guidebooks

INDEX

A

B

C

D

E

F

G

H

N

O

P

Q

R

S

T

U

umbrellas, 70, 152-153
Under the Sea ~ Journey of The Little Mermaid, 81, 90
United Kingdom, 103, 107, 309
Universal CityWalk, 336-337
Universal Studios Florida, 321-329
Universal Studios Orlando Resort, 321-337
Universal's Islands of Adventure, 321-322, 329-335
Universal's Volcano Bay, 335-336
UP! A Great Bird Adventure, 145-146

V

Via Napoli Ristorante e Pizzeria, 239
Victoria & Albert's, 269, 297-298
Virtual Line Pass, 334
virtual queue, 14, 17, 40, 74-77, 82, 104-105, 338-339
Voyage of the Little Mermaid, 114-115

W

Walt Disney, 11-12
Walt Disney World Mobile App, 18, 18, 38, 40-41, 49, 51, 55-56, 70, 72, 75-83, 86, 127, 196, 205-206, 210-211, 216, 306, 339
Walt Disney World Railroad, 85-86, 98, 204
Walt Disney's Carousel of Progress, 101
Walt Disney's Enchanted Tiki Room, 95
water bottles, 69, 149
water parks, 11-12, 16, 28-30, 48-49, 53, 56, 64, 72-73, 150-159
weather, 11, 13, 23-24, 27-3577, 151, 156, 208, 287, 323
websites, 10, 21
Wilderness Lodge, Disney's, 175-176, 182, 275-276, 301
Wildlife Express Train, 148
Wizarding World of Harry Potter, The, 121, 328-329, 334-335
Wonderful World of Animation, 111-112
World of Disney (store), 206-207
World Celebration, 103
World Discovery, 103
World Nature, 103
World Showcase, 103

Y

Yacht Club, Disney's, 53, 170-171, 261-263, 300-301, 312
Yachtsman Steakhouse, 214, 262, 298-299

Z

zebra, 141-142, 167, 260

DINING NOTE: We did not index most restaurants as they are available in alphabetical order by resort area in the Dining Guide chapter.

GET UPDATES!
Walt Disney World 2022

Sign up for our FREE e-mail list!

www.magicguidebooks.com/signup
(We will never spam your information)

Wishing you a magical vacation!
Magic Guidebooks

Was this book helpful?

If so, can you please leave us a quick review on
Amazon.com?

Your reviews GREATLY help us out!
THANK YOU!

Wishing you a magical vacation!
Magic Guidebooks

Printed in Great Britain
by Amazon

76569701R00220